Wes Craven: Interviews

Conversations with Filmmakers Series
Gerald Peary, General Editor

Wes Craven
INTERVIEWS

Edited by Shannon Blake Skelton

University Press of Mississippi / Jackson

The University Press of Mississippi is the scholarly publishing agency of
the Mississippi Institutions of Higher Learning: Alcorn State University,
Delta State University, Jackson State University, Mississippi State University,
Mississippi University for Women, Mississippi Valley State University,
University of Mississippi, and University of Southern Mississippi.

www.upress.state.ms.us

The University Press of Mississippi is a member of the Association of University Presses.

First printing 2019
∞

Library of Congress Cataloging-in-Publication Data available
LCCN 2019032095
Hardback ISBN 978-1-4968-2596-4
Trade paperback ISBN 978-1-4968-2610-7
Epub single 978-1-4968-2611-4
Epub institutional 978-1-4968-2612-1
PDF single 978-1-4968-2613-8
PDF institutional 978-1-4968-2609-1

British Library Cataloging-in-Publication Data available

Contents

Introduction

Wes Craven (1939–2015) stands as a unique figure in post-1960s American cinema. With a career spanning four decades, his work has been an instrumental bridge between independent exploitation cinema and Hollywood big budget horror. His films mix intellectual concerns with political ideas, utilizing both high-tension suspense and devastating visual brutality.

Craven's pedigree is also unusual. Raised in a strict Baptist home, Craven attended Illinois' conservative Wheaton College to study literature. Following graduation, he pursued a graduate degree at Johns Hopkins with an eye toward a career in academia. While there, Craven gravitated toward cinema and became a regular consumer of films by François Truffaut and Ingmar Bergman. Though he would spend a number of years in academia teaching literature and humanities, he would eventually leave education in favor of pursuing a career in cinema. Still, many of Craven's films, including the most exploitative, are infused with a scholarly intelligence and often display the director's affinity for post–World War II art house and international cinema. Indeed, as Caetlin Benson-Allott argued in 2015 within the pages of *Film Quarterly*, "Few directors change a genre by being in it but not of it. Wes Craven did. He brought a new ideological relevance and self-referential poetics to US horror filmmaking precisely because he never identified with the genre in the way audiences identified it with him."

Craven began his career in filmmaking toiling as a New York film editor and then, under pseudonyms, as an adult film director. But it was 1972's *The Last House on the Left*, a visceral tale of countercultural criminals who murder two teens and in turn find themselves the victim of familial vengeance, which gained the attention and ire of many film critics. Yet a few, recognizing the film as an homage to Bergman's *The Virgin Spring*, came to Craven's defense. Roger Ebert in the *Chicago Sun-Times* famously hailed the film as "a tough, bitter little sleeper of a movie. . . . [with] a powerful narrative, told so directly and strongly that the audience . . . was rocked back on its psychic heels . . . This movie covers the same philosophical territory as Sam Peckinpah's *Straw Dogs*, and is more hardnosed about it." But most reviews were like that of Howard Thompson, writing in the *New York Times*, "When I walked out, after 50 minutes (with 35 to go), one girl had just been dismembered with a machete . . . The party who wrote this sickening tripe also directed the inept actors is Wes Craven. . . . [it is a film] for anyone interested in paying to see repulsive people and human agony."

Perhaps somewhat agreeing with Thompson, Craven later distanced himself from the film and its brutality. That said, in 1972 the film struck a cultural chord. Following the Manson Family murders and the disaster at the Rolling Stones' free concert at Altamont (both 1969), it seemed to many that the counterculture had devolved, like the antagonists of *The Last House on the Left*, to a nihilistic collection of sadistic and homicidal libertines.

This interrogation of the American family would also be central to Craven's subsequent horror film, 1977's *The Hills Have Eyes*. As with *The Last House on the Left*, *The Hills Have Eyes* would once again reconsider and realign components of the horror genre. Seeking inspiration not in a cultural product from Sweden but rather in the Scottish tale of the cannibalistic Sawney Bean clan, Craven crafted a harrowing fright film concerning the dissolution of a "traditional" American family. In the bleak deserts of the American southwest, a family travels across the terrain—with mobile home in tow—seeking a respite from civilization. They encounter a cannibalistic family living in the desert who quickly dispatches the tourists one by one through gruesome methods. As with *The Last House on the Left*, Craven analyzes the traditional American family, and by the conclusion of *The Hills Have Eyes*, the survivors of the middle-class family have embraced violent codes similar to that of the cannibalistic clan.

Though certainly not as cruel as *The Last House on the Left*, Craven's second credited feature is shot with a distinct visual style, and its improved production values and use of elaborate locations certainly indicate Craven's ambition to not simply churn out another exploitation film. Indeed, the ideas at the center of the film also reveal Craven once again attempting to wrestle with larger, philosophical concerns. His intellectual ambition did not go unnoticed. Horror writer Ed Gorman noted that *The Hills Have Eyes* "is an existentialist's notion of a Saturday matinee." Further, critic John Stanley argued that the work possesses a powerful social commentary, stating that "[w]hen innocent people resort to violence, they become no better than their nemeses."

Craven struggled with his follow-ups, namely *Stranger in Our House*, *Deadly Blessing*, and *Swamp Thing*. However, in 1984 Wes Craven revolutionized modern horror and cemented his reputation as a director with *A Nightmare on Elm Street*. Blending teen horror with surrealism and further examinations of the failure of the American family, the film was not only a box office hit, it earned critical acclaim. It also spawned multiple sequels, a remake, and a television series and birthed Freddy Krueger as the ultimate modern-day matinee monster. With its utilization of dream imagery, Craven's employment of state-of-the-art special effects captured the attention of mid-1980s Americans. *A Nightmare on Elm Street* was the first major financial success for the then-fledgling New Line Cinema, which would eventually be known as "The House that Freddy Built." The studio would increase its budgets and improve its reputation throughout the ensuing decades, resulting in the critically lauded, Oscar garnering *Lord of the Rings* trilogy. The success of *A Nightmare on Elm Street* and its sequels allowed an independent studio to eventually become a major motion picture player in Hollywood.

A Nightmare on Elm Street explores the sins of parents and the residual impact those sins have upon their children. Also, the film pushes beyond the standard fare of horror cinema of the 1980s, which was overwhelmed by numerous *Halloween* and *Friday the 13th* slasher imitations. By cleverly playing with notions of reality and wisely centering upon a (somewhat) liberated heroine, Craven's invention found critics lauding his new work. Francis Wheen in the *New Statesman* observed that Craven "uses many of the conventional tricks of the trade . . . but wields them with verve" and succeeds in proving "that horror needn't be synonymous with misogyny." Kevin Thomas in the *Los Angeles Times* complimented the film as being "[a]s skillful as it is sickening." *A Nightmare on Elm Street* does push at the borders of the genre, yet it does not fully deconstruct the genre's conventions. That deconstruction of the genre would be left to Craven's late career masterwork, 1996's *Scream*.

Following *A Nightmare on Elm Street*, Craven accepted invitations from an eager Hollywood, but his projects became victims of studio tampering. His work vacillated between compromised visions (1986's *Deadly Friend*) and esoteric, yet highly imaginative and intellectual fare (1988's *The Serpent and Rainbow*). However, in 1996 Craven achieved with *Scream* commercial and critical success, even surpassing that of *A Nightmare on Elm Street*.

Originally titled *Scary Movie*, *Scream* was written by Kevin Williamson, who would become synonymous with rapid fire dialogue and characters interjecting intriguing popular references. *Scream* is a clever horror film that also acts as a whodunit and serves as a deconstruction of the horror film, specifically the slasher subgenre. Critics were appreciative of the film. Thomas of the *Los Angeles Times* commended it as "terrific entertainment that also explores the relationship between movies and their audiences, specifically—but hardly exclusively—teenagers who love the kind of horror pictures Craven specializes in."

Craven continued to work on the *Scream* franchise until his death, yet he would never again reach the critical heights and commercial acclaim as he did with the original film. That said, a post-*Scream* Craven sought to explore avenues outside of the horror genre. These cinematic explorations included 1999's *Music of the Heart* (an inspirational drama featuring Meryl Streep), the 2005 Hitchockian thriller *Red Eye*, and a romantic short in 2006's anthology *Paris, je t'aime*. In the wake of *Scream*'s success, Craven also published a novel (1999's *Fountain Society*), branched out into assisting younger filmmakers by placing his "Wes Craven Presents" on titles, and even wrote a comic book series. In all, Craven was a master of '70s, '80s and '90s horror and left an indelible mark on the genre by forever altering expectations of—and approaches to—the cinema of fear.

The interviews contained within this volume trace Craven's reflections upon his work and his place within cinema history. Indeed, from these exchanges, we can gauge not only Craven's evolving reputation, but also the light in which he views himself and his work. One of the challenges of locating published interviews with Craven prior to the mid-1980s has less to do with his productivity as a filmmaker and more to do with the cultural status of horror. Though films such as *Rosemary's Baby* and *The Exorcist* had certainly raised the cultural and critical status of horror amongst the public, the vast majority of the horror genre was considered by many as simply exploitation cinema, existing in the same realm as biker films, raunchy sex comedies, and trashy subcultural romps. Granted, Craven's debut film *The Last House on the Left* features not only the fear and dread associated with horror, but also the viciousness and degradation emblematic of the roughest of exploitation fare.

The audiences of so-called "highbrow" cinema had very little use for the films and filmmakers associated with horror. As Craven found his initial foothold in horror exploitation—and pornography—and gradually built a reputation with more accessible, acceptable, and popular mainstream films, perhaps it is surprising that his first substantial interview appears in the fall 1980 issue of the decidedly nonfannish, yet firmly academic, *Journal of Popular Film and Television*. Tony Williams's interview includes a few characteristics that would reappear in subsequent pieces, namely Craven's quiet, calm demeanor that seemingly contrasts with his films and his academic background which, to some, seems paradoxical in connection to work such as *The Last House on the Left*. Williams also aligns *Last House on the Left* with Francis Ford Coppola's *Apocalypse Now*, Bob Clark's *Dead of Night* (also known as *Deathdream*), and George A. Romero's *The Crazies* as "an allegory of America's traumatic experience of the Vietnam War" while explaining that *The Hills Have Eyes* is "a prime example of the radical implications of the seventies horror film." Indeed, Williams's academic and scholarly engagement with Craven's work critically elevates the films and legitimizes a director whose work at this time was either ignored or derided by many in the critical establishment. Craven places his work within the cultural and political strife of the 1960s and '70s while also indicating his inclination toward interrogating and dismantling the assumptions about—and dynamics of—patriarchal, heterosexual families. This obsession with the concept of family would continue to haunt future films.

In 1982, *Starburst*, the revered and longstanding English magazine catering to fans of science fiction, fantasy, and horror cinema and television, included a revealing interview. Craven, who was just finishing a taxing shoot of the mainstream *Swamp Thing*, speaks about *Last House on the Left* and *The Hills Have Eyes*, offering insight into the filming and his reactions to the violence. Of *Last House*, Craven explains, "I can't go back and find a film earlier than that in the genre that became so established of breaking barriers of what is allowed to be shown. *Psycho*, I suppose. . . . Sometimes I think it was a terrible film to make, other times I'm glad I was that angry," but also confesses that "I never want to get back into that level of opening up violence on the screen." Of note in the interview are discussions of Craven's unfulfilled projects, including films about atrocities in Vietnam (*Mustang*), children in the circus (*Circus Gang*), and drug smuggling (*Marimba*). Craven's move to more legitimate, nonexploitation fare, such as the TV movie *Summer of Fear* (aka *Stranger in Our House*), indicates his desire to turn away from being specifically a horror director, but his next project, as Craven explains, "is called *Nightmare on Elm Street* . . . So, it looks like I'll be toiling in the horror field for a little while longer."

Tom Seligson, interviewing Craven for *Rod Serling's Twilight Zone Magazine* also in 1982, prefaces the exchange by noting Craven is "so pleasant-looking, good-natured, and soft-spoken that it's hard to imagine Craven as the director of two of the most violent films ever made." The extensive interview also indicates that early in Craven's career he was looking to shake off the restraints of being a genre director, explaining that he spent "two or three years after [*Last House*] writing and developing scripts of social importance. However, no one was interested in them." Craven explains that he's drawn toward "dreams and nightmares . . . I think films are dreams. They're manufactured realities that we created to help allay our fears and deal with our terrors in a magical way." By referencing Bergman, Luis Buñuel, Alfred Hitchcock, and Truffaut, Craven indicates that even though he works in the horror genre, his influences are decidedly more European and more consciously artistic. As with the previous interview, Craven previews his next project, "*A Nightmare on Elm Street* . . . I wrote it myself. It's about a teenage girl who has nightmares that start to come true."

By 1986, Craven's career as a horror auteur had been cemented through the colossal success of *A Nightmare on Elm Street*. With that capital, Craven worked in television, directing six episodes of *The Twilight Zone* and a Disney television film, *Casebusters*. Interviewed in *Fangoria*—a periodical that would consistently publish features on him and his work for the subsequent decades—Craven is an artist in transition, moving from the low-budget world of horror into the mainstream with television and, finally, into the studio system with *Deadly Friend*. What Craven does not know in this interview is that *Deadly Friend* would be a commercial and critical disaster, reviled by horror fans and mainstream audiences alike. His vision of the work, more aligned with its source material (the novel *Friend*), was quite different from the final, released film. Attempting to exploit Craven's name and association with *A Nightmare on Elm Street*, Warner Bros. demanded a title change and the addition of outrageous gore. The resulting product seems to be a mélange of *ET* sentimentalism, the teen romance genre, the "cute robot" fad of the 1980s, and cartoonishly absurd violence. Recognizing the demands as a studio director, Craven confesses that he's "willing to go along" and that "I don't think [adding gore is] going to ruin that progression in my career at all." In fact, he would remain a director associated with horror for the remainder of his life. At the time, Craven finds himself satisfied with his newfound status as a studio director, explaining, "It's nice being on a lot with other filmmakers. My office is two doors from Sydney Pollack's. It's a great feeling. I'm far from being comfortable or smug, but it's like I'm finally in the industry, part of that moviemaking tradition."

Dennis Fischer's lengthy 1988 interview, "Wes Craven, Director of Nightmares," reflects the cultural fascination with the *A Nightmare on Elm Street* franchise and, specifically, the Freddy Krueger character. *Monsterland's Nightmare on Elm Street, The Freddy Krueger Story* is a standalone magazine serving as a companion of sorts to the *Nightmare* films. The interview within recounts in detail Craven's shooting of *Last House*, the development of *Deadly Blessing*, and the agonizing challenges of filming *Swamp Thing*. This is the first interview in the collection that chronicles the filming of *A Nightmare on Elm Street* and aligns Craven with genre masters such as Brian DePalma, John Carpenter, David Cronenberg, and Joe Dante.

Michael Banka's 1990 exchange with the director in the revered *Cineaste* reveals that Craven's oeuvre is also worthy of discourse amongst cinephiles and intellectuals. The thoughtful discussion focuses primarily on his recent releases *Shocker* and *The Serpent and the Rainbow*, while Craven once again reveals his sophisticated influences such as "Buñuel . . . the Europeans such as Bergman, Fellini, Cocteau, Truffaut. Also writers like Tolstoy, Dostoyevsky, Kafka . . . the Theatre of the Absurd. American movies, though not so much Hitchcock as Howard Hawks and John Ford, especially for their well-rounded characters, which you usually don't find in horror movies." Revealing how graphic horror and so-called "splatter movies" had moved into the mainstream, the *Fangoria* offshoot publication *Toxic Horror* catered to "gore hounds" who desired a more shocking type of cinema. David Henry Jacobs's interview, upon the release of 1990's *Shocker*, finds Craven struggling with the MPAA, while also explaining the "reality" of zombies and the primal urges of the early humans that gave birth to Freddy's famed clawed hand. Craven also previews his next projects, *The People Under the Stairs* and a film entitled *Cold Eye*. Of course, *Cold Eye* was never developed into a Craven film. What is interesting is that Craven explains, "*Shocker* was done with complete artistic control. There was no interference whatsoever aside from the MPAA. This is exactly the film I set out to make." Though *Shocker* did not establish a franchise à la

A Nightmare on Elm Street, Craven's pleasure with the process and product seemingly proves that the studios not only trusted Craven as a competent director, but also viewed him as a craftsman whose best work could be produced with minimal interference. Unfortunately, for Craven, studio interference with his work would reemerge in the 2000s.

Returning to *Fangoria* to speak to Marc Shapiro about *The People Under the Stairs* in 1992, Craven "appears poised for a new beginning, one that finds him in a creative and personal sense, in a state of grace." Craven contextualizes the film within the continuum of his other family horror projects and is enthusiastic about his upcoming TV series *Nightmare Café*. Once again Craven revels in the freedom that he has working as a studio director, albeit one working in the horror genre. Craven gleefully notes, "I'm typecast as a horror filmmaker . . . But that's not necessarily bad . . . I've got a lot of power within the genre that has not been afforded me outside of it. Look what I've got when I'm doing genre films, I've got my own production company, script and cast approval, and I don't have to show dailies to anybody." Seemingly, Craven has accepted the confines of the horror genre knowing that the agency and freedom he has attained is rare in Hollywood.

After years away from the *A Nightmare on Elm Street* franchise, Craven unleashed a postmodern, meta-commentary regarding horror and the Freddy Krueger mythos in *Wes Craven's New Nightmare*. Anticipating fan enthusiasm, *Fangoria* released a one-shot *Official Movie Magazine* chronicling the development and production of the film. In an interview included in this volume, Craven has accepted his role as "Freddy's father," yet *New Nightmare* pushes at the dynamics of artistry, creation, evil, and legend. Aware of his fans, Craven also speaks about the long-developing *Freddy vs. Jason*, which not only creates an old-fashioned "monster mash" of the horror icons, but would theoretically reunite Craven with his former collaborator Sean S. Cunningham, creator of *Friday the 13th*. Eventually that film would be made in 2003, but without Craven's direct involvement.

Between the existential and artistic explorations in *Wes Craven's New Nightmare* and his later popular and critical success with *Scream*, Craven helmed a large Hollywood film anchored by a blockbuster, A-list actor: Eddie Murphy. Serving as essentially a director for hire for *Vampire in Brooklyn*, Craven worked with an impressive group of performers, including Angela Bassett, but the project itself was doomed by an inadequate script, the considerable weight and influence Murphy brought to the project, and a studio who wanted to capitalize on its comedic leading man to the detriment of the film's more horrific elements. Marc Shapiro's interview with Craven captures the filmmaker as a dutiful and supportive director promoting a project. There are indications within this interview of some of the film's weaknesses, namely an inconsistent tone, yet Craven remains faithful to the project, commenting that "there's a strength in the marketplace that comes from working with actors with known names. It gives you more leverage, and it gets your projects out there." Aware of the horror fan legions consuming *Fangoria*, Craven comments on the long developing *Freddy vs. Jason* film, while also noting that he is days away from a greenlight on *The Haunting*, a film eventually developed by DreamWorks for Jan de Bont. What Craven did not know was that his next project about a certain Ghostface killer terrorizing high school horror fans would reanimate the slasher subgenre, reinvigorate the horror genre, and prove once again that Craven was a relevant and important filmmaker.

Craven's status as a filmmaker could not be better evidenced than being selected to be the subject of an hour-long documentary for the American Film Institute's *The Directors* series. The 1999 program features extensive interviews with Craven as well as with actors from his productions. Craven's elevated artistic reputation in the wake of *Scream* is evidenced by other directors who received their own installments in the series, namely Steven Spielberg, Clint Eastwood, Spike Lee, and Martin Scorsese. The comprehensive interview chronicles Craven's fundamentalist upbringing, his time working in exploitation as well as the challenges of studio interference, and the success of *Scream*. At the time of the documentary's filming, Craven had completed his first major non-horror film for a studio. *Music of the Heart*, starring Meryl Streep, who would receive an Academy Award nomination for her performance, not only explores the dynamics of artistry and education, but also demonstrates Craven's ability to work outside the genre. Yet, the film was not too dissimilar from Craven's other work. As scholar Will Dodson has noted, "*Music of the Heart* was, for Craven, a chance to leave the horror genre for a straight, middle-of-the-road drama. Craven's common themes made their way into the film, however. *Music of the Heart* is a film about fractured families, children coping with abuse, parents and children alike coping with trauma, and dreams. Not the nightmares and dreamscapes of Craven's horror films, but dreams nonetheless, conveyed and articulated through music." Most notable within the American Film Institute interview is the testimony provided by Craven's actors about his ability to support and collaborate with performers, often creating a family atmosphere on set, serving as a surrogate father figure to many. From these adulations, including praise from Streep, by this time, Craven has not only strengthened his reputation as a filmmaker, but has emerged as an "actor's director" who understands the dynamics and demands of performance.

The two subsequent interviews, J.M. and Randy Lofficier's 1999 exchange and 2001's "Last Housemates" by David A. Szulkin focus on Craven's exploitation roots and his work on *Last House on the Left*. Of note, "Last Housemates" is a joint interview with Craven and his longtime friend and former collaborator, Sean S. Cunningham. From their conversation, we encounter two filmmakers attempting to make sense of the financial expectations of filmmaking in the new century, while also reflecting on the implications of such successful horror films as *The Sixth Sense* and *The Blair Witch Project*.

In 2005, in an excursion beyond the expectations of the horror genre, Craven directed the suspense/thriller *Red Eye*. With radio host Andrea Chase on PRX's *Behind the Scenes*, Craven speaks about the fear of flying, the strength of women in his films, and the constant struggle with the MPAA. Within the interview, Craven—in academic mode—explains that

> in a horror film you're dealing with things that are almost oceanic, these kind of primal fears that we have as human beings, as bodies. I always tell film students you know it is about that fact that there's ⅛ of an inch of skin between you and bleeding to death, and so the edged weapon, knives are just iterations of the claws of animals that chased us around as we were first emerging. That's what horror films are about.

Marc Shapiro's 2005 "The *Cursed* Is Over" chronicles the mishaps and Miramax's interference in the notorious and troubled production of *Cursed*. Billed as a reunion between Craven and *Scream* screenwriter Kevin Williamson that would reinvent the werewolf subgenre, the studio demanded reshoots and recasting while in production, resulting in a completely different film from the one initially written. As Shapiro writes, "it's painful for [Craven] to discuss *Cursed* on any level."

Similar to the American Film Institute's *The Directors* documentary, *Fangoria Screamography: Wes Craven* is an hour-long filmed conversation between *Fangoria* editor Anthony Timpone and Craven. More than in any other interview, Craven narrates the challenges of desert filming for *The Hills Have Eyes*, the development of *A Nightmare on Elm Street*, and the effect *Scream* had upon audiences, while also reflecting upon films, such as *Shocker*, that pleased him as a filmmaker, yet were unable to locate a sizable audience. By now, as an elder statesman of the genre, Craven concludes the interview reveling in his longevity, laughing that he's "just an animal that makes films and maybe they won't let me do it after a while but as long as I can, I'm going to keep making films."

In 2006, Wes Craven stepped outside of the horror genre once again, contributing a segment to the anthology film *Paris, je t'aime*. His short piece joined others directed by such respected filmmakers as Joel and Ethan Coen, Alfonso Cuarón, Tom Twyker, Gus Van Sant, Alexander Payne, and Olivier Assayas. Bilge Ebiri's thoughtful interview probes Craven's involvement with the film, his admiration for Oscar Wilde's writings, the presence of romance in Craven's films, and the challenges of directing outside of one's primary genre. Jason Zingale's "A Chat with Wes Craven," also from 2007, continues Craven's reflections upon *Paris, je t'aime*.

Steven Prokopy (writing as "Capone") converses with Craven at length about the film *25/8* (later retitled as *My Soul to Take*) as well as his struggles with *Cursed* and Hollywood's obsession with remakes. Scott Tobias's interview with Craven for the *AV Club* (2009) focuses upon an artist reflecting on his filmography and development as a director, while Mike Marano's piece in *SciFi Magazine* finds Craven eager to discuss his new project, *My Soul to Take*. Though the film would later fail both critically and commercially, Craven's pleasure in the project indicates that he still retains artistic freedom in his directing ventures.

Returning, along with screenwriter Williamson, to the *Scream* franchise in 2011, Craven speaks to Perri Nemiroff and then Christina Radish about the resurrection of the franchise. Craven contemplates *My Soul to Take*'s failure—"When you do a film like *My Soul to Take* and people think it sucks, that hurts. We put a lot of work into it and it's a good film, but you go on"—while celebrating his return to *Scream*: "The good feeling about doing this film was getting back with old friends, working on something that I thought was really good."

That same year, Jeremy Smith (writing as "Mr. Beaks") questions Craven about the *Scream* legacy, the influence of the internet upon filmmaking, and working with Williamson over the years. In *MovieMaker Magazine*, Craven shares with Bryan Reesman his reactions to the *Scary Movie* spoof films and the devastation he felt with the failure of *My Soul to Take*, and provides a candid assessment of the horror genre: "I think . . . in some ways the material [for horror films] isn't that deep."

Following the completion of *Scream 4*, Craven spoke to Eric Walkulski, reacting to the intersections of film, television, and the internet; the possibly of a *Scream 5*; and the development of his first comic book series. In his final interview with *Fangoria*, W. Bruce McVicar's "Father of Freddy," Craven narrates the origin and development of *A Nightmare on Elm Street*, its cultural reverberations, and how the film shaped him as a filmmaker. Hip-Hop artist R.A. the Rugged Man conducts a rollicking conversation with Craven that moves from Cronenberg, turning *Music of the Heart* into a horror film, and the hazards of playing with Freddy's notorious glove. In his final published interview, Craven invited Jennifer Juniper to his home for an extended exchange. Craven—who does not reveal his declining health—speaks at length about the role of women in his films and ends the interview in the way that he began many—addressing his childhood and upbringing in a fundamentalist family.

With Craven's 2015 death, fans and scholars alike mourned the passing of a filmmaker whose singular vision of horror and terror shaped cinematic nightmares for thirty years. Craven's legacy continues, be it through the *Scream* TV series (2015–2016), the various reboots and revisits, the countless fansites and fanfilms, or simply the unfettered popularity of Freddy Krueger and Ghostface costumes each Halloween. Undoubtedly, Craven's visions of deranged hippies, cannibalistic desert dwellers, a metal-clawed madman, and a cinephiliac serial killer will forever haunt film aficionados.

Craven has been the subject of three full length books: John Kenneth Muir's *Wes Craven: The Art of Horror*; Brian J. Robb's *Screams and Nightmares: The Films of Wes Craven*; and John Wooley's *Wes Craven: The Man and His Nightmares*. These works have contributed enormously to considerations of Craven's films. *Wes Craven: Interviews* is the first volume dedicated to interviews with the director. As Craven was also a public personality known through the popular success of his films, especially *A Nightmare on Elm Street* and *Scream*, he granted numerous interviews, from magazines and newspapers to television and radio programs. That said, Craven himself was persona non grata (as a result of his association with the notorious *Last House on the Left*) amongst most film journalists and critics until the 1990s, resulting in a scarcity of early career interviews. This volume provides the transcripts for two extensive interviews that have never been published previously. *The American Film Institute's The Directors: Wes Craven* is a career-spanning video interview with Craven as well as many of his collaborators. *Fangoria's Screamography* of Craven also chronicles the director's rise from exploitation filmmaker to a position as a "Master of Horror." These interviews are important components of Craven's legacy, and I hope their inclusion within will further provide Craven scholars with a wealth of material from which to construct more projects.

As with other installments in University Press of Mississippi's Conversations with Filmmakers Series, this volume includes interviews drawn from a wide variety of publications, journals, and websites. It is my intention to most accurately represent the writers, interviewers, and Craven himself in hopes to better analyze, historicize, and theorize the director's work.

Of course, the completion of such a volume as this relies on the support, goodwill, and patience of many individuals and institutions. I would first like to thank Emily Bandy at University Press of Mississippi for her encouragement and tireless correspondence. Her enthusiasm for the project has been a constant. Her colleagues at the press, especially project manager Shane Gong Stewart and intern Kjirsten Whitsell, have also been supporters of this endeavor. I have longed to compile a work such as this, and I could not be any happier with their collaboration and guidance. I also thank all the writers, publishers, and editors who worked with me in bringing these materials together into a volume. The writers within this work have created an amazing array of interviews that will forever solidify Craven's standing as a filmmaker. It is because of their provocative questions and their writing that Craven—an erudite, philosophical artist—was able to share his thoughts on his craft and artistry.

On a personal note, Keaton and Kieran are impressively patient children, understanding that their father's toiling away at the computer is not only a component of his occupation, but is also an important expression of his yearning for knowledge. Gretchen Hedrick has remained a loyal friend and source of support through this process. Don and Artyce Hedrick have been loyal supporters as well. Kansas State University's theatre program (especially Jennifer Vellenga, David Mackay, and Jerry Jay Cranford) and the film and media studies certificate program have all been tireless supporters of my research and teaching. The Popular Culture Association has been my scholarly family of choice of the past decade, especially the Horror Area (Text, Media, Culture), led by Tiffany Bryant and Jim Iaccino. They have fostered conversations and panels that have truly propelled Horror Studies forward, and I am grateful to them. Scholar Carl Swanson has been a constant contributor to my approaches to horror, always challenging me to engage with the genre in new and unique ways. My parents Danny and Diane accepted my horror-obsessed childhood and my identity as an early-age-bona-fide "Horror Geek" without any qualms, forever setting the standard for parental support and guidance.

I must also thank my English, film, and theater teachers throughout the years (John Tibbetts, George Wedge, Steve Grossman, Kae Koger, Mark Medoff, Chuck Berg, Mike Vanden Heuvel, Jan Jones, and Robert Wyche) who have all shaped me as a person and scholar. I also thank the many scholars, journalists and writers who granted permission to reprint their work. It is their words and interactions with Mr. Craven that are published in this volume. Without their labor, this project—obviously—would not exist.

Finally, I dedicate this volume to all the students with whom I have worked over the years—from teaching middle and high school in Texas and New Mexico to instructing college in Oklahoma, Wisconsin, and Kansas—it is impossible for me to imagine my life without you and your conversations. You will never know how impactful you have been on my life and scholarship. I know it is a cliché, but my love for teaching comes from my love of learning—and I am able to learn from my students on a daily basis. For that, I am fortunate.

SBS

Chronology

1939	Wesley Earl Craven born on August 2 in Cleveland, Ohio.
1957–1963	Attends Wheaton College in Illinois, studying literature.
1964	Earns master's degree in writing at Johns Hopkins University.
1964	Marries Bonnie Broecker.
1965	Teaches humanities, literature, and writing at Westminster College in New Wilmington, Pennsylvania.
1966–1968	Teaches humanities at Clarkson College in Potsdam, New York.
1968	Collaborates with students at Clarkson College on *The Searchers* (also known as *Pandora Experimentia*), a 16mm forty-five-minute film inspired by *Mission: Impossible*. Spends summer exploring New York City's thriving underground filmmaking scene.
1969	Divorces Bonnie Broecker.
1971	Associate produces *Together* (also known as *Sensual Paradise*) and edits *You've Got to Walk It Like You Talk It or You'll Lose That Beat*.
1972	In July, *The Last House on the Left* screens in select locations under the title *Krug & Co.* and *Sex Crime of the Century*. By August, the film opens under *The Last House on the Left* and is immediately hailed by some and condemned by others for its brutality and graphic violence.
1973	Edits *It Happened in Hollywood*.
1975	Directs *The Fireworks Woman* (as Abe Snake).
1976	Directs segment in *Tales That Will Tear Your Heart Out*; film abandoned.
1977	Releases *The Hills Have Eyes*. Edits *Car Hops* (also known as *California Drive In Girls*). *The Hills Have Eyes* receives the Critics Award in the Sitges Film Festival.
1978	*Stranger in Our House* (also known as *Summer of Fear*) premieres on television. Craven serves as cinematographer for *The Evolution of Snuff* and *Here Come the Tigers*.
1981	Releases *Deadly Blessing*.
1982	Releases DC Comics–based film *Swamp Thing*.
1984	Marries Millicent "Mimi" Meyer. *The Hills Have Eyes Part II*, long

shelved after many financial issues, is released. The television film *Invitation to Hell* premieres. Releases *A Nightmare on Elm Street*.

1985   Directs six episodes for TV's *The Twilight Zone*. The television movie *Chiller* premieres. *A Nightmare on Elm Street* earns the Critics Award at the Avoriaz Fantastic Film Festival.

1986   *Deadly Friend*, based on the novel *Friend*, is released to withering reviews. Directs *Casebusters* for television.

1987   Divorces Mimi Meyer-Craven. Co-writes *A Nightmare on Elm Street 3: Dream Warriors*.

1988   *The Serpent and the Rainbow*, based on the research and writings of anthropologist Wade Davis, is released. The film earns positive notices.

1989   *Shocker* releases. Derided by critics and ignored by audiences, it is widely viewed as a disappointment. Creates *The People Next Door* for television.

1990   Television film *Night Visions* premieres.

1991   *The People Under the Stairs* is released. Creates and executive produces *Laurel Canyon* for television.

1992   *Nightmare Café* runs on television. *The People Under the Stairs* wins a Special Jury Award at the Avoriaz Fantastic Festival and the Pegasus Audience Award at the Brussels International Festival.

1994   *Wes Craven's New Nightmare* is released to rave reviews.

1995   Releases *Vampire in Brooklyn*. *Wes Craven's New Nightmare* awarded Best Screenplay at the International Fantasy Film. Craven presented with Life Career Award from the Academy of Science Fiction, Fantasy and Horror Films. *Wes Craven's New Nightmare* nominated for Best Feature at the Independent Spirit Awards.

1996   *Scream*, written by Kevin Williamson, becomes a sensation, revitalizing both the horror genre and the slasher subgenre. *Scream* wins Movie of the Year Award at MTV Movie Awards.

1997   *Scream 2* is released.

1999   Directs *Music of the Heart*, earning Meryl Streep an Oscar nomination. Publishes the novel *Fountain Society*.

2000   *Scream 3* is released. Craven awarded Lifetime Achievement Award from the Amsterdam Fantastic Film Festival. Receives Cinequest Film Festival Maverick Tribute Award.

2004   Marries Iya Labunka. The troubled and long delayed werewolf film *Cursed* is released after studio interference and extensive reshoots. It is a box office and critical disaster.

Filmography

Editor's Note: Beyond being a writer and director, Wes Craven also produced and executive-produced a number of films and television projects. The entries in this filmography include only works that he directed and/or wrote.

THE LAST HOUSE ON THE LEFT (aka SEX CRIME OF THE CENTURY, NIGHT OF VENGEANCE, KRUG & CO., OR THE MEN'S ROOM) (1972)
Producers: Sean Cunningham
Associate producer: Katherine D'Amato
Director: **Wes Craven**
Screenplay: **Wes Craven**
Director of photography: Victor Hurwitz
Editing: **Wes Craven**
Music: David Alexander Hess
Special effects: Troy Roberts
Cast: Sandra Cassell (Mari Collingwood), Lucy Grantham (Phyllis Stone), David A. Hess (Krug), Fred J. Lincoln (Weasel), Jeramie Rain (Sadie), Marc Sheffler (Junior), Gaylord St. James (Dr. John Collingwood), Cynthia Carr (Estelle Washington), Ada Washington (Ada), Marshall Anker (Sheriff), Martin Kove (Deputy)
Color, 88 minutes

THE FIREWORKS WOMAN (aka ANGELA IS THE FIREWORKS WOMAN) (1975)
Producer: Peter Locke
Director: **Wes Craven** as Abe Snake
Screenplay: Hørst Bardörties and **Wes Craven** as Abe Snake
Director of photography: Hørst Badörties
Editing: **Wes Craven** as Abe Snake
Music: Jacques Urbont
Cast: Sarah Nicholson (Angela), Helen Madigan (Celeste), Erica Eaton (Elizabeth), Eric Edwards (Peter), Ellis Deigh (Roger), Lefty Cooper (The Mad Fisherman)
Color, 78 minutes

THE HILLS HAVE EYES (1977)
Producer: Peter Locke
Director: **Wes Craven**
Screenplay: **Wes Craven**
Director of photography: Eric Saarinen
Art direction: Robert Burns
Editing: **Wes Craven**
Music: Don Peake
Costume design: Joanna Jaffe
Special makeup: David Ayres
Special effects: Greg Auer, John Frazier
Cast: Susan Lanier (Brenda Carter), Robert Houston (Bobby Carter), Martin
Speer (Doug Wood), Dee Wallace (Lynne Wood), Russ Grieve (Big Bob Carter),
James Whitworth (Jupiter), John Steadman (Fred), Virginia Vincent (Ethel
Carter), Lance Gordon (Mars), Michael Berryman (Pluto), Janus Blythe (Ruby),
Cordy Clark (Mama)
Color, 89 minutes

STRANGER IN OUR HOUSE (aka SUMMER OF FEAR) (1978)
TV Film
Producers: Bill Finnegan, Patricia Finnegan
Executive producers: Max A. Keller and Micheline H. Keller
Director: **Wes Craven**
Screenplay: Glenn M. Benest and Max A. Keller, based on the novel by Lois
Duncan
Director of photography: William K. Jurgensen
Art direction: Joe Aubel
Editing: Howard A. Smith
Music: John D'Andrea, Michael Lloyd
Cast: Linda Blair (Rachel Bryant), Lee Purcell (Julia Trent), Jeremy Slate (Tom
Bryant), Jeff McCracken (Mike Gallagher), Jeff East (Peter Bryant), Carol
Lawrence (Leslie Bryant), Macdonald Carey (Professor Jarvis), Fran Drescher
(Carolyn Baker)
Color, 100 minutes

DEADLY BLESSING (1981)
Producers: Patricia S. Herskovic, Max A. Keller, and Micheline Keller,
Associate producers: Matthew Barr and Glenn M. Benest
Executive producer: William Gilmore
Director: **Wes Craven**

Screenplay: Glenn M. Benest, Matthew Barr, and **Wes Craven**, based upon the story by Benest and Barr
Director of photography: Robert Jessup
Production design: Jack Marty
Editing: Richard Bracken
Music: James Horner
Special effects: Jack Bennet
Cast: Maren Jensen (Martha Schmidt), Sharon Stone (Lana Marcus), Susan Buckner (Vicky Anderson), Jeff East (John Schmidt) Coleen Riley (Melissa), Doug Barr (Jim Schmidt), Lisa Hartman (Faith Stohler), Ernest Borgnine (Isaiah Schmidt), Michael Berryman (William Gluntz), Kevin Cooney (Sheriff)
Color, 100 minutes

SWAMP THING (1982)
Producers: Benjamin Melniker and Michael E. Uslan
Director: **Wes Craven**
Screenplay: **Wes Craven**, based on the comic book by Len Wein and Bernie Wrightson
Director of photography: Robbie Greenberg (as Robin Goodwin)
Production design: Robb Wilson King and David Nichols
Editing: Richard Bracken
Music: Harry Manfredini
Special effects: Art Brewer
Makeup: William Munns (Designer), Steve LaPorte, David B. Miller, Wren Boney, Ken Horn, Tonga Knight, Tony Marrero, Esther Mercado, and Deborah Shankle
Cast: Louis Jourdan (Arcane), Adrienne Barbeau (Alice Cable), Ray Wise (Dr. Alec Holland), Dick Durock (Swamp Thing), David Hess (Ferret), Nicholas Worth (Bruno), Don Knight (Ritter)
Color, 91 minutes

THE HILLS HAVE EYES PART II (1984)
Producers: Barry Cahn and Peter Locke
Associate producer: Jonathan Debin
Director: **Wes Craven**
Screenplay: **Wes Craven**
Director of photography: David Lewis
Production design: Dominick Bruno
Editing: Richard Bracken

Music: Harry Manfredini
Costume design: Taryn De Chellis
Special effects: Dick Brownfield, Frank Monroe, Mark Stimpson
Makeup: Ken Horn
Cast: Robert Houston (Bobby), David Nichols (The Psychiatrist), Michael
Berryman (Pluto), Janus Blythe (Rachel/Ruby), Tamara Stafford (Cass), Penny
Johnson (Sue), John Laughlin (Hulk), Willard Pugh (Foster), Kevin Blair (Roy),
Peter Frechette (Harry), Colleen Riley (Jane), Edith Fellows (Mrs. Wilson), John
Bloom (The Reaper)
Color, 86 minutes

INVITATION TO HELL (1984)
TV Film
Producer: Robert Sertner
Executive producer: Frank von Zerneck
Director: **Wes Craven**
Screenplay: Richard Rothstein
Director of photography: Dean Cundey
Art direction: Hub Braden
Set decoration: Bill Harp
Editing: Ann E. Mills, Gregory Prange
Music: Sylvester Levay
Special effects: Ken Pepiot
Cast: Robert Urich (Mat Winslow), Joanna Cassidy (Patricia Winslow), Susan
Lucci (Jessica Jones), Joe Regalbuto (Tom Peterson), Kevin McCarthy (Mr.
Thompson), Patricia McCormack (Mary Peterson), Bill Erwin (Walt Henderson),
Soleil Moon Frye (Chrissy Winslow), Barret Oliver (Robbie Winslow)
Color, 96 minutes

A NIGHTMARE ON ELM STREET (1984)
Producers: Robert Shaye and Sara Risher
Associate producer: John Burrows
Executive producers: Stanley Dudelson and Joseph Wolf
Director: **Wes Craven**
Screenplay: **Wes Craven**
Director of photography: Jacques Haitkin
Production design: Greg Fonseca
Editing: Pat McMahon, Rick Shaine
Music: Charles Bernstein

Special effects: Jim Doyle
Makeup: Kathy Logan, David Miller, Mark Wilson
Cast: Heather Langenkamp (Nancy Thompson), John Saxon (Lt. Thompson), Ronee Blakley (Marge Thompson), Robert Englund (Fred Krueger), Amanda Wyss (Tina Gray), Nick Corri (Rod Lane), Johnny Depp (Glen Lantz)
Color, 91 minutes

CHILLER (1985)
TV Film
Producers: J. D. Feigelson
Associate producer: Anderson G. House
Executive producer: Richard Kobritz
Director: **Wes Craven**
Screenplay: J. D. Feigelson
Director of photography: Frank Thackery
Art direction: Charles L. Hughes
Editing: Duane Hartzell
Music: Dana Kaproff
Cast: Paul Sorvino (Reverend Penny), Michael Beck (Miles Creighton), Beatrice Straight (Marion Creighton), Laura Johnson (Leigh Kenyon), Dick O'Neill (Clarence Beeson), Alan Fudge (Dr. Stricklin), Craig Richard Nelson (Dr. Collier)
Color, 94 minutes

THE TWILIGHT ZONE (1985–1986)
TV Series
Director: **Wes Craven**
Episodes: "A Little Peace and Quiet," "Shatterday," "Wordplay," "Chameleon," "Dealer's Choice," "Her Pilgrim Soul," and "The Road Less Travelled."
Color, 22–45 minutes

DEADLY FRIEND (1986)
Producer: Robert M. Sherman
Director: **Wes Craven**
Screenplay: Bruce Joel Rubin, based upon the novel Friend by Diana Henstell
Director of photography: Philip H. Lathrop
Production design: John Loggia and Daniel A. Lomino
Editing: Michael Eliot
Music: Charles Bernstein
Makeup: Michael Hancock, Lance Anderson (Special Makeup Effects)

Cast: Matthew Laborteaux (Paul Conway), Kristy Swanson (Samantha Pringle), Michael Sharrett (Tom 'Slime' Toomey), Anne Twomey (Jeannie Conway), Anne Ramsay (Elvira Parker), Richard Marcus (Harry Pringle), Charles Fleischer (voice of BB)
Color, 91 minutes

CASEBUSTERS (1986)
TV Film for The Magical World of Disney
Producers: John Garbett
Associate producer: Gordon Wolf
Executive producers: Paul Aaron and Erwin Stoff
Director: **Wes Craven**
Screenplay: George Arthur Bloom and Don Roos
Director of photography: George Koblasa
Art direction: James Shanahan
Editing: Duane Hartzell
Music: David Frank
Cast: Pat Hingle (Sam Donahue), Noah Hathaway (Jamie), Virginya Keehne (Allie), Gary Riley (Anthony 'Ski' Zabrowski), Sharon Barr (Loretta Bonner), Nicholas Worth (Riker), Tim Russ (Dixon)
Color, 45 minutes

A NIGHTMARE ON ELM STREET 3: DREAM WARRIORS (1987)
Producers: Robert Shaye and Sara Risher
Associate producers: Niki Marvin and Steve Thompson
Line producer: Rachel Talalay
Executive producers: **Wes Craven** and Stephen Diener
Director: Chuck Russell
Screenplay: **Wes Craven**, Bruce Wagner, Frank Darabont, and Chuck Russell, based on a story by **Wes Craven** and Bruce Wagner
Director of photography: Roy H. Wagner
Art direction: C. J. Strawn and Mick Strawn
Editing: Terry Stokes and Chuck Weiss
Music: Angelo Badalamenti
Makeup: Greg Cannom and Kevin Yagher, Screaming Mad George, Lou Manigan, Kelly Mann, Matthew W. Mungle, Brian Penikas, Christa Reusch, and Mark Shostrom
Cast: Heather Langenkamp (Nancy Thompson), Patricia Arquette (Kristen Parker), Larry Fishburne (Max), Priscilla Pointer (Dr. Elizabeth Simms), Craig

Wasson (Neil Gordon), Robert Englund (Freddy Krueger), Ken Sagoes (Kincaid), Rodney Eastman (Joey), Jennifer Rubin (Taryn), John Saxon (Lt. Thompson), Dick Cavett (Dick Cavett), Zsa Zsa Gabor (Zsa Zsa Gabor)
Color, 90 minutes

THE SERPENT AND THE RAINBOW (1988)
Producers: Doug Claybourne and David Ladd, Robert Engelman
Associate producers: David B. Pauker and Victoria Kluge
Executive producers: Keith Barish and Rob Cohen
Director: **Wes Craven**
Screenplay: Richard Maxwell and A. R. Simoun, inspired by the book by Wade Davis
Director of photography: John Lindley
Art direction: Dave Brisbin
Production design: David Nichols
Editing: Glenn Farr
Music: Brad Fiedel
Makeup: Dave Anderson and Lance Anderson
Cast: Bill Pullman (Dennis Alan), Michael Gough (Schoonbacher), Paul Guilfoyle (Andrew Cassedy), Dey Young (Deborah Cassedy), Francis Guinan (American Doctor), Cathy Tyson (Marielle Duchamp), Zakes Mokae (Dargent Peytraud), Paul Winfield (Lucien Celine), Brent Jennings (Louis Mozart), Conrad Roberts (Christophe Durand), Aleta Mitchell (Celestine), Badja Djola (Gaston), Philogen Thomas (Priest), Evencio Mosquera Slaco (Old Shaman)
Color, 98 minutes

SHOCKER (1989)
Producers: Barin Kumar, Marianne Maddalena, Bob Engelman, and Peter Foster
Executive producers: **Wes Craven** and Shep Gordon
Director: **Wes Craven**
Screenplay: **Wes Craven**
Director of photography: Jacques Haitkin
Art direction: Randy Moore
Production design: Cynthia Kay Charette
Editing: Andy Blumenthal
Music: William Goldstein
Makeup: Lance Anderson, Rosalia Altamura, David L. Anderson, David Atherton, Scott Coulter, Jeffrey S. Farley, Laura Gorman, Roger McCoin, and Suzanne Parker Sanders
Cast: Michael Murphy (Lt. Don Parker), Peter Berg (Jonathan Parker), Mitch

Pileggi (Horace Pinker), Camille Cooper (Alison Clemens), Sam Scarber
(Sidney Cooper), Richard Brooks (Rhino), Theodore Raimi (Pac Man),
Heather Langenkamp (Victim), **Wes Craven** (Man Neighbor), Jessica Craven
(Counterperson), Jonathan Craven (Jogger), Timothy Leary (Television
Evangelist), John Tesh (TV Newscaster)
Color, 109 minutes

NIGHT VISIONS (1990)
TV Film
Producers: Thomas Baum, Marianne Maddalena, and Rick Nathanson
Executive producer: **Wes Craven**
Director: **Wes Craven**
Screenplay: **Wes Craven** and Thomas Baum
Director of photography: Peter Stein
Art direction: Wm. L. Pomeroy
Production design: Vincent M. Cresciman
Editing: James Coblentz and Mark Melnick
Music: Brad Fiedel
Cast: James Remar (Sergeant Thomas Mackey), Loryn Locklin (Dr. Sally Powers),
Penny Johnson (Luanne), Francis X. McCarthy (Commissioner Nathan Dowd),
Mitch Pileggi (Captain Keller), Jon Tenney (Martin), Bruce MacVittie (Starks),
Angela Alvarado (Aura), Kristen Corbett (Young Sally), Timothy Leary (New Age
Minister)
Color, 92 minutes

THE PEOPLE UNDER THE STAIRS (1991)
Producers: Marianne Maddalena, Stuart M. Besser, and Dixie Capp
Associate producer: Peter Foster
Executive producers: **Wes Craven** and Shep Gordon
Director: **Wes Craven**
Screenplay: **Wes Craven**
Director of photography: Sandi Sissel
Art direction: Steven Lloyd Shroyer
Production design: Bryan Jones
Editing: James Coblentz
Music: Don Peake
Special makeup supervisors: Robert Kurtzman, Greg Nicotero, and Howard
Berger
Cast: Brandon Adams (Poindexter "Fool" Williams), Everett McGill (Man),
Wendy Robie (Woman), A. J. Langer (Alice), Ving Rhames (Leroy), Bill Cobbs

(Grandpa Booker), Kelly Jo Minter (Ruby), Sean Whalen (Roach), Jeremy
Roberts (Spenser), Conni Marie Brazelton (Mary), Joshua Cox (Young Cop),
John Hostetter (Veteran Cop), John Mahon (Police Sergeant), Yan Birch
(Stairmaster)
Color, 102 minutes

NIGHTMARE CAFÉ (1992)
Episode: "Aliens Ate My Lunch"
Producers: Thomas Baum and Bruce A. Pobjoy
Coordinating producer: Joseph Patrick Finn
Supervising producer: John Leekley
Senior producer: Marianne Maddalena
Executive producer: **Wes Craven**
Series creators: **Wes Craven** and Thomas Baum
Director: **Wes Craven**
Teleplay: **Wes Craven**
Director of photography: Rodney Charters
Production design: Richard Kent Wilcox
Editing: Patrick Lussier
Music: J. Peter Robinson
Cast: Jack Coleman (Frank Nolan), Lindsay Frost (Fay Peronivic), Robert
Englund (Blackie), Jimmy Briscoe (Earl/Earth), Don S. Davis (Sheriff Dan
Filcher), Adrien Dorval (Elmore), Arturo Gil (Winston/Wind), Stephen E. Miller
(Deputy), Kevin Thompson (Fred/Fire)
Color, 46 minutes

WES CRAVEN'S NEW NIGHTMARE (1994)
Producers: Marianne Maddalena and Jay Roewe
Associate producer: Jeffrey Fenner
Executive producers: **Wes Craven**, Robert Shaye, and Sara Risher
Director: **Wes Craven**
Screenplay: **Wes Craven**
Director of photography: Mark Irwin
Art direction: Diane McKinnon, Troy Sizemore
Production design: Cynthia Charette
Editing: Patrick Lussier
Music: J. Peter Robinson
Special makeup effects: Robert Kurtzman, Howard Berger, Gregory Nicotero,
and Mike J. Regan
Cast: Heather Langenkamp (Heather Langenkamp/Nancy Thompson), Robert

Englund (Robert Englund/Freddy Krueger), Miko Hughes (Dylan Porter), John Saxon (John Saxon /Lt. Donald Thompson), Tracy Middendorf (Julie), David Newsom (Chase Porter), Fran Bennett (Dr. Christine Heffner), **Wes Craven** (Wes Craven), Robert Shaye (Robert Shaye), Marianne Maddalena (Marianne Maddalena), Sam Rubin (Sam Rubin), Sara Risher (Sara Risher)
Color, 112 minutes

VAMPIRE IN BROOKLYN (1995)
Producers: Eddie Murphy, Mark Lipsky, Ray Murphy Jr., and Dixie J. Capp
Associate producer: Jeffrey Fenner
Executive producers: Stuart M. Besser and Marianne Maddalena
Director: **Wes Craven**
Screenplay: Charles Murphy, Michael Lucker, and Christopher Parker, based on a story by Eddie Murphy, Vernon Lynch, and Charles Murphy
Director of photography: Mark Irwin
Art direction: Cynthia Charette and Gary Diamond
Set design: Henry Alberti and Philip Dagort
Editing: Patrick Lussier
Music: J. Peter Robinson
Cast: Eddie Murphy (Maximillian / Preacher Pauly / Guido), Angela Bassett (Detective Rita Veder), Allen Payne (Detective Justice), Kadeem Hardison (Julius Jones), John Witherspoon (Silas Green), Zakes Mokae (Dr. Zeko), Joanna Cassidy (Captain Dewey), W. Earl Brown (Police Officer), Simbi Khali (Nikki)
Color, 102 minutes

SCREAM (1996)
Producers: Cathy Konrad, Cary Woods, and Dixie J. Capp
Associate producer: Nicholas C. Mastandrea
Executive producer: Marianne Maddalena, Bob Weinstein, Harvey Weinstein, and Stuart M. Besser
Director: **Wes Craven**
Screenplay: Kevin Williamson
Director of photography: Mark Irwin
Art direction: David Lubin
Production design: Bruce Alan Miller
Editing: Patrick Lussier
Music: Marco Beltrami
Special makeup effects: Greg Nicotero, Howard Berger, and Robert Kurtzman
Cast: Neve Campbell (Sidney Prescott), David Arquette (Dewey Riley), Courteney Cox (Gale Weathers), Skeet Ulrich (Billy Loomis), Matthew Lillard

(Stu Macher), Rose McGowan (Tatum Riley), Jamie Kennedy (Randy Meeks), Drew Barrymore (Casey Becker), Joseph Whipp (Sheriff Burke), W. Earl Brown (Kenny), Liev Schreiber (Cotton Weary), Henry Winkler (Principal Himbry), Kevin Patrick Walls (Steve Orth), Lawrence Hecht (Neil Prescott), Roger L. Jackson (Voice of Ghostface)
Color, 111 minutes

SCREAM 2 (1997)
Producers: Marianne Maddalena, Cathy Konrad, Daniel Lupi
Associate producers: Dan Arredondo, Nicholas C. Mastandrea, and Julie Plec
Executive producers: Bob Weinstein, Harvey Weinstein, Kevin Williamson, Richard Potter, Andrew Rona, and Cary Granat
Director: **Wes Craven**
Screenplay: Kevin Williamson
Director of photography: Peter Deming
Art direction: Ted Berner
Production design: Bob Ziembicki
Editing: Patrick Lussier
Music: Marco Beltrami
Special makeup effects: Greg Nicotero and Howard Berger
Cast: Neve Campbell (Sidney Prescott), David Arquette (Dwight "Dewey" Riley), Courteney Cox (Gale Weathers), Jamie Kennedy (Randy Meeks), Jerry O'Connell (Derek Feldman), Elise Neal (Hallie McDaniel), Timothy Olyphant (Mickey Altieri), Sarah Michelle Gellar (Cici Cooper), Roger L. Jackson (Voice of Ghostface), Liev Schreiber (Cotton Weary), Laurie Metcalf (Debbie Salt), Duane Martin (Joel Jones), Jada Pinkett (Maureen Evans), Omar Epps (Phil Stevens), David Warner (Mr. Gold), Rebecca Gayheart (Lois), Portia de Rossi (Murphy)
Color, 120 minutes

MUSIC OF THE HEART (1999)
Producers: Susan Kaplan, Marianne Maddalena, Alan Miller, Walter Scheuer, Stuart M. Besser, Sandy Gallin, and Meryl Poster
Associate producers: Dan Arredondo and Nicholas C. Mastandrea
Executive Producers: Amy Slotnick, Bob Weinstein, and Harvey Weinstein
Director: **Wes Craven**
Screenplay: Pamela Gray, based on the documentary Small Wonders
Director of photography: Peter Deming
Art direction: Beth Kuhn
Production design: Bruce Alan Miller
Editing: Gregg Featherman and Patrick Lussier

Music: Mason Daring
Cast: Meryl Streep (Roberta Guaspari), Aidan Quinn (Brian Turner), Angela
Bassett (Janet Williams), Gloria Estefan (Isabel Vasquez), Cloris Leachman
(Assunta Vitali Guaspari), Josh Pais (Dennis Rausch), Jane Leeves (Dorothea
von Haeften), Kieran Culkin (Alexi Tzavaras), Michael Angarano (Nick
Tzavaras), Jay O. Sanders (Dan Paxton), Jean-Luke Figueroa (Ramone Olivas),
Olga Merediz (Ms. Olivas), Charlie Hofheimer (Nicholas Tzavaras)
Color, 124 minutes

SCREAM 3 (2000)
Producers: Marianne Maddalena, Cathy Konrad, Kevin Williamson, Julie Plec,
Dixie J. Capp, Dan Arredondo
Associate producer: Nicholas C. Mastandrea
Executive producers: Bob Weinstein, Harvey Weinstein, Andrew Rona, Cary
Granat, and Stuart M. Besser
Director: **Wes Craven**
Screenplay: Ehren Kruger
Director of photography: Peter Deming
Art direction: Thomas Fichter
Production design: Bruce Alan Miller
Editing: Patrick Lussier
Music: Marco Beltrami
Cast: David Arquette (Dwight "Dewey" Riley), Courteney Cox (Gale Weathers),
Neve Campbell (Sidney Prescott), Patrick Dempsey (Detective Mark Kincaid),
Parker Posey (Jennifer Jolie), Scott Foley (Roman Bridger), Deon Richmond
(Tyson Fox), Emily Mortimer (Angelina Tyler), Matt Keeslar (Tom Prinze),
Jenny McCarthy (Sarah Darling), Lance Henriksen (John Milton), Patrick
Warburton (Steven Stone), Liev Schreiber (Cotton Weary), Kelly Rutherford
(Christine Hamilton), Roger L. Jackson (Voice of Ghostface)
Color, 117 minutes

CURSED (2005)
Producers: Kevin Williamson, Marianne Maddalena, Dan Arredondo, Julie Plec,
Jennifer Breslow, and Dixie J. Capp
Associate producer: Nicholas Mastandrea
Executive producers: Andrew Rona, Bob Weinstein, Harvey Weinstein, Brad
Weston, David Crockett, and Stuart M. Besser
Director: **Wes Craven**
Screenplay: Kevin Williamson
Director of photography: Robert McLachlan

Art direction: Andrew Max Cahn, Jeff Knipp
Production design: Chris Cornwell, Bruce Alan Miller
Editing: Patrick Lussier, Lisa Romaniw
Music: Marco Beltrami
Cast: Christina Ricci (Ellie Myers), Jesse Eisenberg (Jimmy Myers), Joshua Jackson (Jake Taylor), Judy Greer (Joanie), Milo Ventimiglia (Bo), Kristina Anapau (Brooke), Portia de Rossi (Zela), Shannon Elizabeth (Becky Morton), Mýa (Jenny Tate), Michael Rosenbaum (Kyle), Eric Ladin (Louie), Michelle Krusiec (Nosebleed Co-Worker), Nick Offerman (Police Officer), Derek Mears (Werewolf)
Color, 97 minutes

RED EYE (2005)
Producers: Marianne Maddalena and Chris Bender
Executive producers: Bonnie Curtis, Jim Lemley, Mason Novick, and J. C. Spink
Director: **Wes Craven**
Screenplay: Carl Ellsworth, based on a story by Carl Ellsworth and Dan Foos
Director of photography: Robert Yeoman
Art direction: Andrew Max Cahn
Production design: Bruce Alan Miller
Editing: Patrick Lussier and Stuart Levy
Music: Marco Beltrami
Cast: Rachel McAdams (Lisa Reisert), Cillian Murphy (Jackson Rippner), Brian Cox (Joe Reisert), Jayma Mays (Cynthia), Jack Scalia (Charles Keefe), Robert Pine (Bob Taylor), Teresa Press-Marx (Marianne Taylor), Angela Paton (Nice Lady), Laura Johnson (Blonde Woman), Loren Lester (Irate Passenger), Max Kasch (Headphone Kid), Kyle Gallner (Headphone Kid's Brother), Brittany Oaks (Rebecca), Colby Donaldson (Keefe's Head Bodyguard), Marc Macaulay (Coast Guard Officer), Jenny Wade (Coffee Shop Girl)
Color, 85 minutes

PARIS, JE T'AIME (2006)
("Père-Lachaise" Segment)
Producers: Emmanuel Benbihy, Claudie Ossard, Stefan Piech, Matthias Batthyany, and Burkhard Von Schenk
Executive producers: Chris Bolzli, Gilles Caussade, Rafi Chaudry, Samuel Englebardt, Ara Katz, Maria Köpf, Frank Moss, and Chad Troutwine
Director: **Wes Craven**
Screenplay: **Wes Craven**
Director of photography: Maxime Alexandre

Production design: Bettina von den Steinen
Editing: Stan Collet
Cast: Rufus Sewell (William), Emily Mortimer (Frances), Alexander Payne (Oscar Wilde),
Color, 5:18 minutes

PULSE (2006)
Producers: Anant Singh, Brian Cox, Michael Leahy, and Joel Soisson
Associate producer: Stephen Maloney
Executive producers: Bob Weinstein, Harvey Weinstein, and Vlad Paunescu
Director: Jim Sonzero
Screenplay: **Wes Craven** and Ray Wright, based on a screenplay by Kiyoshi Kurosawa
Director of photography: Mark Plummer
Art direction: Michael Barton and Sorin Popescu
Production design: Ermanno Di Febo-Orsini, and Gary B. Matteson
Editing: Bob Mori, Robert K. Lambert, and Kirk M. Morri
Music: Elia Cmiral
Cast: Kristen Bell (Mattie Webber), Ian Somerhalder (Dexter "Dex" McCarthy), Christina Milian (Isabelle "Izzie" Fuentes), Rick Gonzalez (Stone), Jonathan Tucker (Josh Ockmann), Samm Levine (Tim Steinberg), Octavia L. Spencer (Landlady), Ron Rifkin (Dr. Waterson), Joseph Gatt (Über Phantom), Kel O'Neill (Douglas Ziegler), Zach Grenier (Professor Cardiff), Riki Lindhome (Janelle), Robert Clotworthy (Calvin), Brad Dourif (Thin Bookish Guy)
Color, 90 minutes

THE HILLS HAVE EYES 2 (2007)
Producers: **Wes Craven**, Peter Locke, Marianne Maddalena, Samy Layani, Tina Anderson, Jonathan Craven, and Cody Zwieg
Executive producer: Jonathan Debin
Director: Martin Weisz
Screenplay: **Wes Craven** and Jonathan Craven
Director of photography: Sam McCurdy
Art direction: Alistair Kay
Production design: Keith Wilson
Editing: Sue Blainey and Kirk Morri
Music: Trevor Morris
Cast: Michael McMillian (PFC David "Napoleon" Napoli), Jessica Stroup (PFC Amber "Barbie" Johnson), Jacob Vargas (PFC "Crank" Medina), Flex Alexander (SGT Jeffrey "Sarge" Millstone), Lee Thompson Young (PFC Delmar Reed),

Daniella Alonso (PFC Marisol "Missy" Martinez), Eric Edelstein (CPL "Spitter" Cole), Reshad Strik (PFC Mickey Elrod), Ben Crowley (PFC "Stump" Locke), Michael Bailey Smith (Papa Hades), Derek Mears (Chameleon), David Reynolds (Hansel), Jeff Kober (Colonel Lincoln Redding), Jay Acovone (Dr. Wilson), Philip Pavel (Dr. Paul Foster), Archie Kao (Dr. Han), Tyrell Kemlo (Stabber), Gáspár Szabó (Grabber), Cécile Breccia (Pregnant woman), Jason Oettle (Letch)
Color, 89 minutes

MY SOUL TO TAKE (2010)
Producers: **Wes Craven**, Anthony Katagas and Iya Labunka
Associate producer: Carly Feingold
Executive producers: Ryan Kavanaugh, Andrew Rona, and Tucker Tooley
Director: **Wes Craven**
Screenplay: **Wes Craven**
Director of photography: Petra Korner
Art direction: Jack Ballance and Brianne Zulauf
Production design: Adam Stockhausen
Editing: Peter McNulty
Music: Marco Beltrami
Cast: Max Thieriot (Adam "Bug" Hellerman), John Magaro (Alex Dunkelman), Denzel Whitaker (Jerome King), Zena Grey (Penelope Bryte), Nick Lashaway (Brandon O'Neil), Paulina Olszynski (Brittany Cunningham), Jeremy Chu (Jay Chan), Emily Meade (Leah "Fang" Hellerman), Raúl Esparza (Abel Plenkov), Jessica Hecht (May Hellerman), Frank Grillo (Det. Frank Patterson), Danai Gurira (Jeanne-Baptiste), Harris Yulin (Dr. Blake), Shareeka Epps (Chandelle King), Dennis Boutsikaris (Principal Pratt), Felix Solis (Chela), Trevor St. John (Lake), Lou Sumrall (Quint), Alexandra Wilson (Sarah Plenkov), Michael Bell (Podcast Guest)
Color, 107 minutes

SCREAM 4 (2011)
Producers: Kevin Williamson, **Wes Craven**, Iya Labunka, and Carly Feingold
Executive producers: Cathy Konrad, Ehren Kruger, Marianne Maddalena, Ron Schmidt, Matthew Stein, Bob Weinstein, and Harvey Weinstein
Director: **Wes Craven**
Screenplay: Kevin Williamson
Director of photography: Peter Deming
Art direction: Gerald Sullivan
Production design: Adam Stockhausen
Editing: Peter McNulty

Music: Marco Beltrami
Cast: Neve Campbell (Sidney Prescott), David Arquette (Dewey Riley),
Courteney Cox (Gale Weathers), Emma Roberts (Jill Roberts), Hayden
Panettiere (Kirby Reed), Rory Culkin (Charlie Walker), Erik Knudsen (Robbie
Mercer), Nico Tortorella (Trevor Sheldon), Marley Shelton (Judy Hicks), Alison
Brie (Rebecca Walters), Mary McDonnell (Kate Roberts), Marielle Jaffe (Olivia
Morris), Anthony Anderson (Anthony Perkins), Adam Brody (Ross Hoss), Aimee
Teegarden (Jenny Randall), Britt Robertson (Marnie Cooper), Anna Paquin
(Rachel), Kristen Bell (Chloe), Lucy Hale (Sherrie), Shenae Grimes (Trudie),
Roger L. Jackson (Voice of Ghostface)
Color, 111 minutes

Wes Craven: Interviews

Wes Craven: An Interview

Tony Williams / 1980

From *Journal of Popular Film & Television*, October 1, 1980. Reprinted by permission of Taylor & Francis Ltd, http://www.tandfonline.com.

Unlike his films, Wes Craven is a quiet, retiring youthful forty-year-old who left the world of higher education to pursue filmmaking. Meeting him at the 1979 Toronto Film Festival Retrospective on the Horror Film proved quite a rewarding experience. Like many of the contemporary generation of young filmmakers, he began in exploitation movies, editing, co-producing, and directing many he would now care to forget. His TV movie credits include *Summer of Fear* and *Stranger in Our House* where he enjoyed the advantages of high budget technical facilities, but at the expense of creative freedom.

Last House on the Left is banned in Britain and has been severely censored in North America. Despite the initial traumas of first watching it, there is no doubt that it and its consciously designed partner *The Hills Have Eyes* are masterpieces of the seventies renaissance of the horror film. Although based on Bergman's *The Virgin Spring*, *The Last House on the Left* is not only a classic illustration of the horror genre's "return of the repressed" theme (articulated by Robin Wood in *Film Comment*, 1978) but also an allegory of America's traumatic experience of the Vietnam War. It is a key companion of other Vietnam horror movies such as Bob Clark's *Dead of Night*, George Romero's *The Crazies*, and Francis Ford Coppola's *Apocalypse Now*. The fellow product, *The Hills Have Eyes*, is as much a prime example of the radical implications of the seventies horror film as its distinguished predecessor.

Both films belong to the despised category of "exploitation," a genre where radical statements can be made with much more force than within the so-called creative confines of art cinema. They also shed incisive light on the sociological and psychological roots of American cinema which crucially deserve examination.

Tony Williams: What's your background, and how did you become a filmmaker?

Wes Craven: I'm from a midwest working-class family, the only member to go to college, study literature. I wanted to be a writer. So I went to study at Johns Hopkins' writing seminars. I left school, began to teach college, married, had a couple of kids, and taught for about five years. Everything was going along slowly until a student came along to me saying, "Professor Craven, how would you like to be advisor on a film?" I accepted without thinking about it. I had been joking with friends that we ought to make a movie. Although I had various images floating around in my head, I essentially saw myself as a frustrated artist, writing poetry and short stories.

Anyway, I advised on this film and had so much fun doing it. It was a forty-five-minute rip-off of *Mission: Impossible*. We shot it in the college town, so everyone came to see themselves in it. I then realized that I was not particularly happy teaching. It was during the Vietnam War. I was teaching in an engineering college. Most of my students were male and most of them wanted education to get a B average so they would not have to go into the war. My department chairman was always coming to me saying, "Don't give these kids Bs just because they ask you," "You've got to get your PhD," "You've missed two department meetings." The whole thrust seemed to be not teaching, not learning anything at all, just keeping the wheels running smoothly. I began to suspect this more and more. So I told my department chairman he could keep his contract and went to New York to break into the film business.

There I learned everything about making films. Initially, I didn't really know anything. But I got more work, edited a small sex education documentary, *Together*, as well as directed additional scenes. The film was a big hit, playing in all the drive-in and supermarket theaters. Its distributors then came to the producer, Sean Cunningham, suggesting we make a really violent film. Neither of us had really done a feature before. I went home and wrote *Last House on the Left* (originally titled *Night of Vengeance*), the most shocking schlock B-movie I could think of. I'd been writing for ten to twelve years—artistic, poetic things—but oddly enough never anything like this. Suddenly, I was working in an area that I'd never really confronted before. It was almost like doing a pornographic film if you'd been a fundamentalist. I found that I was writing about things I had very strong feelings about, drawing on things from very early in my childhood, things I was feeling about the war. They were pouring into this very simple B-movie plot—two girls taken into a woods, tortured, and killed, and the parents finding out—using the Bergman format of *The Virgin Spring* quite consciously.

The first indication I had that I touched on something was when I walked on to the set. I went to pick up the script Xeroxes I'd handed in two days ago, but I was told, "It's not ready yet. Each time we give it to a secretary she starts reading it and passes it around. Everyone here has read this thing. It's really disgusting!" But I said, "But you *read* it!" That was the pattern of *Last House*. People could not look away. After seeing it they were very furious—not the people I worked with, but the ones who came to peer. Especially in the editing I began to become aware of how strong it was just for me to work with it. I felt, "I don't like what's happening to these people but at the same time I do like it." I had to be not only the victim but the murderer, to be the person who could get into somebody being tortured enough to make it sound like she was really suffering. At the same time part of me felt, "I've been tortured like that; I've felt like that, totally isolated from everybody else. I've seen people take pleasure in my own personal discomfort." All sides of me were coming in at the same time, but there were sides of me I never knew existed, did not recognize, or ever want to see revealed. I think that was the key to it.

One of the things that offended me in films was that the bad guy would be bad in a safely bad way. Then John Wayne would come and shoot him. Everybody would be happy. I never once saw the bad guy cry, "Hey, Jesus. You really hurt me," or relate to anyone in a really human way. Neither was he afraid, sorry, or embarrassed. Now the thing that was then happening in the United States in a very subtle, deep, and terribly frightening way for many Americans was that for the first time they saw themselves as bad guys. John Wayne was still trying to tell us we were the Green Berets. But the young people knew that our government, and more terrifyingly, the foot soldiers in Vietnam, were doing things we never dreamed that we would ever do. Although they denied it, word on the streets was that horrible things were happening in Vietnam, things that were so terrible that when people came back they didn't want to talk about them. They couldn't even relate to society anymore.

In *Last House* I was trying to relate to that side of us that we like to externalize, the guy in the black hat. I tried to find out whether that was coming from my own soul, how it could get so loose, how it could happen like that. And the thing that seemed to be was (without getting into pat psychological explanations) that those terribly violent parts of humanity which we like to externalize—especially with Americans who say, "They were the Indians, Russians, dope addicts, blacks"—were *us*. They were in all of us, part of our fiber. Although we were a very civilized nation, it was really a hollow lie. We were specialized. The part of our specialty we liked we showed. On TV we had pap, *Ozzie and Harriet*, everybody was nice and nobody threatened. The bad guy was just a cowboy in a black hat. We had other specialities we didn't know about. Sometimes they were concealed in our government, the CIA. But they spilled over in many strange ways: Lee Harvey Oswald, Manson, Wounded Knee, Vietnam, the Bay of Pigs. There were places we could have orgasms of violence and then deny what was happening.

In *Last House* even the girl who was into the peace and love generation was into something violent. Putting aside the straight American culture and the Vietnam War, it was always ironic to me that the peace generation (of which I was a part) was also very violent. When I lived on the lower East Side of New York in the sixties, the street culture was very violent, as was Haight Ashbury.

People came into the theater to be amused and entertained by violence, the right amount of blood and killing. They certainly expected the director to have the taste to cut away at the right moment. They certainly would not want you to be joking at the same time you were killing people or show sympathy for the murderers. So *Last House* upset everybody, outraged projectionists, was cut by censors and distributors, and set upon by armed groups who forced their way in the cinemas.

Both *Last House* and *Hills Have Eyes* had the knife killings censored. The knife has an overt phallic quality. There are obvious parallels between killing someone with a knife (especially in an orgiastic way like the Manson group) and the sexual act. In the killing of Phyllis in *Last House* and Mars's death in *Hills* both bad and good guys get off on the stabbing until they realize what they've done. Kilgore in *Apocalypse Now* says he likes the smell of napalm because of its victory associations. He really gets off on killing people. The term "get off" is very significant because it reveals the sexual side to violence. Most societies get round to sexual repression sooner or later, and violence is a good way of controlling culture. A lot of violence percolates down the cracks, but it comes out in a very sexual way. Phyllis's death is very sexual in feeling. The man and the woman stab her repeatedly. But the murderers stop after an intestine loop is pulled out. They become disgusted. It was like they were playing with a doll, or a prisoner they thought was a doll, and it has broken or come apart and they did not know how to put it back together again. There were parallels between what I was seeing in our culture where the same sort of thing was happening.

In *Hills* the people outside the trailer and those inside are extremes. But they merge. I was not aware of it when I did *Last House*, but I was then. The outsiders are one's darker side that one does not know or care to face. Although they are separate in a movie I'm really talking about the same people, two sides of the same coin.

Williams: Could you elaborate on the parallels between *Last House on the Left* and *The Hills Have Eyes*, particularly the family motif in relevance to Vietnam?
Craven: The family is the best microcosm to work with. If you go much beyond that you're getting away from a lot of the roots of our own primeval feelings. Let's face it, most of the basic stories and feelings involve very few people—Mommy, Daddy, me, siblings, and the people in the other room. I like to stay within that circle. Our strong emotions and gut feelings come from those very early experiences and how they are worked out. I grew up in a white working-class family that was very religious. There was an enormous amount of secrecy in the general

commerce of getting along with each other. Certain things were not mentioned. If there was an argument it was immediately denied. As I got older I began to see that as a nation we were doing the same thing. Most of us grew up thinking that the Indian was the bad guy who mysteriously disappeared. We never thought that we might have exterminated all indigenous nations in the United States in order to get their land. Most of us did not look very carefully at what we were doing. We didn't look at how we got Puerto Rico and most of Texas and what happened in the Bay of Pigs. So it was a nation that was very much kept secret. I doubt that there's a single person in the United States to whom you could say, "Do you really think you know what went on behind the assassination of Kennedy?"—and get a positive answer. We all think there are enormous amounts of things kept from us and there are. In *Hills* nobody even tells anybody what they saw. Everybody's trying to protect everyone else, so nobody tells the truth. Truth costs you in time and preparedness because you're not psychically facing what really is happening. I feel there are all these things within the family. The outsiders are really us. It lies in the sixties. "We are not the enemy. They are us." We have done the most violent things. I'm talking about the civilized middle class that has done the most uncivilized acts. Animals don't have all these psychoses and external fears. It's characteristic in this country to sort out the civilized in one section and put the violence either in prison, another country, or part of the subconscious so we don't think about it. But as soon as you leave a door open it comes racing in and something happens. Then you suppress it. "It didn't really happen. Let's not look at it. Let's not bring these things up again. Why do we have to talk about Vietnam again? It's over." It's not over with. It's going to come in through another door.

Williams: In both films you reverse the opposition you initially make between the normal pacifist family and its dark alter ego.
Craven: In *Hills*, you have the whitebread family, Bobby and his family and the dogs Beauty and Beast. There's a little clue with the dogs. They're joking about how their dog killed a poodle in Miami. That actually came from a conversation with a friend. He had a big German Shepherd dog. We sat 'round the dinner table one night. He and his wife were very straight people, and they joked about how their dog killed a poodle in Miami. It's these little things, these little glimpses which are fascinating. You go to California and every road sign you see is perforated by bullets. When I was shooting *Hills*, I found a gas tank from a motorcycle. I wanted to have it mounted but it disappeared. It had about 10,000 bullet holes in it, so perforated that I could just keep it structural. This could have been of great significance for our culture, like the Rosetta Stone. All the working class does is go out there with their guns, shotguns and Magnums, and shoot the shit out of everything that moves. There's an enormous violence. I think it's a part of life. It's

an exertion of one's will over something else that is going in another direction. When it becomes extreme, it gets to you and you say, "Stop. This is too much. It's too much that I want to kill people or torture them for pleasure." We should not deny that we get pleasure from torture. We do. We do. You just have to be aware of it. It's when you deny it that the problem occurs. I'm not saying, "Go out and torture people because we all get off on it." It's when you say that you could never get off on it that it builds up. It comes out in some godawful way because you were afraid of the manifestation of violence in yourself. Extreme examples are quite visible. Some Eagle Scout climbs up a tower in Texas and starts picking off people with his telescopic rifle. We all do it in little ways. We do it to our children. We do it to ourselves. We do it in our relationships.

Williams: In contrast to *Last House* the evil characters in *Hills* seem evil from the start.

Craven: There were several scenes where you have more sympathy for them cut out because they didn't fit into the action. But I still think you do. It's like *The Deerhunter* where Cimino was dealing with characters we don't comprehend. In *Hills* I dealt with people I don't comprehend but still apprehend. During summer I travelled throughout Europe, South America, and west Colombia. I went up to the hills which had the worst slums ever and found people there with a totally different existence.

These people are not going to be there forever. They want what we have, and the only reason they don't have it is because we won't give it to them. I know that most of those people want to kill me to get what I have. It's something I can't resolve. That's what I'm trying to deal with. There are people on the outside kept there by our armies, our borders, our sophistication with weaponry, while we've been living off the raw products of their country for many years. That's what colonization was all about. We come in and say, "Don't cry. We'll take care of you." But in the meantime we help ourselves to all these things. Now they say, "Get the hell out of our country." What's going to happen? That's up to you.

Williams: Would you say that it's more or less an uprising of the oppressed against the oppressors since the first person to be killed in *Hills* is the ex-policeman father?

Craven: Yes. It is very much. They're living on a bomb range, which is as significant as you can get. We don't even allow our own citizens to go in there because the weapons are so sophisticated; they don't even know who or what is defending them.

Williams: In both films you have children trying to break out of the savage parental group—Junior Stillo and Ruby?

Craven: Junior is successful, but it costs him his life. What he should have done
was shoot his father. The image in my mind for that scene was the Goya painting
of Kronos devouring his children. One of the conscious things in *Last House* was
the primal event: the mother bites off the cock of the man who raped her daughter
while the father cuts off the head of the other rapist.

There was a whole milieu of hatred and prejudice in the world I grew up in,
that I was able to get away from. When I return to Cleveland, the people are in a
totally different world to me. It always fascinates me how people progress, spiri-
tually or consciously, so that they attain a different level from that of the people
they emerged from. It's fascinating. It happens at great cost and very rarely. But
it is possible. Change is something that is very important to me. It's possible to
arrive at the end of certain films with the feeling that nothing is going to change
and we're trapped into whatever we are. Something I've been wrestling with for
a long time is the possibility of really changing yourself. If you change yourself in
the most significant way, you can change the society or world you live in. That's
why I'm interested in Ruby and Junior. They come out of the worst sort of families
and do make decisions. It's what you decide at this moment. We can anesthetize
ourselves with saying, "We don't have any choices here," or "I can't cope with it."
So we don't take responsibility for our lives. Every second of our lives people make
decisions. That's where the significance is.

Even the Stillos attempt to change in *Last House*—the idea of being in a popular
home and changing clothes. They set out to escape, but every time they keep getting sucked back into their old violent patterns. That's why Weasel keeps saying,
"This isn't getting us out of the state." They were practically out of the state when
they took the two girls into the woods and precipitated the events. Ruby continu-
ally attempts to change herself both culturally and socially.

Wes Craven. . . . Who's Made Nightmares Come True

Tom Seligson / 1982

From *Rod Serling's The Twilight Zone Magazine*, February 1982. Reprinted by permission of Tom Seligson.

Considering the countless horror films made in recent years, it's not surprising that few survive their initial release to become classics of the genre. But classics do exist; one thinks of George Romero's *Night of the Living Dead* and Tobe Hooper's *Texas Chainsaw Massacre*, both of which have achieved cult status over the years. Another horror film that has developed a special reputation is *The Last House on the Left*. Made in 1971 at a cost of only $90,000, the film was a grisly update of Bergman's *The Virgin Spring* and depicted a family's revenge upon a murderous teenage gang. What distinguished the film, even more than the millions it's grossed, was its graphic violence. *The Last House on the Left* was the first horror film to present violence in a realistic, almost documentary fashion. Filmgoers at the time were deeply shaken by it.

The director, Wes Craven, had never made a movie before. In fact, he had little background in films. Raised in an orthodox Baptist family in a suburb of Cleveland, his religious upbringing was so strict that as a boy he was forbidden to see movies, and it wasn't until he was a junior in college that he saw his first movie in a theater. The film was *To Kill a Mockingbird*, and he was "bowled over by it"—though not in quite the same way audiences were later affected by his first film.

Though surprised and perhaps even alarmed by what he had produced, Craven returned to the horror genre in his next film, *The Hills Have Eyes*. Once again the film concerned a family fighting for survival, once again the violence was graphically realistic, and once again his film became a box office success. Since then, Wes Craven has not wanted for work. He followed *The Hills Have Eyes* with a television movie called *Stranger in Our House*, a witchcraft thriller starring Linda Blair. His next feature, *Deadly Blessing*, was released last summer. Set amidst a fanatical religious sect, the film starred Maren Jensen, Lois Nettleton, and Ernest Borgnine.

Craven's latest film is *Swamp Thing*, a screen adaptation of a popular DC comic book. It stars Louis Jourdan and Adrienne Barbeau. Appropriately enough, the film was shot in the swamps of Charleston, South Carolina, and it was on location that we caught up with its director.

Wes Craven is forty-one years old, divorced, and the father of two teenagers. He's so pleasant-looking, good-natured, and soft-spoken that it's hard to imagine Craven as the director of two of the most violent films ever made. But he's extremely articulate, especially on the subject of films as a means of exploring both fantasies and nightmares.

TZ: Tell us a bit about your background and how you got involved in films in the first place.

Craven: I was born and raised in Cleveland, and I began writing at a very early age. I wrote short stories when I was a teenager. I wrote for the high school newspaper and the college literary magazine, and I ended up getting a scholarship to the writing seminars at Johns Hopkins. I studied for a master's degree there under the poet Elliot Coleman, who was a friend of E. E. Cummings and T. S. Eliot. It was a very eye-opening experience for me because all we did under the program was read—modern novelists, Theatre of the Absurd, modem poets—and then write work of our own. I wrote a novel, and the comment on it was "This would make a hell of a movie." It was very strange because before that I had absolutely no idea of going into films.

TZ: What was the title of the novel?
Craven: *Noah's Ark: The Diaries of a Madman.*

TZ: Did you try to get it published?
Craven: Yeah, but nothing ever happened with it. I went through years of writing stuff and sending it off, but without much success. So after graduate school, I got married and began teaching college. I taught humanities and modern drama at Clarkson College, which is in upstate New York. About four years later, just for the hell of it, I made a little film with some of my students. It was a *Mission: Impossible* type story, and we got all the townspeople in on it and a lot of the student body. It was forty-five minutes long and cost about three hundred dollars. We started showing it, charging fifty cents, and funnily enough, everybody started coming. We ended up making about three thousand dollars on it. More importantly, I got bitten by the bug. So I quit my job and went down to New York City to try to get into the film business. I spent the whole summer going around to all the

documentary places, but I couldn't get a job. I went back upstate and taught a year of high school, then went back down the next year. But this time I had a contact; a brother of a student friend of mine was Harry Chapin, the singer.

TZ: How did he help you?

Craven: At that time, Chapin was a real hotshot film editor, and he let me work with him while he explained how film was edited. Of course, I wasn't getting paid or anything. However, while I was there, the office we were in fired its messenger, a seventeen-year-old kid. Chapin came in and asked me if I knew any kids who wanted to work as a messenger. I said, "I'll do it." So even though I was thirty at the time, I took the job as a messenger. Meanwhile, I was learning how to sync up dailies. About a year later, I got a chance to switch jobs and actually work at syncing up on a little film that Sean Cunningham was doing. Cunningham was twenty-nine years old, and he was doing some little pasted-together picture with one cameraman and himself. They called me in as an assistant, and during the next ten months he and the cameraman would keep having fallings out and the cameraman would leave. I'd say, "Well, I can edit a little." And I'd start cutting the picture. Then I'd say, "Well, I can write a little." And I'd get to write some.

TZ: Was this Cunningham's film *Together*?

Craven: Right. It cost about seventy thousand dollars and made, I think, around seven million. The distribution company was Hallmark Producing, up in Boston. They said to us, "You know, you guys should do a real knock-down drag-out horror film. We'll give you fifty thousand dollars to do it." Sean came to me and said, "Listen, I think we can do this in about three weeks for forty thousand, and we'll pocket the rest. Can you come up with anything? I said I'd try. I was going out to Long Island for the weekend, and while I was there, I wrote the first draft of *Last House on the Left*. It was about fifty pages long.

TZ: Were you a horror buff yourself at this point?

Craven: No, not at all. I was just given the genre and told to come up with a story that takes place mostly out of doors and uses a very small cast. We were going to shoot it in sixteen millimeter with all amateur actors. That's how it started. So I wrote the script, and when I went to pick it up at the Xerox place, two days in a row it wasn't ready. The guy confessed that everybody was reading it. I realized then that it was good. We sent it off to Boston, and they loved it too. They even gave us another forty thousand. So for ninety thousand dollars, we made *Last House on the Left*. It's still playing today. In fact, I think it's number ten on the top-grossing fifty this week in *Variety*.

TZ: Were you surprised by the film's success?

Craven: Absolutely. I never expected anybody to go see it. We were doing it on a ten-cent budget, and I'd never made a film before—never directed, not even edited a whole feature. We never expected anything that big. But all of a sudden it just took off. I was living in a commune on the Lower East Side, living on seventy-five dollars a week, and all of a sudden I got a check for twenty thousand dollars. The next week it was another big check. It was all very unreal. Very strange.

TZ: What about the audience response to *Last House on the Left*? How did you react to that?

Craven: In a way, it's haunted me for a long time. As you know, the film is very violent. Not in a gory way, but because it's human. You know, the characters really suffer. The film gripped and upset a lot of people. Consequently, Sean and I spent two or three years after that writing and developing scripts of social importance. However, no one was interested in them. I finally went out to California and made *The Hills Have Eyes*.

TZ: How many years were there in between?

Craven: *House* came out in '71 and *The Hills Have Eyes* was produced in '75.

TZ: So you tried to break out of the horror genre in between but found there was no interest on the part of producers?

Craven: Right. I wrote Liz Torres's cabaret comedy act two times. I edited a lot of films, edited trailers. Wrote a lot of scripts for pay. But I didn't get anything produced until *The Hills Have Eyes*.

TZ: Tell us about the origin of that film.

Craven: *The Hills Have Eyes* was originally written as a near-future drama, taking place during the 1984 presidential primaries. People were trying to get out of New York because it was too terrible to live there anymore. They had to have passports to cross the George Washington Bridge and state passports to cross from one state to another. Everybody was trying to get to the Sun Belt. The family in the original script decided to sneak along back roads to get to California. It was like *Grapes of Wrath* set in 1984. However, we ended up moving it back to the present because the producers felt it would be too expensive to set it in the future.

TZ: *The Hills Have Eyes* concerns a civilized family confronting a barbaric one. The theme of families living on the outskirts of civilization is one you often find in American literature as well as in films. Were you deliberately working in that genre?

Craven: In a way. I was very much interested in dealing with mirror images of people. The two families actually were mirror images of each other, the darker side and the lighter side. Each family had its own integrity and its own system of values, but ultimately, they became very similar. The All-American family, the white bread family, became progressively more and more vicious. They bragged about their dogs. They had guns secreted away. And their paranoia eventually turned them violent. What I'm saying in the film is that there's a brutal, barbaric nature in all of us.

TZ: I can see that. Especially since you never once asked us to really dislike either family.

Craven: No. I don't want the audience to totally dislike anyone in my films. Even the villains in *Last House on the Left*. After they've killed those girls and done horrible things, the next minute they're doing something very human, like washing up in the lake or trying to be gentlemanly at the table, trying to pass for middle class. Despite what they did, suddenly you sympathize with them again.

TZ: What effect did *The Hills Have Eyes* have on your career?

Craven: Quite a lot. It was written up in a lot of magazines, so I got a chance to direct a television show with Linda Blair and Carol Lawrence—*Stranger in Our House*. It was the first time I'd worked with name stars. We had a twenty-one-day shooting schedule and turned out a really nice film. It's played all over the world as a feature, under the title *Summer of Fear*. Linda Blair plays a girl whose aunt and uncle are killed in a crash out of state, and her cousin comes to live with her. In subtle ways, things start going wrong for her, and she begins to realize that the cousin's a witch. Of course, nobody believes her. But her horse goes crazy, her father falls in love with the new girl, and everything goes wrong, until eventually in the last act, she takes the cousin on as a witch and does battle with her. What I like most about the film is the paranoid angle. Is it all her imagination, like everybody's telling her? Or is the girl really a witch? The uncertainty continues through most of the film.

TZ: Your most recent picture was *Deadly Blessing*. Tell us about its origin.

Craven: The same producer that I did *Stranger in Our House* for, Max Keller of Interplanetary Productions, owned a property called *Deadly Blessing*. It was sort of a *Charlie's Angels* rip-off about three girls in the country, one of whom was married to an Amish fellow who was murdered in the first act. The two girlfriends come to stay with her, more murders occur, and they solve the crime and survive. I did a one-week rewrite on it as a favor for him. I think I charged him five hundred dollars for what I did. It floated around for a year, and all of a sudden Polygram picked it up. So I went down to Texas, and after three weeks of preproduction we did the picture. It turned out very well. Polygram is very excited about it because it looks like about a five- to eight-million-dollar picture, although it cost only about three million. It stars Ernest Borgnine and Lois Nettleton, and a guy from *The Hills Have Eyes*, Michael Berryman, plays a part in it.

It's my kind of film. It has wonderful dream sequences, which I love. One of the girls is a little crazy and half the time experiences horrors that turn out to be nightmares. And there's a lot of use of animals, which I like to do in my pictures. There's a great scene in a bathtub where Maren Jensen is taking a bath, and you see somebody sneak in. It's the Hitchcock shower scene updated. Instead of using a knife, her assailant puts a water moccasin on the floor. Of course, she's still bathing, and as she's covering her face with a washcloth and singing, you see the water moccasin crawl across the bathroom floor, up over the tub, and down into the water. It swims right between her legs and disappears. I won't tell you the rest of it, only that it sends everybody right up the wall.

TZ: I can imagine. You said, "My kind of film." What do you consider your kind of picture?

Craven: I like pictures that deal with situations that at first seem real and tame, but gradually turn more and more nightmarish. They're sort of half fantasy, half real and deal with very deep-seated subconscious fears. I'm very interested in dreams and nightmares. I think films are dreams. They're manufactured realities that we created to help allay our fears and deal with our terrors in a magical way. I find that the mixture of dreams within films does precisely that.

TZ: Is *Deadly Blessing* as graphically violent as your two previous films?

Craven: No, it has very little actual violence. There's a lot of tension and suspense and scares, but it has very little graphic violence in it. I'm very interested in getting away from that. I think it's a dead-end street. Sean Cunningham's picture, *Friday the 13th*, helped to revive that kind of horror picture, but otherwise it's been exhausted for some time. Right now I'm more interested in Hitchcockian kinds of terror and suspense.

TZ: Would you list Hitchcock as one of your prime influences?

Craven: Definitely. Along with Buñuel and Bergman. My whole background in film came quite late in life because I wasn't allowed to see films when I was a kid. I didn't start to see them until I was in the university. So I saw all the "foreign film club" type classics: Truffaut, Buñuel, Hitchcock. They became my inspiration.

TZ: This brings us to *Swamp Thing*, your current film. How did you come to make it?
Craven: I had been working on a film for a year in Colombia, South America. It was about dope smuggling and had an Italian producer. I'd just gone to Rome, where our preproduction had fallen through. We'd set up offices and hired the cast, only to find out that the producer didn't have his money. Coming back through New York, my agent told me about these two producers, Michael Uslan and Ben Melniker, that I should stop in and see. I went to see them, and they showed me the *Swamp Thing* comic books. We talked about what would happen if a man were half-plant and half-human. I said, joking around, "Well, maybe he would be photosynthetic and get weak if he were kept in the dark a long time." We started tossing around ideas, and they said, "Why don't you write up a treatment?" On the plane to LA, I wrote it up and mailed it back to them. They liked it. I did a first draft, and they liked that, too. It just took off from there.

TZ: Were you familiar with the *Swamp Thing* comic book before?
Craven: Not at all. I had read comic books as a kid, but mostly *Superman*, *Batman*, and *Blackhawk*. But what fascinated me about *Swamp Thing* in terms of a movie was that he was a monster who had a human being inside. A monster that maintains all of his human capabilities, mental capabilities, and emotions. It had what I saw as a *Beauty and the Beast* feeling that would enable me to explore how a human being feels about his darker side or his ugly side being exposed, and whether or not someone can love that. That was the really interesting thing to me—the love story. One of the major changes I made from the comic book was to change Cable from a male character to the part now played by Adrienne Barbeau. She provides the love interest for the monster.

TZ: Another change seems to be the creation of a second, villainous monster. I'm talking about Arcane, who I gather also becomes transformed.
Craven: Right. What I've done is to take characters from throughout the many stories in the comic books. Arcane is a villain who appears in one of them; I simply took that name and created a character. But there is a sequence in the comic book where one of the villains changes into a werewolf-type monster, so in fact there is precedent for it.

TZ: What about the look of the comic book? Do you plan on somehow trying to translate that?
Craven: Sure. We're going for a sort of stylistic low angle. Strange shadows, weird colors, and fogs. Very much of a comic-book look, but in tandem with a very realistic human approach. For example, everybody who's in contact with the monster reacts to it very much like you and I would—with unbelief. We're trying to keep all

the emotions very human, rather than making them camp or exaggerated. We're generally underplaying it a lot. Louis Jourdan, for instance, is playing Arcane as a very aristocratic and subtle villain, not the moustache-tweaking villain of yore.

TZ: Why do you think *Swamp Thing* caught on as a comic and became a cult?

Craven: I think because he's sort of a green James Dean, an outsider you can iden-tify with. There's a part of all of us, I think, that feels that we're the ugly duckling, that nobody can really relate to the real us, and that we're sort of a creepazoid just wandering around in a world of our own making. And I think *Swamp Thing* has that feeling to it. Inside this monster there's this beautiful person he knows is there, but which he can't convey to anybody else. It's like when people look at Wes Craven, the filmmaker, and say, "How can you make those terribly violent films?" It's like I'm a Swamp Thing. All of us have this, but especially kids. They're still forming their personalities and have a lot of unfettered urges and wishes. Their parents think they're monsters anyway, so they can easily relate to someone who rushes into a room and smashes the whole thing to smithereens or who goes out and gets completely muddy. There's a likability about a monster who's very primitive and direct in all his needs and desires. He feels different from everyone else around him, and that's how kids feel. They're in an adult world, and they're expected to conform.

TZ: When a comic book comes to life, everyone has his own preconceived ideas as to whom they would cast. How did you come to choose the stars in *Swamp Thing*—for example, Louis Jourdan as Arcane?

Craven: Louis Jourdan actually came across the table at a late date. He wasn't a first choice. We went through a long list of typical villains—Telly Savalases—and we were turned down by a lot of people who didn't want to do a horror film, es-pecially one with a monster. Christopher Lee, for instance, liked the script a lot but didn't want to do something where he'd have to be a monster. But when we eventually thought of Louis Jourdan, he suddenly seemed a natural. And he saw something in the script that fascinated him. I often get that reaction to my scripts. An actor might not want to do a horror movie, but he'll read the script and see that the character gets a lot of good moments. I like to write solid dramatic moments for all the characters in my film.

TZ: Was Adrienne Barbeau a first choice for the female Cable?

Craven: No. Again the producers had their sights on some of the foremost names in the business. Adrienne Barbeau we came to later—but what a fantastic choice she's been! She's a real trooper. She does all her own stunts, including drowning scenes in water I wouldn't want to stick my hand in.

TZ: The film seems to have more special effects and stunt sequences than any of your earlier films. Has that made it more of a challenge?

Craven: Definitely. It's a very difficult shoot, the most difficult I've ever done. I'm working quite often up to my ass in alligators and water snakes. There's a lot of deer flies and bugs, a lot of sickness in the crew. We're working with costumes that tend to fall apart in the water after a take or two, and big elaborate sets that make it hard just getting off a shot. So we're behind schedule and a little over budget. It's been very arduous. You know, I run a lot, five to six miles a day, sometimes even fifteen, and this has taxed my physical limits.

TZ: What are your future projects after *Swamp Thing*?

Craven: The first thing I'm going to do is go lie on a beach somewhere. After that I have a project called *A Nightmare on Elm Street*, which I'd like to do next. I wrote it myself. It's about a teenage girl who has nightmares that start to come true. Everybody thinks she's insane. But she takes on the person in the nightmares and tries to bring him out into the real world, where she can prove to people that he is alive and that he is committing murders.

TZ: As a director, you seem to prefer to write your own scripts. Are there any books in the horror genre or other novels that you'd be interested in adapting?

Craven: I'm not at the stage where I can possess those properties. I'd love to do a Stephen King novel, but someone else would have to buy it and approach me about it. However, I don't mind writing my own scripts. I like my ideas, and I'm more interested in solving my own problems than in trying to solve someone else's.

TZ: What other horror or suspense filmmakers do you like?

Craven: Hitchcock, as I said earlier. And I like many of Roman Polanski's films, *The Tenant* and *Repulsion*, for example.

TZ: What about some of the other classics of the genre? I would guess that *Freaks* might be a favorite of yours. Is that true?

Craven: Not so much. I consider *Texas Chainsaw Massacre* to be a brilliant film. And *Night of the Living Dead* I enjoyed immensely. I'm interested in films that go below the surface of madness or insanity. When I saw *Texas Chainsaw Massacre*, it frightened me so much that I felt the people who made it must have been insane. Of course, I also like *Last House on the Left*. In terms of low-budget scary films, I think those three are my favorites.

TZ: Some critics have claimed that the extreme violence of a film like *Texas Chainsaw Massacre* may help to inspire the tremendous amount of violence we have in our society. Do you think that's true?

Craven: I don't think a movie inspires violence any more than a flash of sunlight in a windshield might cause someone to flip out. I think it's the nature of our society that produces such violence—the overcrowding and pressure that causes some people to crack. If anything, these films offer a pressure release, the same way a nightmare operates physiologically: they take you into a space that in your normal, rational state, you would not take yourself. They seem to have some therapeutic function. Also, you have to remember, people were assassinating presidents long before television and movies. John Wilkes Booth didn't see *Texas Chainsaw Massacre*.

TZ: One final question. Is there anything that frightens Wes Craven?

Craven: Yes. My shooting schedule.

Wes Craven

Alan Jones / 1982

Original feature written by Alan Jones and published in *STARBURST* Magazine, Issue No. 44, April 1982. Reprinted by permission.

"Can a movie go too far?" said the catch-line for one of the watershed gore movies of the early '70s. And for once a film lived up to its advertising in many people's eyes. It was for *The Last House on the Left*, and it made such an enormous impact that its effect still reverberates with anyone who has seen it. Depending on your point of view, it is either a moving and violently deromanticized look at America during the Vietnam era or a despicable and utterly degrading voyeuristic experience. I happen to be in the latter school of thought, and along with other aspects of his career, I put my feelings to director Wes Craven when he was in London recently, just as he finished the arduous filming of his latest movie, *Swamp Thing*.

"I have to be honest, even for me now it isn't a pleasant film to watch, but I genuinely felt I portrayed what it actually felt like to kill somebody for real. The killing is absolutely heartless, the protracted violence was very human to me. I wanted to make a statement about violence and American movies at the time. You must remember that I made the film at the time when people were watching villages being burned on the news as they ate their dinner. Nobody comes out of *The Last House on the Left* looking noble after they have killed somebody, even though it may have been for the right reasons."

The producer of *The Last House on the Left* was Sean S. Cunningham, now better known to contemporary audiences as the director of *Friday the 13th*. The photographer (super 16mm) was Steve Miner, who made his directorial debut with that successful film's sequel. This talented collective were able to make *The Last House on the Left* when Cunningham's previous film became extraordinarily successful. It was a pornographic sex instruction film called *Together* and featured an actress called Marilyn Briggs, who later changed her surname to Chambers. This led to one of the top exploitation-releasing companies, Hallmark, showing interest in the film that was to become *The Last House on the Left*. The story was a virtual remake of Ingmar Bergman's *The Virgin Spring* as it told of two girls on their way to a rock concert who are kidnapped and sexually tortured by a quartet of sadists. After murdering both girls, the killers wind up in the home of one of the dead girl's parents who, upon finding the disemboweled body of their daughter floating in a nearby pond, exact an equally horrendous assault on the killers themselves. The film was the first to feature that recent icon of horror movies, the chainsaw as the epitome of the murderous weapon, but according to Craven, Tobe Hooper says he has never seen the film. The disemboweling, the attempted lesbian rape, and the carving of initials on one of the girl's stomachs is disgusting and disturbing to watch. But it is precisely this emotion that Craven was after. "The film never leaves anybody unmoved. They are either fascinated, upset, drained, or very angry. The film has such an undeniable strength that to discuss it, it really is like a war; you don't want to go back to it. When I think about it, I thought I was adding a cartoon dimension to offset the onscreen carnage but . . ."

Craven expected the film to have a small circulation and was surprised that the film became the popular success it did. It was recently rereleased in America in a slightly cut version and once again did very good box-office. Cunningham apparently wanted even more blood in the film, but Craven's directorial restraint meant he didn't shoot the heroine's feet being singed by cigarettes and a scene featuring a rat that even I am not prepared to describe. After the film's success Craven was approached to do more of the same, but he refused. "'Why not two disembowelings?' they would say. I decided that when I did go back to doing a film like that again I would be less intense and use suspense rather than raw emotion. I never want to get back into that level of opening up violence on the screen. *The Last House on the Left* was an apocryphal film. I can't go back and find a film earlier than that in the genre that became so established of breaking barriers of what is allowed to be shown. *Psycho*, I suppose. . . . Sometimes I think it was a terrible film to make, other times I'm glad I was that angry."

Craven then spent three years trying to move into other areas but was always turned down because of the very strong typecasting of *The Last House on the Left*. "I wrote a very ambitious film called *Mustang*, which was based on the true life story of a colonel who was court-martialed for reporting American atrocities in Vietnam. All I wanted was a half-million dollars, but nobody wanted to listen. So I wrote *The Hills Have Eyes*."

The simple story of *The Hills Have Eyes* has the Carter family on holiday in their trailer. When they break down in the Californian desert, they are attacked by a family of savage cannibals, and after one of their number is killed and another kidnapped, they find the only course open to them is to retaliate on the same violent level. The film has a very effective nightmare reality, and as he purposely set out to thrill and shock and consciously appeal to a demanding audience, Craven succeeds admirably. As with *The Last House on the Left*, *The Hills Have Eyes* dealt with family microcosms. "Well they do say that you write about what you're closest to and what you experienced first. My deepest impressions come from my family, so a lot of that works its way out through my movies. I didn't have a particularly horrendous childhood, but I did suffer severe emotional stresses. A lot of things are planted deeply in the mind. The family to me is a very potent amalgam of what we later experience in the broadest sense. I set out to have the two families in *The Hills Have Eyes* be mirror images of each other just so I could explore the different sides of the human personality—the two brothers being the antipodes of each other within the bounds of popular entertainment. I wanted that sort of complexity within the framework of something more sophisticated than *The Last House on the Left*. I didn't want to ever feel uncomfortable again about making a statement about human depravity—and then engaging in it to make the point."

For his next film, Wes Craven proved he was working along the same lines as John Carpenter, whose *Halloween* had just opened to eventual worldwide acclaim. It was an NBC-TV movie of the week called *Stranger in Our House*, and it was considered good enough to release theatrically outside the USA as *Summer of Fear*. The subject matter appealed to Craven as much as American television's strict censorship code meant that he would have to make the film a study in unseen terror. As he says, "I wasn't allowed to have any violence, and the story didn't need it anyway."

Based on the novel by Lois Duncan, *Summer of Fear* continued in the same thematic territory of his previous films, that of an All-American family under threat, although this time it comes from within the actual family circle. The Bryants give a home to their cousin Julia, a relation they have never seen, when her parents are killed in a car crash. In reality, Julia is a witch practicing a form of Ozarkian Black Magic, and before long she has alienated their daughter Rachel from her family, stolen her boyfriend, killed her favorite horse, and threatens to take over as Mrs. Bryant by having the mother killed in an accident. The film contains an exceptional performance by Linda Blair as Rachel and some fine imagery, like Julia, eyes blazing, bursting out of a dark room in slow-motion. With *Summer of Fear*, Craven lost his exploitation tag and his next film. *Deadly Blessing* was his step into mainstream cinema. Before *Deadly Blessing*, however, things looked a little bleak. "I had written a script called *Marimba* about drug smuggling. Dirk Benedict and Tim McIntyre were cast, but the money I was promised from Italy never came through. The same people had asked me to write a script on the Guyana tragedy, and I wrote it thinking, "My God, I'm going from being a director of horror films to a director of horrifying true incidents." I was really thankful when that was scrapped. I was really anxious to be working again. I hadn't done a feature since *The Hills Have Eyes*, and I began to think I would never work again. I quickly latched

onto the first thing I could, and it turned out to be *Swamp Thing*. So I started working on that when the scriptwriters of *Summer of Fear* asked me to do a rewrite on
a script they had had some interest in. It was called *Deadly Blessing*, and while the
producers of *Swamp Thing* decided about the script I had done for them, I did the
rewrite and from that moment on jumped between the two projects until I filmed
them virtually on top of each other."

Deadly Blessing is a psychological thriller in the vein that Craven likens to
Hitchcockian and is about three women being terrorized in rural Pennsylvania
by a fanatical group of religious zealots called Hittites. The film works best in its
quieter, moodier moments, something that Craven realized when he took on the
film. "*Deadly Blessing* had a very complex story, and to my mind not a good one,
but the money was there. The film would have a good distributor, and it was a
chance to work with some interesting people. So I did it. I tried to minimize the
problems with the script due to all those red herrings, and I thought I clarified it
as much as I could. I guessed the film would live or die on its images rather than
rely on great storytelling coherence. I'm pleased with the film. It came off looking
pretty good, as if it cost a lot of money, but it only cost $2.5 million dollars. It made
its money back in the first three weeks of release, and it is now well into profit."

One of the best things in the film is the shock ending. Craven was astute
enough to realize that audiences these days are now well prepared for a final twist
in the last seconds of a film and decided to go for broke with an absolutely smash-
ing tongue-in-cheek pyrotechnic firework display. You are guaranteed to leave the
cinema in sheer disbelief in what you've just seen. "I did the ending as a send up.
It became quite apparent early on that having an ending with the girls just saying
goodbye to each other wouldn't be enough. To my astonishment, the producers
gave in to my demand for the new ending, despite it being off-the-wall to say the
least. It cost $200,000 to film as we had to reconstruct the set, but I was really
thankful to them for letting me do it. The only argument we did have was that they
wanted to shake the building before the effect, but I thought that would only alert
the audience that something big was about to happen. I lost."

The finale was solely the work of Everett Alson and Ira Anderson as John Dyk-
sta, who was initially approached, had other commitments. *Deadly Blessing*, despite its complex plot, I thought [was] an easy whodunnit to work out. When I
told Craven that my policy of watching films in this genre very closely for the first
five minutes, as it was those that usually contained the answer, had paid off yet
again, he laughingly promised to make a mental note and fool me the next time
he made a film in that genre.

Craven liked *Swamp Thing* much better as it was his from the start, even though
the producers of the picture made his life hell. "They fired my cinematographer
and the production manager and kept asking me why I needed this shot and that

shot and why I needed all the coverage I was shooting. The reason for this was the film was being done on the cheap, and they were under a completion bond. The film couldn't and doesn't rely on its special effects. As the producers went for the person who did the effects on the basis of who gave the lowest quote, you can understand why I had to make the film more a human experience."

Craven wrote the screenplay as well as directed the $3 million production and was told by DC Comics that he could change the story of their ill-fated comic book character in any way he thought best. "But in actual fact, I changed very little apart from peripheral characters." The story of *Swamp Thing*, for those who have not read the comic books, concerns Dr. Alec Holland, a brilliant scientist who has discovered a formula that stimulates plant growth, which he realizes would solve the world hunger problem. However, a madman named Arcane wants to rule the world with Holland's discovery, and in a fight with his henchmen, Holland is splashed with the solution, which bursts into flames causing him to run and disappear into the surrounding swamp land. The chemical reacts with the swamp waters turning him into a hideous half-man/half-plant being able to regrow severed limbs and take nourishment via his roots. He also finds out he's invulnerable and sets out to avenge his sister who was murdered by Arcane's ruthless men.

"I changed the character of Cable, who is obsessed with finding out who the Swamp Thing is, into a woman so I could add a romantic element and work the story more on a *Beauty and the Beast* level. Then I realized I would have to change Holland's murdered wife into his sister as I didn't think it would be valid that three days after losing his wife he would be running around after Cable. There is also an Arcane character in the original story that was a magician, but here he's just an international villain. In fact, I'm combining all of *Swamp Thing*'s villains into just one, which is where Arcane gets transformed into a monster." The film, which was shot on location in and around Charleston, South Carolina, has been given a distinct comic book style by Craven, "Lots of low angles, strange shadows, weird colors, and fog."

Although he wishes they could have had something equally as spectacular as the transformation scene in *The Howling*, Craven is glad that he turned down the idea of an electronically animated creature. "For the quote we were given, I just knew we would never be able to pull it off. We would still be shooting now! There was also talk of fully motorized heads, but I knew it wouldn't work. The money was all there, but it was an inadequate amount for the picture. *Swamp Thing* is apparently a dry run for the producers to do *Batman*. If it's the same conditions I was working under, I wish whoever will be the director the best of luck."

The complex special make-up requirements were the work of thirty-two-year-old Bill Munns. It was his offer of $80,000 that the producers couldn't refuse, and he built the latex suits in the film. Although the suits were lightweight enough to help the stuntmen move properly and in theory reinforced enough to handle the weight of swamp water, it was discovered that the swamps secreted an acid into the water that corroded the suits after a short while. Bill Munns found he had to spray an antacid solution onto the costumes to reduce this effect. Munns's suit for the amalgam of monsters that Arcane becomes was designed with the mane of a lion, the face of a boar, and a reptilian body, and it was a design that won Craven's full support: "the upshot is that it all came together looking quite nice even though the special effects and make-ups aren't what it's about at all—I kinda like it—it's different. I don't know who's going to pay and see it, but we'll see."

Swamp Thing will be released in March by Avco Embassy in the States and hopefully not long after that in Great Britain by United Artists. As a result of these last two films, more doors have opened for Wes Craven. He is hoping for example that his script called *Circus Gang*, about the children of circus folk, will be filmed shortly by either Disney or Fox. Although he really does want to leave the genre and be known as a director rather than an exploitation director, it looks like his next film will, in fact, be in the genre where he first made his name. "It's called *A Nightmare on Elm Street*, and it is essentially about a girl who dreams about being followed by a man who wants to kill her. She is so frightened by this dream that she tells a girlfriend. The next day she is murdered in her sleep, and then her girlfriend starts to have the same dream. The murderer getting closer and closer every time she falls asleep. So, it looks like I'll be toiling in the horror field for a little while longer." I actually hope for a lot longer. After my talk with Wes Craven, I only have the greatest admiration and respect for the director once dubbed "the hardcore maniac of violence."

Wes Craven's *Deadly* Doubleheader

Lee Goldberg and David McDonnell / 1986

From *Fangoria* 57, September 1986. Reprinted by permission of Joseph A. Sonnier IV, CEO of *Cinestate* and *Fangoria*.

Keep an eye on Wes Craven. He's in the midst of a transformation—and not the kind you would see in one of his movies. The director of such cult horror hits as *The Hills Have Eyes*, *Last House on the Left*, *Deadly Blessing*, *Swamp Thing*, and the enormously successful *A Nightmare on Elm Street* is trying to change his image.

It's a concerted effort that began in earnest last fall, when he helmed six diverse segments of *The Twilight Zone* aimed at showing the entertainment industry he could do more than low-budget splatter films. He even did a segment for *The Disney Sunday Movie*. Well, the campaign is paying off. Craven has just wrapped up his first medium-budget studio film. It's called *Deadly Friend*, it's for Warner Bros., and it tells the story of a teenage boy whose robot gets destroyed by a nasty neighbor and whose girlfriend is killed by an abusive father. So he takes a computer chip from the robot, puts it in his dead girlfriend, and she comes back to life. She starts hunting down the people who did her—and the robot—wrong.

Craven, eager to shift into mainstream moviemaking, likes to call it a love story. Warner Bros., eager to latch onto that *Nightmare on Elm Street* audience, bills it as horror. Whatever it is, it has Craven on the studio lot and out of the ramshackle soundstages of grade-B filmdom. And it's here that he would like to stay. But for old time's sake, he just finished coscripting *Nightmare on Elm Street 3*!

Fango: How did you get involved with *Deadly Friend*?
Wes Craven: The producer, Bob Sherman, sought me out after *A Nightmare on Elm Street*. He had the rights to the novel *Friend*. I liked the fact that it was in the genre, and yet it wasn't the story of a slasher, it wasn't a story of teenagers being victimized by an adult, and it had more well-rounded characters than many of the things I was being offered. It was also with a major studio, which was very important to me.

Fango: Was the script already written when you came on the project?

Craven: No. We got together and selected the writer.

Fango: Why didn't you write it?

Craven: Because I was doing *Twilight Zone* at the time and I just didn't have the time. We selected Bruce Rubin based on his unproduced script *Jacob's Ladder* and on our story meetings.

Fango: Are you happy with the title change?

Craven: I was upset about it. I'm getting used to it now. I really would have much preferred just *Friend*. They went through hundreds of titles, and we had all sorts of meetings. Marketing wanted a title with punch.

Fango: Will *Deadly Friend* satisfy the fans of *The Hills Have Eyes* and *A Nightmare on Elm Street*?

Craven: I think so. It won't satisfy, perhaps, fans looking for a bloodbath, but fans who have been maturing along with me. I had a belated adolescence, and I'm getting a little more sophisticated in my work. Those fans will probably find it intriguing because it has the Wes Craven elements in it, but it also has some interesting human things, too.

Fango: Why is Warner Bros. having you reshoot parts of *Deadly Friend*?

Craven: We're not reshooting as much as shooting additional scenes. We started off doing a picture that Warner Bros. indicated they wanted to do, a macabre love story with a twist. About five weeks into the shoot, they realized who I was and told me not to be inhibited by what they had told me in the past. In a way, I had held back. So in the last week of shooting, I made up one little nightmare scene and put it into the film. It was the big hit of the screening. So, then, they came to me and said, "Well, listen, what we need is more of that stuff." What we're doing is adding to the deaths of a few people, a jump for the beginning, a new closing scene, and two nightmares—that sort of Wes Craven touch.

Fango: Are you trying to make these scenes more graphic?

Craven: It is going to be more graphic. We're killing Anne Ramsey, for example, in another new, different way. The nightmare sequences will sneak up on people. I'm not going to go into the dream state because that's the province of *A Nightmare on Elm Street*. I don't want to twist the story around just to get in that neighborhood. On the other hand, there are nightmares that seem to be real at first, so in that sense, you're in the dream state; but they stay more within the boundaries of hard reality rather than what I call rubber reality—where you can pass through walls. That remains the world of Freddy.

Fango: Originally, doing *Deadly Friend*, *The Twilight Zones* and the Disney movie were a way to try to get one step away from hardcore horror to softer subjects. Do you feel Warner Bros. is now pulling you back?

Craven: To an extent, yes. But I'm willing to go along. The picture still has a lot of elements, nice dramatic scenes. I don't think it's going to ruin that progression in my career at all—the next picture I may do doesn't have any murders in at all. *The Twilight Zones* are out there being seen. I feel more relaxed about it now. If more horror is what the studio and the audience want, I enjoy doing that kind of scene, too. It's not going to ruin the other parts of the picture. It's always fun to have someone say, "Here's some money, go out and do something that's wacky and crazy."

Fango: Are you now a studio director, more of a mainstream name?

Craven: I think I am a more mainstream name, which I became automatically after a hit picture. The six *Twilight Zones* that I did were very, very helpful because they showed a broad range of subject matter that I could do. I never want to lose that crazy edge, but I certainly would like to have a larger audience, bigger budgets, better writers.

Fango: How do you feel about what has happened with your *A Nightmare on Elm Street* idea?

Craven: It's odd. It was astonishing. I found out I had no participation in the sequel. It was very upsetting. I realized I had created this wonderful character that somebody else was going to get fabulously wealthy on. [New Line President] Bob Shaye bought it from me outright.

Fango: You knew at the time that a sequel was a strong possibility. You left the door open for it in your script.

Craven: I assumed I was going to share in the sequels. Sean Cunningham, a good friend of mine, has made a lot of money off those *Friday the 13th* sequels. I just assumed it was in my contract. Then, I went back and looked at my contract and it wasn't.

Fango: So what arrangement has been worked out for *Nightmare 3*?

Craven: Well, I'm going to write it and perhaps direct it. I will actually be co-writing it with another very good writer named Bruce Wagner.

Fango: How does *Nightmare 2* fit into the storyline?

Craven: I'm ignoring it.

Fango: So, in the new one, we won't see any *Nightmare 2* characters or references to events from that film?

Craven: No.

Fango: Freddy just shows up?

Craven: Not quite. The plan is to bring back Nancy and her father [Heather Langenkamp and John Saxon]. I don't want to give away too much here, but basically, the back story is that the father was a very straight guy who never believed any of this stuff was possible. When he glimpses his wife being dragged through a bed and disappearing and sees the rest of what has happened, his entire life is changed. He pursues Freddy back through Freddy's past to the house where Freddy was born. Nancy follows her father who has essentially gone mad and left his job. And they both end up in the house of Freddy. We're exploring not only dreams but other states of altered reality within the human consciousness, and we'll be trailing through all of them. Also, this house will be sort of an architectural portal to that world. It is virtually a limitless world of the human psyche in all of its dimensions, many of which will be explored. So you can enter this other world through the house or dreams or madness or hallucinations or special psychic states that various people have. There will be a group of very special kids who will align themselves with Nancy and her father to fight Freddy. Freddy is about to pass on to a higher level of evil, greater powers, expanded effects on others. Freddy's moving up. These people are the last stand against him before he gets so big that no one can stop him.

Fango: Why are you returning?

Craven: I realized that New Line really wanted a Wes Craven *Nightmare* for 3 and that idea appealed to me in and of itself. It feels like 3 may be lucky somehow. I thought it might be fun to give them a real solid story, and, frankly, I would like to direct it. I'm contractually obliged to a pay-or-play deal on another film, *Haunted*, a love story about a guy, a girl, and a ghost, for Heron Communications, whose parent company is Media Home Entertainment, one of the big funders of the *Nightmare* series. If *Haunted* does fall through, I might well try to jump in at the last minute and direct *Nightmare 3*. But otherwise, it's just being written by myself and Bruce Wagner.

Fango: What is Bruce Wagner bringing to this as a writer that you didn't have when you wrote the first one?

Craven: I wrote that alone, but back then, I had the time. The deadline for delivering the first cut of *Deadly Friend*, with the reshooting included, to Warner Bros., and the *Nightmare 3* script to New Line is virtually the same. The two things crammed in on top of each other. There was no way, physically, I could do both at once. So Bruce and I are writing together, talking through everything. He has been actually putting the stuff down on paper. Bruce has a very strange, bizarre sense of humor. He's a big fan of *Nightmare 1*. He has a real *Nightmare on Elm Street* type of imagination. He's bringing some wonderful ideas of his own to it, so it has been a good collaboration.

Fango: Robert Englund told us that he had also written a treatment for *Nightmare 3* and turned it in. Were you aware of this?
Craven: Oh really? No. I don't talk to New Line Cinema a lot. I heard at one point that they were talking to Bob about directing one. Certainly, they can use his treatment or anyone's for *Nightmare 3* and throw ours out; they have an option to do whatever they want. I've got a treatment for a *Nightmare* script from Bob Shaye's daughters—who are like thirteen and fourteen—and it wasn't bad. I'm sure there are other scripts and treatments floating around and I would suspect the *Nightmares* will be a continuing series.

Fango: Englund says he sees it only as a trilogy.
Craven: That's not true about myself. I think the *Nightmares* can go on and on. But it is hard to expand into new areas. If you do the most outstanding thing you can think of in one film, then to have to sit and think about filling ninety more minutes with new, it gets very tricky. We thought long and hard before we came up with a concept that took this movie into a whole new dimension. But I don't see why you couldn't go on, do *Son of Freddy* . . .

Fango: Will 3 be better than the first sequel?
Craven: I hope so. Bob Shaye keeps telling me that 2 was really a bigger success than 1, but I really don't believe it. I didn't like it.

Fango: I couldn't figure out all that stuff with the bus.
Craven: Neither could I, and Bob Shaye loves those scenes. At the end of *Nightmare 1*, Bob was determined that Freddy should be at the wheel of the car. He thought that would be the most terrifying thing. I absolutely refused. Freddy was defeated as far as those kids were concerned. So I decided to have Freddy at the wheel for the sequel's beginning. There are many creative differences that Bob and I have, but I think we can still work together and make a much better *Nightmare 3*.

Fango: Is *Deadly Friend* left open for a sequel?
Craven: Sure.

Fango: Then can we look forward to twenty-four more *Deadly Friends*?
Craven: Yeah. What I would like to do sooner or later is produce a film myself so I can benefit from sequels more than just watching them.

Fango: How does it feel to be on the Burbank Studios backlot making a film for Warner Bros., instead of being out in the middle of nowhere working on a shoe-string budget?
Craven: Very, very good. It's nice being on a lot with other filmmakers. My office is two doors from Sydney Pollack's. It's a great feeling. I'm far from being comfortable or smug, but it's like I'm finally in the industry, part of that moviemaking tradition.

Fango: Will people be watching this film closely to see if you can hack it in the major leagues?
Craven: I've already been feeling those results. Cannon Films approached me for *Superman IV*, and that had a $30 million budget. So the answer is yes.

Fango: *Superman IV* would have been terrific for you. What happened?
Craven: Chris Reeve and I had creative differences. He and I didn't see eye-to-eye, and he decided I wasn't the director for it. But there's a strong chance that I'll go on and do that kind of picture.

Fango: *Swamp Thing* producers Mike Uslan and Ben Melnicker are working on the *The Batman* movie. They're looking for a new director.
Craven: They've been talking about putting my name in the ring for that job. If *The Batman* was done right and had a good budget. I mean, it was my favorite comic book as a kid. I would like to go back and do *The Batman* right as a period piece.

Fango: Are you looking forward to the day when the interviewers who come knocking on your door are from *Esquire* and the *Los Angeles Times* and not genre magazines like *FANGORIA*?
Craven: I don't want to get away from anybody. I would like to include more people, though. It's always frustrating to me that large sections of the press and public are unaware of my work or haven't taken it seriously. Yeah, I would also like those people to be aware of me, but to not lose touch with the genre press and the fans I started with.

Fango: What happened to *Flowers in the Attic*?
Craven: They finally came up with the money, and they sent me a pay-or-play offer on the day after I accepted *Friend*. It was simply impossible to do. Plus, we had big creative differences.

Fango: What has happened with Roger Corman's *Frankenstein*?
Craven: I don't know. I wrote it, turned it in, and they were all happy with it. I think Tri-Star put it into turnaround and last I heard Corman's company was going to try to do it themselves.

Fango: Do you have a piece of the sequel deal on *Deadly Friend*?
Craven: I'm sure I do.

Fango: What'll it be—*The Deadlier Friend*? *The Deadlier, Bloodier Friend*?
Craven: The way my career is going, it'll be *The Nicer Friend*.

Wes Craven, Director of Nightmares

Dennis Fischer / 1988

From *Monsterland's Nightmares on Elm Street: The Freddy Krueger Story* by James Van Hise, 1988. Reprinted by permission of Dennis Fischer.

Wes Craven seems like such an unassuming, quiet, soft-spoken man that it is often difficult to believe that he was the creative force behind some of the cinema's greatest shockers. He seems more like a New England college teacher, which in fact he was and which was where he caught the filmmaking bug after having helped some students make a film.

"I quit teaching," he recalled, "and to make a long story short, I spent about a year looking for work in New York and ended up in a lower-echelon job as a messenger. I worked my way up in a postproduction house, so I learned all of the postproduction side of films.

"One of the things that I did on the side, sort of moonlighting, was the syncing of rushes for documentaries and various small films in the area. So there was this job syncing up rushes for this guy Sean Cunningham (the man who later directed the original *Friday the 13th*). I went in and did that. They had just done a reshoot on this film that they were working on, *Together*, and then after doing that for about a week, he said, 'Why don't you be an assistant editor to this guy?' There was one man who shot it, helped write it, helped direct it, and was cutting it. So I became Roger Murphy's assistant editor.

"Roger Murphy kept having fights with Sean and leaving. So then I said, 'Well, let me try to do something.' Sean and I would sit down, so by the end of the picture, I had become 'additional writing, additional editing, and additional directing by.' And by then Sean and I were close friends.

"When the film made money, the people who backed it gave us money to make a horror film of some kind. Sean suggested that we do it together, so that's how *Last House on the Left* came about. I wrote it, directed it, and cut it. Sean produced it and provided the editing facility. He had a Steenbeck. We virtually made the film together. We taught each other how to make a film by making one. *Together* was much more of a semidocumentary. *Last House* was our first feature film.

"That accounts for its rough look. I didn't know what a master was or coverage. I didn't know any of that. It was shot much more like a documentary; a lot of continuous takes with multiple coverage. We'd stage a scene three times and cover it from three different angles. It was like reinventing the typewriter. It was after that that I read all the books on coverage and masters and work prints and all that. I hadn't studied film or anything. I was going into it as sort of a hobby. I had no formal training whatsoever, so *Last House* is a very rudimentary film in some ways, but a very visceral film in other ways. Not knowing what the classic techniques were probably made it original in a way."

Last House on the Left started filming with a budget of $40,000. The people backing the film were pleased with the rushes and the ante was upped to $90,000, which still was not a great deal of money. The film is very crudely put together. It contains some noticeable lapses in continuity including a phone that stops working so constantly that it seems like the actors have to keep reminding the audience as to the phone's current status every other scene.

The basic plot is that on Mari's seventeenth birthday, she decides to go to a rock concert rather than stick around her parents' isolated country home, though her parents do not approve of her choice of a companion: a low-life teenaged girl from the wrong side of the tracks. Together the pair try to score some grass before the concert only to find four more-than-slightly deranged escaped convicts.

The sheriff's deputies try to warn Mari's parents, but the phones aren't working. They spend the entire film and almost a day in time just to travel twenty miles (the squad car runs out of gas halfway there) and arrive too late. Their ineffectiveness and bumbling incompetency make them almost as contemptible as the killers in the film.

Craven's documentary approach does, however, accentuate the killers' nightmarish attack on the two girls. There is no style or flair given to the proceedings, leaving a feeling of absolute realism as the audience must helplessly watch the prolonged torture and demise of young female victims. Part of Craven's premise is that it's tough to kill a human being, and so the horrors continue and continue as if it might never end. Mari's friend tries to escape and is finally trapped by three of the convicts in a cemetery. The scenes that were to follow were, in 1972, the grisliest, goriest scenes ever included in an American horror film. (I'm excepting Herschell Gordon Lewis's blood-splattered epics for the reasons that his films a) never managed to be convincing, and b) were defused by the addition of cornball humor and ineptness of execution.)

Commented Craven, "I think that without question that was the most powerful scene that I ever put on film. I think it was much too powerful for people to bear. You did not see her actually being stabbed, but they (the killers) went into a frenzy of stabbing. At the end, they suddenly stop. Once they started stabbing the girl and holding her, it was very sexual and murderous. It was very upsetting and strange.

"At the end, they lay her down, and the girl, Sadie, bends down and picks up a loop of intestine, and Fred says something like, 'Well, we broke her,' but he says it like she's a broken doll or something. And for a while, it looks like they're going to throw up, and they walk away. It just never stops. It's like walking into a real killing where people kill and they go into a frenzy, and then they suddenly realize what they've done, literally just broken the person open.

"It was just too intense. Everybody just seized it. Projectionists would cut it, then theater owners and distributors, until there wasn't an intact print of the film left. It was really a very early telling lesson in the vulnerability of film. It's not like you print a book and there's an intact copy of it someplace. It is a series of physical objects that are printed and go out and are attacked by everybody from projectionists to theater owners. Some prints might have escaped pulverizing. I have a friend in New York that has a complete 16mm print.

"And then Mari's death was more of a tragedy. The shooting was not, but the rape was crude and horrible. Krug carved his name on her chest. It was really horrendous. It really went on and on. A lot of it was based on things that I was reading that were going on in Vietnam, you know, cutting off the ears and carving the unit name into the dead Cong's chest, but it was just too intense, too much. The original concept was to make a film that broke barriers, and we broke too many."

Craven decided to reprise the plot of Ingmar Bergman's *Virgin Spring* which itself was based on a violent folk tale. After killing Mari, the killers go to her parents' house and claim to be friends of Mari's. Slowly, the parents discover just who their houseguests are and then take a revenge that is almost as gruesome and just as repulsive as the killers' own acts. The film as shown lacks a key scene where the parents finally realize who their visitors are. The scene would have stretched the audience's credulity to the breaking point in that the audience is asked to believe that Mari, after being raped, having her chest carved up, shot, and drowned in the lake, was still living in the middle of the night when the parents run down to the lake shore.

Said Craven, "The scene's still in where they (the parents) run down the driveway, but in most prints, there is no following scene or it is very truncated, but originally what happened was they pulled her out of the water—she was half in the water and half out. There was a scene where the mother says, 'Who did this, baby?' And she says, 'Two men and a woman. I don't know why they did it.' The father picks her up and starts carrying her back to the house, and they put her down on the couch. The father turns to the mother and says, 'I'm going down into the basement and get something to get them.' But all the acting was so bad. That was the problem. It was impossible, and the acting was bad, the directing was bad. It just had to go."

The killers' deaths include a fellation/castration and a chainsaw to the chest (a possible influence of Tobe Hooper?). Craven established what was to become one of his trademarks, the setting up of a complicated booby trap, this time of electrical leads wired up to a doorknob and under a wet rug to prevent the killers from escaping by the front door. There was also a very effective nightmare sequence. Weasel dreams that the mother and father pry his mouth open and take a chisel to his teeth. Overall, the film is neither pleasant nor entertaining, but as amateurishly made as it is, the film is unquestionably unsettling.

The title of the film remains a bit of a puzzle. The house is always on the right whenever anyone drives up, for example. It is ironic that the killers' car breaks down in front of Mari's and that she and her friend die only a few hundred yards from her door (and perhaps might have been saved if only they dared scream loud enough). Some people have seen the title as a reference to Stanley Kubrick's *A Clockwork Orange*, where the writer F. Alexander (Patrick McGee) lives on the last house on the left of a dead-end street. But that isn't how the title was chosen at all.

Said Craven, "The original title was *Night of Vengeance*, and when we came to release it, somebody said, 'Well, that title doesn't really fit.' What should we call it? It was called *Grim Company* and *Sex Crime of the Century*. Broadway Frack, this guy who did publicity on little pictures, came up to us and said, *Last House on the Left*.

"We looked at him and said, 'What's that got to do with anything?' It's the only house on the road, but, well, we'll try it. So we opened with three different titles, three different prints, and three geographically similar towns. The other two did so-so business, and the one with *The Last House on the Left* had lines around the block, so we all agreed that it would be *The Last House on the Left*.

"Everybody insists that it's a great title, but it means nothing. It was one of those cases where you realize that a title doesn't have to do anything but get people into the theater. Now interestingly enough, what this guy said was, 'Titles with "house" in them are always hits.' And it's true. A lot of very good films have the word 'house' in the titles. There is something very relevant about the concept of house. *The House of Usher*. *House Calls*. 'Left' has always been used to signify the radical, the unusual, the side of death. The left side has always been a bit more suspect. And 'last,' of course, implies death in the end, so it's a very canny combination of buzz words."

Despite the excesses that the film has been accused of, Craven considers the film to be moralistic in the sense of warning that when one gets in over his or her head. The fact that the teens died because of people they tried to buy drugs off of also has a moralistic twinge.

Said Craven, "At the time, I happened to be doing every drug available, but I think at heart I felt that drugs were not such a great idea for kids to get into. I think it is very moralistic in a sense, but I'm not ashamed of that. I don't think the great, sort of libertarian, opening of the floodgates of morality in the '70s has done the next generation a great amount of good. I think there was some sort of balance that had to be attained. The pendulum had to swing back the other way and come back. If nothing else, the film says be careful, the world is not all full of sweetness and light."

Craven's technical proficiency improved greatly with his next film five years later, *The Hills Have Eyes. The Last House on the Left* was shot on Super-16 and looks it, while *The Hills Have Eyes* was filmed using 16 mm negative and lacks the telltale graininess that typically gives away films that have been blown up from 16 mm. Still, *The Hills Have Eyes* is a very static picture as Craven's budget did not allow for the use of dollies or cranes.

Part of the inspiration for *The Hills Have Eyes* came from an account of the Sawney Bean family (recounted in *Historical and Traditional Tales Connected with the South of Scotland* by John Nicholson. It also appears in the "Human and Inhuman Stories" portion of *The Omnibus of Crime* by Dorothy L. Sayers.). This was a family of robbers and cannibals that perpetuated itself by incest. They waylaid unsuspecting passersby and took them to a secret cave where the victims were pickled for later consumption. Though it was estimated that over a thousand people had disappeared in the area they were not discovered until a man and his bride were attacked. The groom watched horrified as his bride's throat was slit and her body disemboweled. Fortunately for him, 20 or 30 men came upon them, and the Sawney Bean family made a hasty retreat, leaving their handiwork behind. The group went to Glasgow to notify the magistrates who in turn summoned the king. With several hundred men and a large number of bloodhounds, the Beans' hideaway was discovered along with evidence of their ghastly crimes. Under strong guard, the men were taken to Leith, dismembered, and bled to death in a few hours. The women and children were afterwards burned to death. Craven had decided to combine a modern version of the Sawney Bean family with a dream he had had. "I had a dream, a sort of *Beauty and the Beast* dream, and it ended with two dogs named Beauty and Beast, one very gentle and the other savage. There was the idea of the two families who mirrored each other with parents and children on both sides, one civilized and the other not civilized. That was the genesis basically.

"What I tried to do was start with civilized man and all the trappings of his civilization. It's mobile (i.e. they travel in a mobile home), but it's there. They have the dogs, they have the CBs, they have this and that. Then say, what happens when you destroy all that? What do they do with the remnants of that civilization and whatever is inside of them? It was a feeling like, well, this is the last days of

American civilization, the decline and fall of Western civilization. What's going to come out of it? Would the generation that had to deal with the remnants of be able to survive? Will they survive with their savageness and conquer, or will we just go back into a dark ages? There was that sort of philosophical inquiry behind it, if you will. This was done in 1975, so it was set ten years in the future. New York was uninhabitable and you had to have a passport to travel between states because states had become very territorial. The family was supposed to be stationed in Sun Valley. But they didn't have a passport to get into California, so they were trying to sneak in through the desert. That was the original premise.

"The producers then decided that maybe that was too futuristic, so we had them go out for a silver mine. The basic notion was, and still is, what do you do with the pieces? How do you improvise with the pieces that are left of your civilization? And it answered the same thing. How tough are we or can we be if the chips are down? I think it was saying that the college generation has it in them. They can improvise with what they have, and they have the motivation to survive. It was also another way of saying we're not so gentle as we like to think we are. There is the savage in all of us, and there's the civilized in most savages too. I always try to show villains that are at least partially civilized. The wild family thinks about their family members and have things about them that are jealous or insecure or are humorous. In *Last House*, I have the scene where the killers don't know what utensils to use and they get embarrassed and talk about it later."

Apart from doing a stunt for Sean Cunningham's *Here Come the Tigers* in which Craven appears as a man reading a newspaper who leans against his car door just as the car door is pulled off by a prankish trickster, Craven's last bit of film work in the '70s was a made-for-tv movie called *Stranger in Our House*. Despite the fact that *The Last House on the Left* and *The Hills Have Eyes* were both great financial successes, there was not much demand for Craven's talents. Craven did welcome the opportunity to work with the better equipment that his television debut afforded him.

Stranger in Our House also introduced Craven to Max Keller and Glenn Benest, both of whom worked on *Deadly Blessing*, Craven's next project. *Stranger* is based on Lois Duncan's novel, *Summer of Fear*, and was released under that title in Europe. Lee Purcell played a teenaged witch who comes to live with her cousin, played by Linda Blair, and her family. She drives the whole family into chaos until finally Blair figures out what is going on and has it out with her at the end. Craven did some uncredited rewriting on the final screenplay.

The producer of *Stranger in Our House* called on Wes Craven to do a rewrite on the script for a film titled *Deadly Blessing*. Pleased with the rewrite, the producer offered Craven a chance to direct the project, which he eagerly accepted. Initially, the film was no more violent than, say, "Charlie's Angels Go to the Farm," so it gave Craven a chance to do a less "intense" type of horror film. And since the film was financed by Universal, Craven would have the kind of equipment that he had heretofore lacked on his productions, so *Deadly Blessing* would at last give him a chance to show off his technical proficiency.

Said Craven, "I wanted to show, first of all, that I know how to do it (make a slick film), and second of all, it was a very different kind of picture. I wanted a big, smooth, sort of Philip Wylie look to it. We very consciously went in with that intention. Robert Jessup, the cinematographer, and I went through Philip Wylie's books and paintings by Van Gogh for the looks of the house down the lane and young woman's paintings. I directed the artist to paint like a combination of Van Gogh and Walter Lance. I wanted it to look very cartoony, but sort of strange and twisted, reflecting her own mentality. That was the girl who was killed, who turned out to be a hermaphroditic painter whose paintings kept changing and getting more distorted."

An attractive young woman (Maren Jensen) marries a Hittite farmer and joins him in his repressive, religious community, which in turn disapproves of the marriage. Things go from bad to worse when Jensen's husband is mysteriously crushed by a tractor, and the village elder (Ernest Borgnine) declares it the work of an incubus, that is an evil spirit who entices people with sex and then leads them to their doom. Jensen calls on a couple of her friends (Susan Buckner and Sharon Stone) to keep her company.

The isolated farm community begins to seem even more ominous, and the three women become terrified. Stand-out scenes include a dream where Sharon Stone dreams that a tarantula is dropped into her mouth; Maren Jensen gets an unexpected visitor while bathing—a snake which slithers up between her thighs; and Susan Bruckner falls for one of the village lads, played by Jeff East, and initiates him into sex. Unfortunately, East is dispatched at the end of the scene by an outside force as if the director suddenly remembered this was a horror film and in a horror film, anyone who makes love is doomed.

Commented Craven, "I've had a lot of people ask me if this is sort of repressive sexuality or something, but I think the real reason is in horror, if you look at the bald mechanics of it, in order to scare somebody or spring out fear or pity for victims, you put them in a very vulnerable, sort of 'passed out' situation. One of the key places where we are totally preoccupied is when making love, where you drop your shield and become very unprotected. When people are sleeping, making love, in their bathtubs, listening to music through earphones—when their traditional defenses are down—are the best times to strike. I probably should do one where somebody is on the toilet."

The film has many of the hallmarks of Craven's films: dream sequences, shocks piled on shocks, Michael Berryman in a small but important role, etc. The most peculiar thing about *Deadly Blessing* is that after the hermaphroditic killer is revealed and dispatched, a real incubus suddenly appears and carries Jensen away. It is the only supernatural element in the film, and it is a surprise since the audience assumed that the Hittites' claptrap about an incubus was meant to be a designation for Jensen and the outside evil of sexuality she was bringing into the community. Sometimes, this last ironic twist is omitted from the film by distributors or theater owners. The effects for it were originally to have been done by John Dykstra, but he had to bow out when *Firefox* had its schedule moved up and so the effects were actually performed by Everett Alson and Ira Anderson with an assist from costumer Tony Masters. *Deadly Blessing* works well in some of its segments, but overall the plot just clunks and chugs along from incident to incident. While it is enjoyable, instead of being an explosion which demonstrated what Craven could do with a bigger budget, it was more of a fizzle. It looked good for the money spent, but even with Craven's script surgery, the story was weak.

Unfortunately, the same thing could be said of Craven's next project, *Swamp Thing*. Originally, the *Swamp Thing* was the creation of Len Wein and Berni Wrightson for DC Comics. It was a beautifully drawn, sensitively written episodic series of stories about a scientist named Dr. Alec Holland who, in a lab accident, becomes a monstrous-looking half-man, half-plant type creature. The Swamp Thing itself was a very sympathetic character, treated cruelly by the outside world because of his unprepossessing features. The character has much in common with Frankenstein's monster of Shelley's classic tale and, as such, seemed a good bet to translate well to the movies.

One of the central problems with the film was created when the producers decided to go with the lowest make-up bid, that of Bill Munns's for $80,000. (The next-lowest bid was a more realistic $250,000). Adding to Munns's headaches were the facts that he wasn't given a full go-ahead until six weeks before production, had created one Swamp Thing body suit only to have a taller, thinner actor take over the role, and the head intended for close-ups was discarded when it was felt that it didn't match the body suit head well enough. (Actor Ray Wise, who played Dr. Holland in the film, was to have played the Swamp Thing in close-ups, but he had the wrong kind of nose and face to perfectly match up with the look of the Swamp Thing that had already been established, and so Dick Durock ended up playing the Swamp Thing throughout the movie with a head mask that was only intended to be seen in long-shot.)

Said Craven, "*Swamp Thing* had a lot of problems with the body and a rough schedule. The costume was a real problem. The designer was not given an adequate amount of lead time. He showed up on the set the day before we had to shoot it. It was virtually, 'Well, do we stop production?' and there was no money to do that, so the attempt was to do something that would sort of transcend the costume. In a sense, it has. The film plays for kids all right, but it doesn't play for teenagers or adults. Because the technical abilities are so high these days, people have a hard time getting past that; but on the other hand, it does play for a lot of people—women like it, a lot of parents like it, a lot of young kids like it. It played very, very strongly on HBO and other cable and cassette releases. It's a Wes Craven movie which children can enjoy and laugh at, you know?"

Craven reworked the original story in the comic book, changing the person in charge protecting Dr. Holland from Matt Cable to Alice Cable (played by Adrienne Barbeau) so that Craven could give the story a love interest and add a *Beauty and the Beast* type overtone to the story.

"It was very much a *Beauty and the Beast* tale," he said. "It was clearly an attempt to do a variation on the *Beauty and the Beast* theme. You have a beast that you know inside is a handsome prince, but you see him as a toad. You've seen him before, and you know he was amorous and humorous and very, very scientifically brilliant, yet outwardly now he's a monster.

"On the other hand, you have Louis Jordan's character Arcane, who is someone who looks very nice on the outside, but when you see his true self, it's monstrous and ugly. Then there is the character of Bruno, who turns into a giant mouse. I like exploring the idea that there are antipathies to everything. Beneath the surface, there is another side. That theme has run through all of my films."

In addition, Craven added the character of Jude (Reggie Batts), a young black kid who seems intended to act as a spokesman for the kids in the audience. "Jude was somebody that the kids could identify with," Craven admitted. "We wanted somebody that could ask the questions that only an uninformed person would ask, and who would add humor. That's basically it. He just came out of me, and we all liked him. Originally, he was an old man, but in the second or third draft (of the screenplay), he switched to being a kid. Overall, I kept the basic character names and sort of combined them, and then I created the kid and created the story. I would say up to the formula exploding in Holland's face, it was pretty much along the lines of the comic, and everything after that was just made up. It was a fun picture. I met my wife on it, so it was successful," Craven said with a smile.

Swamp Thing does have a very dreamlike feel to it, but it fails to evoke the same beauty and unease that Walter Hill was able to achieve with a similar location in the film *Southern Comfort*. Rather than a classic monster tale or an inspired adaptation of a very fine comic book, *Swamp Thing* is a kiddie matinee film that is unlikely to attract audiences other than the younger audience for which it appears to have been intended.

Because of the success of *The Hills Have Eyes* on videotape, particularly in Europe, the European video distributors offered to finance a sequel to the original film, and so *The Hills Have Eyes 2* was born. However, since the video rights had already been sold, it became difficult for a distribution deal to be struck in the United States. Increasingly, today's films have become more and more dependent upon so-called ancillary rights (such as cable and videocassette sales) to break even overall. Films were no longer breaking even at the box office domestically, partially because of declining attendance and partially because it was simply costing more for films to be made. But while Craven had mostly finished *The Hills Have Eyes 2*, the film was not released until after his next two projects.

The first was a telefeature called *Invitation to Hell*. Craven was called in after the script had been completed, but he ended up doing an uncredited polish job on it. The basic premise of *Invitation* (originally titled *The Club*) was that a family moves in to a new location that is situated near the gates of hell. The family is lured into hell by a mysterious club comprised of members of the local community. As luck and the screenwriter would have it, the father (Robert Urich) has been working on a special fireproof suit that allows him to enter hell to rescue his family. Any relationship to Greek mythology is purely coincidental.

Overall, the film is very tame. Said Craven, "When television is dealing with me, they say, 'We can't do violence, so we must be able to do witchcraft because that's something else, that's a little off-the-wall.' Whenever I get approached by television, it is usually for something supernatural. I think *Invitation* turned out well for what it was. It was a very fast job. They were having to rush to make it because it was designed to fill a hole that suddenly opened up. I think there were about two weeks preproduction and something like three-and-a-half weeks postproduction. We got the second-highest ratings for the week and swept the ratings for the night. I beat *Simon and Simon* and *Magnum*, so for the time we had, we did very, very well."

However, Craven really hit his stride with *A Nightmare on Elm Street*. In its original opening, the film did very well, climbing to a profit position even before it reached wider release. More importantly, it was an unexpectedly stylish and energetic film while Craven's latest films seem to have suffered from tired blood. Craven had a real dedication to the project and had tried to get it made for years. Unlike his projects since the original *The Hills Have Eyes*, it was one that he originated rather than coming in on a project that somebody else had written and prepared first. Craven had shown the scripts for *Nightmare* for several years without success. It had been turned down virtually everywhere, but once it was released, it was evident that his faith in the project was justified.

Despite the use of the overly-prevalent "teenagers in peril" approach to horror, the film did not ape overused clichés, but rather the world of dreams to strike out into some fresh territory, proving to be first-class horror filmmaking. The film recapitulated all of Craven's interests. It had dreams (long one of his fortes), clever booby traps, and clearly defined forces battling for survival. *Nightmare* gives clear evidence that Craven has learned from his previous experiences and is refining his craft.

He is still able to manage ably on a small budget. *A Nightmare on Elm Street* was shot in thirty-two days on a budget of under $2 million. The film almost didn't come off when the financial backing fell out three days into shooting, but fortunately a deal was struck and New Line Cinema agreed to distribute the picture once it was completed. The actors and the crew were paid scale, that is, guild minimum. Said Craven, "There were a lot of very talented people working on it. Nobody took much money on it. We improvised like mad. Our special effects guy, Jim Doyle, did a magnificent job. We had a very small crew. The entire special effects crew was somewhere around a half a dozen people. They built an entire revolving room so that Tina could go up the walls and the ceiling. The room is revolving in that shot. We were strapped into chairs. The camera was strapped into a chair. We had to keep blood off the lens because it would have totally ruined the shot.

"Actually, when it started to go sideways, it felt like the room was going out of control. We started screaming. It was the best ride since Disneyland, strapped into a room with 250 gallons of blood flying around.

"There were certain things that we were going to do with the revolving room that we couldn't afford. The fact was that the special effects people had so much to do, they needed to have control of the set, and we ended up having this room and not being able to do all as much with it as we could have done because we were so rushed. Towards the end, we were shooting in every corner of the set. I was literally running from one end of the stage to the other, shooting these little inserts. We'd have a camera crew over here shooting inserts, and we'd have a camera crew over there shooting Rod being dragged across the floor. And a camera crew up here shooting where he went. It was just total insanity. It was like a test of how resourceful and resilient we could be. There were a lot of things we could have done with the special effects room, but he didn't have time to do them."

Craven feels that he was psychologically prepared for the film because it came at the tail end of what has been, so far, the busiest time ever in his career. He literally walked off the soundstage of one project and onto the soundstage of another. He was also fortunate enough to find a cast largely composed of talented unknowns and beginners. The story mostly focuses on the character of Nancy as she discovers that she and three of her friends all shared the same terrible dream one night. As one by one, her friends begin to get murdered in the most bizarre and inexplicable fashion, she realizes that the razor-clawed horror that has been haunting her dreams will be after her next. To sleep is death, and so she must battle to stay awake while the adults around her cannot believe her incredible story and are all telling her to relax and go to sleep.

The part of Nancy is played by Heather Langenkamp, and in many ways, it is she who must carry the picture, which she does very well. Said Craven, "I think she's fantastic. She was in *Rumble Fish* before her part was cut. I don't think she has a project yet, but I'm sure she will because she's a fine actress. She's about twenty years old, and this was her first major role.

"As a director, you hope after you write a character you can find her. You make up somebody, and then you have to find that person in the real world, and then that person has to be able to act. I really felt that I'd found my Nancy. Heather's very talented, and she really has her head screwed on. She's a very serious actress."

The cloaked, rotting figure with the steel knives for fingers that is haunting the teens' dreams is Fred Krueger (Robert Englund), a child molester who was the victim of some parental vigilantes and who has now returned from the dreamworld to exact his revenge. Just who he was and why he was after these particular teens was clearer in the original cut of the film.

"In the original cut of the film, it was much clearer that all of the parents were in collusion, hiding this secret," Craven recalled. "It was the parents of these four kids who had killed Fred Krueger. There were scenes where various groups of parents talk about it and say they shouldn't have done it or that he couldn't possibly be hurting the children. There was even a line indicating that all the teenagers once had siblings who had been killed when Fred Krueger had originally terrorized the town, but nobody would believe that Nancy could not remember having siblings, so I cut it out."

Craven and his cinematographer, Jacques Karkin, have given a good look to the film which suggests the eerie wrongness of a dream, and it ably communicates the feeling that somehow reality has been skewed. There are a number of memorable sequences in the film including a girl who is lifted out of her bed and onto the walls and ceiling while being attacked by an invisible adversary, a boy who gets sucked into his bed and becomes a torrent of blood, and a telephone mouthpiece that suddenly develops a slavering tongue which tries to French the heroine. "The tongue coming out of the phone is one of my favorite scenes," said Craven, "simply because it cost about five dollars. It's very effective and very cinematic. Since I started off as a writer, I tend to be verbal, so I love it when I can get myself to do something totally visual like the bathtub scene. Tina's death is cinematic, the whole sequence going down the alley and all that. I feel good about the whole picture."

The only exception to the last statement that Craven makes is that he is not totally happy with the final shock at the end. "The ghost of *Carrie* haunts us all, unfortunately. There's hardly a producer alive that will allow a film to end classically—you must have that final shock. The script ended with her going out the door, getting into the car, driving off into the fog, and the mother seeing the girl leave before the credits.

"That, more than any other scene, was fussed over by other people, especially the producer who felt we had to have a strong, 'proper' end. So I said, 'Ok, I'll pull the mother through the door,' and they said, 'Yeah!' I thought of that almost as a joke on the very last night before shooting had to stop. I said, 'Ok, we'll put a cable on this dummy,' and sure enough, we had eight people pulling in the other direction, and by God the thing went through the door like shit through a goose. It was just incredible. We looked at the shot and said we'll go with it. Some people love it; some hate it."

On the whole, *A Nightmare on Elm Street* is the best made, most stylish, and most enjoyable film that Craven has made to date. The audience achieves a rapport with the heroine and empathizes with her plight. The film is presented from a teenage point of view—all adults are noncomprehending but well-meaning dolts. John Saxon, the square-jawed father, does eventually rush to the rescue, but by then, the heroine has finally learned how she can deal with Fred Krueger herself. Overall, this successful film boded well for Craven's future.

The future included *The Frozen Man*, a telefeature written for CBS as a Movie of the Week and which aired under the title *Chiller*. Craven's next theatrical release was *The Hills Have Eyes II. Hills II* was shot at Joshua Tree National Monument under the auspices of the Forestry Service. The production was able to use an old abandoned ranch where rustlers used to hang out as a location and near an old gold mine, a place called Hughes Ranch, which is off-limits to the public. The film was intended to be less intense than the original but with plenty of action and stunts to appeal to the exploitation crowd that loves these films. In addition to the actors who play Ruby and Bobby, the film also has Michael Berryman, another important member of the original cast. This was followed by the film *Deadly Friend*, a flawed adaptation of the novel *Friend* by Diana Henstell, and a successful collaboration on *A Nightmare on Elm Street 3: Dream Warriors*.

Craven can always be counted on to come up with creative ways to scare people. As his position firms up and his work receives more attention, he should be able to enter the pantheon of most-talked-about horror film directors—a distinction he would share with Brian De Palma, John Carpenter, George Romero, David Cronenberg, Joe Dante, and a few others.

Interview on Elm Street

Michael Banka / 1990

From *Cinéaste*, vol. 17, no. 3 (1990), 22–25. Reprinted by permission of *Cinéaste*.

The "shock troops" of popular culture—as one might refer to the directors of the wildly popular horror and thriller films—often elude the intellectual grasp of film critics. Why do they want to splatter blood across the screen? Are they endemically sexist? What do they think of attempts to censor their violence? Where do they come from, and where do they go after dark?

Wes Craven is an acknowledged master of the genre, and is himself versed in genres, having once taught English literature. No longer the professor, his education still shows in his methodical approach to making horror films. His name may sound like an invention of Edgar Allan Poe, but at the age of fifty-one, with twenty years of box office hits behind him, Craven has not shed the Midwestern normalcy of his Cleveland, Ohio, background.

The controversial nature of these movies does not concern Craven as much as the choices within his job of directing a horror film, and he speaks with professional pride and awareness of how he has achieved a certain renown and precise effect. He first surfaced as a filmmaker with *Last House on the Left* (1972) and received critical notice with the *vérité*-style *The Hills Have Eyes* (1977). The forgettable *Deadly Blessing* (1981) preceded the intelligently amusing adaptation of a comic book hero in *Swamp Thing* (1982).

In 1984, Craven made the original *Nightmare on Elm Street*, which launched a cottage industry of sequels and paraphernalia, as Freddy Krueger became a cult hero. Although Craven was involved in none of the sequels, he did direct *The Hills Have Eyes Part II* (1985), *Deadly Friend* (1986), and the atmospherically interesting *The Serpent and the Rainbow* (1988), which he acknowledges as an ambitious but not overtly violent film. Some interpreted his unaccustomed subtlety as a sign that violence was in remission, possibly as a result of the controversies raised by citizens' groups about its effects on youth.

Craven's next movie reinforced the genre. Clearly, horror is here to stay. For *Shocker* (1989), Craven polished up the conventions of splatter movies in the story of a serial killer who survives being electrocuted and returns to provide de rigueur mayhem. Craven and his colleagues are often accused of exploiting the basest emotions of a not-too-discriminating public. Seldom do we hear what demands are made of them by the film industry or the expectations of an audience increasingly immune to the shock therapy that Craven sees in his own movies. The following interview offers a glimpse of this engaging, unassuming refugee from Elm Street.

Cinéaste: A New York movie critic wrote that *Shocker* plays like *A Nightmare on Elm Street* meets Marshall McLuhan.
Wes Craven: Well, there's a lot of television in it. I suppose a lot of McLuhan's ideas could be applied to what goes on. The point is that Pinker is a villain out of television. He represents the whole violence of civilization as seen through and perpetuated by television. And when he and Jonathan [the teen hero] literally leap into the television set, the images they battle are elements of the coercion of the twentieth century on the human spirit. That includes everything from war to Alice Cooper to supposedly suitable paradigms for American family life like *Leave It to Beaver*. The media rocket us from one extreme to another and bludgeon rather than educate us, not allowing us to make up our own minds.

Cinéaste: *Shocker* shows us a lot of television screens, video images, and cameras, as if to call attention to the artifice involved in any visual entertainment. The effect is very distancing.
Craven: My intention is to make people aware of the media. By hypnotizing or involving them at one point and then distancing them at another, I can make them aware of the various states they're in while watching a movie, states they might not ordinarily recognize. It's like that old saying: the fish can't be aware of the water; the birds can't be aware of the air; and man can't be aware of consciousness. I think there's a fourth axiom now that says Western-civilized beings can't be aware of television. Watching television or movies is like being unconscious. And by cutting back and forth in *Shocker* I'm able to show that. I tried for the same effect in *The Serpent and the Rainbow* by just going to total black screen. It's a way of making the audience aware that they're in a kind of altered state when they watch a movie or television so that they can be a little more guarded and volitional. Otherwise, they're just passive receptors.

Cinéaste: So you distrust technology?
Craven: And not just television. The basic nightmare of the twentieth century

is that the most technologically advanced phenomenon has always been coupled with the most primitive and brutal. Look at Vietnam and the weaponry America used. Look at Nazi Germany. The Germans gave us Bach and Beethoven and jet planes and many of the optics used in the movie business. Yet they also invented ways to exterminate eight million people and make lamp shades out of them. There's always been that incredible juxtaposition of high tech and low bestiality.

Cinéaste: In his review of *Shocker*, Roger Ebert objected that you didn't make clear how Pinker survives the electric chair and travels via electric current.

Craven: I think he missed the point. I gave three indications that Pinker was involved in the supernatural. There was the initial glimpse of his back room with hanging cats, evil signs, Egyptian ideograms. Then in the newscast just before [Jonathan's girlfriend] Allison is killed, you hear that the police discovered in the backroom hundreds of mummified cats and that Pinker had been practicing black magic. Then you see in his prison cell an inverted cross, symbols scrawled on the floor, and black candles, and Pinker is doing strange incantations. I had thought of more elaborate scenes of witchcraft, but I'm not dealing with a consensus form of reality anyway. I'm talking about deeper, subconscious realities. What I'm dealing with is a personification of the influence of television and electromagnetism on our culture; Pinker is that personification. To spell that out in the dialog instead of suggesting it visually would have come off as pat and phony. Nobody criticizes a Mickey Mouse movie because Walt Disney never explained how the mice could talk.

Cinéaste: You seem to enjoy the contrast of a rational approach to the world with bizarre, inexplicable events.

Craven: I like exploring the human psyche, especially its uncharted and irrational aspects. There's so much in the realm of human consciousness that doesn't fit into consensus reality. I'm dealing with states of being we're in when we daydream, have a fantasy or orgasm, or call up our memories. There are so many different human mental states we enter into that we don't fully understand and then abruptly come out of and convince ourselves that we're back in reality. I try to bring those states of mind into my movies willy-nilly because that's how they actually occur. So we have Jonathan in *Shocker* walking through the house where Pinker murdered Allison, and she appears before him. She's not physically present, but for Jonathan she's very much there because of his memories of her and the associations that the house has for him. I think the audience gets that; they're in a much more fluid state than critics.

Cinéaste: The scene toward the end of *Shocker*, when Jonathan makes love to Allison's spirit has necrophiliac overtones.

Craven: First of all, I thought the scene was so pristine and dreamlike that it was obvious she wasn't a corpse. What I meant to suggest by her being there was the presence of their relationship in Jonathan's mind. I also wanted to hint at an alternative reality where the two of them could merge, a reality beyond their natural lives.

Cinéaste: The heroes and villains in your movies seem bound in symbiotic relationships.

Craven: I try to devise movies about two sides of a single personality or group, which gives the story a dual structure. I divide the good and bad personality aspects into two characters, and, by the end, the good encompasses the bad, or vice versa.

Cinéaste: Is horror through suggestion still possible, or are audiences so jaded by explicit violence that they won't accept anything else?

Craven: It's very tricky. Sometimes you have to deliver a tremendous amount of violence if you want to appeal to that large audience. That is why people go to horror movies. Even in *Shocker* I had to keep in mind a core audience that wants blood and guts—more than I care to give them. It's really scary sometimes, but I like this core audience's intensity and honesty. It's like they say, "Give me some blood!" For instance, when Jonathan has a knife at Pinker's throat, about eighty percent of the audience wants him to cut his throat right then. That's where that audience is.

Cinéaste: Didn't the ratings board make you cut some scenes?

Craven: The hallway scene where Pinker bites the guard's fingers, Pinker's electrocution, Allison dead in the bathtub, the coach stabbing himself in the hand . . . those are some of the scenes I had to cut from. What bothers the ratings board is not necessarily the explicitness of individual shots, but the overall intensity of a scene. Think of Pinker's electrocution. Electrocution is condoned by several states and conducted by government forces, but movies aren't allowed to show it in anything approaching its actual intensity. I had to remove whole shots of Pinker in the chair. It's a paradox, because to generate the intensity that the ratings board objects to, you have to be an accomplished filmmaker. In other words, you pay for being a polished director. The less skillful director simply inserts shots of graphic gore but without the same polished intensity and rarely has a problem with a rating. It's very painful, especially on a low-budget film where you don't have time to reshoot and reedit.

Cinéaste: Will that kind of forced cutting ever become passé?

Craven: The problem could be solved by having a rating for intensity. Designate a movie *I* if it's too intense for children. The ratings board's argument is that even though an R-rating keeps children out who aren't accompanied by adults it also tells adults that it's safe to take children into the movie, and sooner or later a child will be brought in who's way underage and not prepared for the intensity. It's such a fatuous argument because it leaves no place for an adultly intense, fun movie. They'll tell you that if you want artistic freedom, go outside and release the movie unrated, and when you answer that you'll suffer financial ruin, they say, "Oh, then we're not talking about art here are we? We're talking about profit."

Cinéaste: Just as you are aware of the pros and cons of that argument, your films reveal a split artistic personality, wavering between horror and camp. *Shocker* can be very funny, as in the scene where Pinker takes over the body of a little girl who instantly becomes vicious and foulmouthed.
Craven: I like to think my movies make people laugh at disturbing material, at the ferocity of the world we live in. That's a very legitimate human response. It was fun to show that this little yuppie child had ferocity in her. The reviewer in *People* called me slime for doing that, but the actress had a wonderful time.

Cinéaste: Is it possible to make an effective big budget horror movie, or are higher production values and a glossy look inimical to a frightening horror movie?
Craven: I think it definitely can be done. Friedkin did it with *The Exorcist*. What happens is that as a director works with bigger budgets, a lot of painful things you find in his early work get ironed out. Another thing is that people get to know who you are, and you find yourself not doing certain things to remain a part of their community. The first time you make a movie, you're out to tear down your audience, shock them, and make a name for yourself. I know I'm a lot more restrained these days. You also become a bigger target for censorship. The first movie quite often gets by because no one is looking for you. Now when I come out with a movie, all the red lights go on; I can't get anything by. And it's not always the case that the studios themselves put restraints on what I want to do. When I made *Deadly Friend*, Warner Bros. encouraged me to make it more violent than I intended.

Cinéaste: Why does horror in most of your movies have its roots in the American family?
Craven: *The Hills Have Eyes*' desert family; *A Nightmare on Elm Street*, with Freddy Krueger murdering children because their parents mutilated him; also, *Last House*, whose killers are more like a family than a gang of criminals; and *Shocker*, with Pinker murdering whole families. I've concluded over the second half of my career that the family is at the core of my work. I think horror movies play in the

ballground laid out when people are between the ages of zero and five; that's where their emotions come from. The issue of young people taking over for their parents is particularly key. A lot of the younger audience who either don't know about the terrible things going on in the world, won't admit what's going on, or else are contributing to the problems. That sort of rite of passage where the younger generation triumphs and takes its place over the older is what many horror movies are about. And you find it time and again in my movies. *The Hills Have Eyes* has three generations, with the younger using the dead bodies of the older to trap their tormentors.

Cinéaste: Much has been made of your fundamentalist upbringing. But, with the exception of *Deadly Blessing* and *The Serpent and the Rainbow*, your movies have rarely touched on religion.
Craven: In many ways, I regret ever having mentioned my upbringing because it's been focused on too much. I was raised in a very religious period. I went to high school with Catholics who were in church all the time; they always wore crosses around their necks. But religion is a normal part of a lot of Americans' lives, and I've never felt the need to deal specifically with it in my movies. Religion means different things to different people, but at least in the most literal and fundamental sense, it's concerned with the horror of the strong surviving and the weak perishing. We have to eat other species in order to survive. Whether we admit it or not, it's kill or be killed. Lots of dead cows, right?

Cinéaste: *The Serpent and the Rainbow* reflects a sustained attempt to create horror through atmosphere. Why?
Craven: It's more restrained than my other movies, and there is a great deal of atmosphere. But that's how Haiti [the movie's setting] felt. The movie was a tightrope act. We all wanted to make a scary movie, but we also wanted to reveal something about voodoo other than the usual business about dolls. We tried to combine a love story with a scientific story. It was a big undertaking just in storytelling, and I think it was pretty successful.

Cinéaste: *Last House on the Left* has a lot in common with the mad-slasher genre spawned by *Friday the 13th* in the 1980s. But as Robin Wood has observed, it is more complex because you endow both the victims and violators with "vivid, personalized aliveness."
Craven: I made *Last House* when I was examining the whole sickness associated with Vietnam. It was fascinating to take characters who had killed, who'd done something utterly reprehensible, and make them worry about being dressed properly for dinner at the house or who was going to sleep with whom. It was a strange

turnaround that really snapped people's heads. Western culture has traditionally dealt with barbarism by projecting it outward. There's that old rationalization that we're only dealing with animals, so we have the right—or God has given us the right—to be animals and kill the Aztecs, kill the Indians, enslave the Blacks, drop bombs on the Japanese. One of the healthier notes of the latter twentieth century is that Americans are finally looking in the mirror and seeing that the enemy is in us as well as in others, that there really is no essential difference between the enemy and us. We all have the capacity to be maniacal or go crazy.

Cinéaste: How do you find the balance for your villains—especially those in *Last House* and *The Hills Have Eyes*—who explode with an over-the-top viciousness, although they have been established as unsettlingly realistic?
Craven: That kind of mix owes to a combination of things. One is careful casting. I try to find people who are willing to dwell in that land; many actors aren't able or willing to project that sort of evil. But some actors can get into the minds of these kinds of characters and admit that they have these feelings without destroying their self-image. As a director you have to be committed to a very high level of energy. You can't let up on the pressure; you have to keep the ferocity going because a movie is made in sixty second bursts in the middle of twelve hours of boredom. That ferocity is contagious to the crew.

Cinéaste: What directors and authors have had the greatest impact on you?
Craven: The directors whose work I saw first: Buñuel—very influential; the Europeans such as Bergman, Fellini, Cocteau, Truffaut. Also, writers like Tolstoy, Dostoyevsky, Kafka . . . the Theatre of the Absurd. American movies, though not so much Hitchcock as Howard Hawks and John Ford, especially for their well-rounded characters, which you usually don't find in horror movies.

Cinéaste: Which of today's horror directors do you think produce the most interesting work?
Craven: Sam Raimi, when he gets around to it. Also Cronenberg, although he's moving away from horror. He's definitely mastering film as art. I understand Stuart Gordon is a big fan of mine. But I've seen only *Re-Animator*, and I thought it was shockingly gory. It had great intensity but was gory beyond anything I'd ever do.

Shock-Waves: *Toxic* Interviews Wes Craven

David Henry Jacobs / 1990

From *Toxic Horror,* April 1990. Reprinted by permission of Joseph A. Sonnier IV, CEO of *Cinestate* and *Fangoria*.

Three important, wildly dissimilar filmmakers share the same unlikely background: When they were young, they were forbidden by their parents from seeing any movies but the most innocuous Disney variety. They grew up to become Steven Spielberg, *Taxi Driver* author Paul Schrader, and Wes Craven.

Wes Craven is a unique and original talent, the visionary creator of such intense classics as *Nightmare on Elm Street*, *The Hills Have Eyes*, *Last House on the Left*, and *The Serpent and the Rainbow*. His new hit, *Shocker*, is funny, smart, and tough—an ambitious, densely-textured film filled with ideas and, well, shocks. And who else but Wes Craven would think of making a handheld remote-control unit the ultimate weapon in a video-ized duel to the death?

Shocker opened on Friday, October 29, 1989. Wes Craven was in New York City earlier that week, making the rounds of the TV talk-show circuit and visiting friends. He was nice enough to find time to talk with us, in a wide-ranging conversation focusing on such topics as Horace Pinker's neon-bright jumpsuit, the reality of zombies, the terrifying real-life inspiration for Freddy Krueger, and other items of interest.

In person, Wes Craven is soft-spoken, thoughtful, articulate. His style seems more of the academic world than of Hollywood; it's not too much of a stretch to imagine him as a member of the distinguished faculty of H. P. Lovecraft's Miskatonic University, teaching nineteenth-century literature (one of his passions) to eager young Herbert West wannabes.

Toxic: Thanks for seeing us. Your schedule must be pretty crowded.
Wes Craven: It's been a busy few days, I'm doing *The Larry King Show* tonight. I just did MTV; I was on *The Big Picture*.

Toxic: That's a nice cue-in to *Shocker*'s heavy-metal score.
Craven: That came out of my partnership with Shep Gordon and Alive Films. Shep Gordon manages Alice Cooper and has a real good relationship with Desmond Child, who wrote all those songs. And Desmond in turn has great connections, so we got all the top heavy metal people.

Toxic: Is the soundtrack album due soon?
Craven: I believe the album comes out next Monday. Album, CDs, everything. Actually, it's a very good album.

Toxic: Friday you open nationwide?
Craven: Nationwide, in fifteen hundred theaters.

Toxic: What sparked the creation of *Shocker* villain Horace Pinker?
Craven: You know, it was one of those ideas that came out of a conversation with a friend, and he was saying that he always loved the idea of *The Thing*, where the monster got into people's bodies and you didn't know who it was in. I was working with that basic concept, and I'd always wanted to do something that went into television. So I decided to deal with somebody who was electrically charged and was using all forms of electricity.

He began by invading bodies through the electrical parts of their nervous systems and was able to move on through the wiring system of houses, then into the transmission beam of television and finally was infesting television itself and coming out of TV sets to strike and then going back in. It just sort of formulated around that sort of a person with those abilities.

I said, "I'll make him a television repairman. That'll give him a background in electronics." I knew I wanted him to be a very physical specimen, since he starts off being a real-life killer who batters his way into people's apartments at night . . . and then when the actor was found, a lot was built around his particular idiosyncrasies.

Toxic: Mitch Pileggi as Pinker comes across as a very impressive-looking individual.
Craven: He's very bright, and really a superb actor, so he's able to project that sense of threat and evil and a great sense of intelligence. You really believe this guy is a formidable enemy.

Toxic: Pinker's loud orange jumpsuit is an effective visual.
Craven: There were two reasons for that. One is that I wanted to have a definite color and pattern to represent him no matter where or what shape he was in. The other was that it allowed us to pull mattes more easily because it was so contrasty.

Toxic: How do you see yourself in relation to the Empire of TV?
Craven: I see myself as the usual subversive. (laughs)

Toxic: *Shocker*'s set in Ohio. You come from Ohio. Any autobiographical elements there?
Craven: Some. (laughs) You know, I'm not going to drag my family in here, but it's based on these sorts of people I knew in Ohio.

Toxic: Families, good and evil, are a major motif in your work.
Craven: I found that it's very fertile soil for me to mine. In one shape or another family is a very powerful thing for almost all the audience . . . there's always that need, that longing for the mystery of the family, and what it was or what it could have been or what it really was behind the scenes for the child. I think a lot of horror films are built around that structure without even realizing it. So I just sort of consciously stay in there.

Toxic: You had a little go-around with the MPAA.
Craven: Their logic is that an R-rating designates to a parent that they should feel comfortable bringing a child of any age to the film—a criteria they really only apply to horror films . . . *Shocker* was not hideously damaged as some films I've had, but it certainly had a few shots taken out of it; it required cuts. I really resented it. But on a happier note, the picture still plays very strongly, and it's still a very, very good picture.

Toxic: Going back to *Serpent and the Rainbow*: do zombies exist?
Craven: Oh, yes. I met a zombie and several of the producers met other zombies . . . Basically, what it is, is a process of poisoning that makes you appear dead when you're not, and you're fully conscious while you're buried alive . . . That night, when your family has gone home and considered you gone forever, these people dig you up as you start to revive.

To process you further, there's a severe series of beatings, and then a second drug, datura, which is basically a severe hallucinogen. And the repeated dosages wipe up that person's volitional system. That coupled with a deep interior belief that they are, in being made into zombies—the whole personality just collapses. It's a very real process, and very frightening.

I met a nineteen-year-old girl, by the name of Rosemary, who was in a clinic outside Port-au-Prince. She had been taken ill with a fever, died in about three days, was buried, and returned about twelve days later, wandering through a cane-field. She had done something to irritate one of the village chiefs . . .

Apparently, the system of zombification is done as some sort of a tribal judgement, and quite often is perverted into people just settling personal scores.

One of the other famous cases was a young woman who refused to marry the man that her mother and father had chosen for her, and her mother went ahead and had her zombified—an outrageous form of parental discipline.

Toxic: The poor man's lobotomy, with supernatural overtones.
Craven: Exactly.

Toxic: Charles Bronson once said that for a change of pace he'd like to make a movie where he just stands around and drinks cocktails and doesn't shoot anybody. Any change-of-pace item you would particularly like to do?
Craven: I'd certainly love to do more comedy . . . I'm trying very hard to get work outside of the genre for my next film. I want to establish a basis for myself as a director, period, rather than as a horror director or a genre director. It's very important for me as I'm entering my mature years here that I do more than just horror, although I really like horror and have a lot of fun with it. But I'm feeling the need to do other things, too.

Toxic: Any colleagues in the genre whose work you particularly like?
Craven: Oh sure, a lot of them. I like Sam Raimi's work; I like Cronenberg's work a lot . . . Polanski's work I always watch very carefully; he has the ability to be superb. I mean, he's been on the dark side of the moon.

Toxic: What scares Wes Craven?
Craven: Taxes. Divorce lawyers.

Toxic: What was the seed, the inspiration, for Freddy Krueger?
Craven: Freddy is a little bit based on a man that frightened me when I was a kid. I've told this story before, but basically, I was in my bed and I heard this sort of scraping footstep. And I went to the window, and there was a man, I guess a drunk, dressed very much like Freddy. He just stopped on the sidewalk and looked directly up in my window, into my eyes, and really frightened me. I was a kid, and I was only eight years old.

I jumped back into the shadows and waited for him to go away and didn't hear him go away. I waited and waited, as long as I thought I could, and finally I crept back. And he was just staring right at me, and he turned around and walked into our building, our apartment building. I was absolutely panic-stricken, terrified! It really seemed like he had all the malevolence I could ever imagine in adults. So I woke up my whole family and my brother went down with a baseball bat and the guy disappeared. And that was the sort of kernel, of that sort of man in my mind.

And then there was sort of very methodical things, of deciding I would give him a certain pattern so he could be recognized, like the sweater. I gave him a hat, the kind of hat that that man wore in my memory. The claws were just thinking what the most primitive fear of a weapon would be in the mind of mankind, that it would probably be tooth or claws, so I decided to make it claws.

Toxic: The opening sequence in *Nightmare*, with Freddy sharpening up his finger-knives, has tremendous energy. The quick cuts create a sense of real unease.

Craven: That comes out of my years in the editing room. That's the way I got into the film business, by cutting trailers. That sense of rhythm is very important to film. The time that I spend in an editing room has probably more to do with the way that my films come out than anything else that I do, including directing. It's just that that body of knowledge is absolutely invaluable, you know: how to do cuts and how to do sound and how to structure visually.

Toxic: I believe Joe Dante started that way.

Craven: A lot of people did. Peckinpah was a really skillful trailer editor before he became a director. Hal Ashby, who did *Being There*, was a great editor. It's a really good way to break into it.

Toxic: What's next?

Craven: I have a four-picture deal with Alive and Universal. There certainly will be one more that's already in the writing stages. It's called *The People Under the Stairs*. I'm looking to do an out-of-the-genre film next. I'm developing a project with Larry Turman, who's the producer of *The Graduate*, based on a novel by a New York writer named Giles Blount. The book is called *Cold Eye* and is set in the New York art world. It's sort of a Faustian story with a little twist of *Portrait of Dorian Gray*. If that's ready, I'll do that next; if not, there are several other things that we're talking about.

Toxic: Lucky you signed with Alive rather than MGM. [Note: Not long after Wes Craven inked the deal with Alive, MGM went through some changes that would not have been beneficial to *Shocker*, to say the least.]

Craven: Really. It's amazing, because there was a very real consideration that Alive's just a small company, whereas MGM actually offered us a larger budget. MGM didn't offer us the freedom Alive offered. That was the basis of our decision, and it proved to be by far the best decision . . . *Shocker* was done with complete artistic control. There was no interference whatsoever aside from the MPAA. This is exactly the film I set out to make.

Craven Images

Marc Shapiro / 1992

From *Fangoria* 109, January 1992. Reprinted by permission of Joseph A. Sonnier IV, CEO of *Cinestate* and *Fangoria*.

"Boy! You can't get a good cappuccino when you want one," Wes Craven's request for a highbrow coffee is greeted with howls of laughter. The drink order wasn't out of line, but the incongruity of ordering the brew on the dirty, dusty, and highly claustrophobic set of *The People Under the Stairs* has struck a collective funny bone.

His response, a thoughtful look and a chuckle that lets the crew know he's hip to the madness of the situation, is followed by the setting of this long, lean, and, these days, bearded figure into a director's chair. To anyone who's been following his career, Wes Craven at ease is a bit of a revelation. He's healthier looking than he was shortly after the completion of *The Serpent and the Rainbow* and much more relaxed than he appeared while toiling on *Shocker*.

This just might signal the arrival of a new Wes Craven. The man who scared audiences to death for over two decades does not appear to be the figure in constant creative torment he used to present to the world. This Craven appears poised for a new beginning, one that finds him in a creative and personal sense, in a state of grace.

"I don't know if what I'm going through now is so much a new beginning as it is a transition of sorts," the director contemplates. "I feel more settled and more mature than I did two pictures back, but as far as a new beginning, I don't really know. I'm just continuing to follow that inner voice, whatever it is."

Craven's current expression of his personal concerns is *The People Under the Stairs*, a raw excursion into real-life horror that he discussed in the last two issues of *Fango*. The odyssey of creating *People* began twelve years ago, but the origin of this particular nightmare has been in his head much longer.

"This movie is really getting at something that's been in and out of my dreams for years," Craven reveals. "They were visions of houses, finished and unfinished, that branch off into long, winding galleries. *Nightmare on Elm Street* got into that dream to a certain extent, but this film is taking it all the way."

Craven does not view *People Under the Stairs* as being a new step in horror for him. On the contrary it's a return to the themes of the films that made his early reputation. "I see it as being more along the lines of my earlier work like *Last House on the Left* and *The Hills Have Eyes*," he comments. "It's a very real and primitive situation that is not dreamlike and does not rely on electrical circuits. I see it as something very symbolic. The kids going up against Man and Woman are representative of small groups standing up for larger groups. The house with all its claustrophobic spaces in hiding places, stands for civilization run amok. The generations that have lived in that have gotten more and more crazy until the present one is totally locked into madness."

Man and Woman (Everett McGill and Wendy Robie), the extremely bad couple who imprison and torment the people under the stairs of their dark abode, are the latest in a long line of distinctive villains created by Craven. And as with such previous fiends as Freddy Krueger and Horace Pinker, the writer/director invested them with distinctive personalities.

"Woman had to be very manipulative and clever," he explains. "She's someone who has taken neatness to maddening heights. Man was a much more beastly creation, a wily and brutal person. I'd like to say that their creation was all in the script, but Everett and Wendy came up with some very strange twists that enhanced what I wrote."

While Craven was putting the finishing touches on *People*, another of his projects, the television series *Nightmare Café*, was shooting in Canada: at press time, it is slotted as a midseason replacement for NBC. The supernatural anthology, which features Robert Englund, Jack Coleman, and Lindsay Frost in recurring roles, is described as *"Cheers* meets *The Twilight Zone."*

"The show takes place in an all-night restaurant that is in the netherworld between life and death," he elaborates. "Each week, people from this world end up in the café for one night to encounter the turning point in their lives. It could be their worst nightmare or their ultimate breakthrough.

"The three characters who run the place observe the ongoing story of each person [whom they watch on the eatery's TV set] and bet on how it's going to come out," Craven continues. "From time to time they will enter the action and, at some point, the story will be as much about the people who inhabit the café as it will be about the people who come into it."

According to Craven, working with Robert Englund post–*Elm Street* has been a strange but enjoyable experience. "Robert approach me about the role of Blackie in the show," the director reveals. "At first I didn't think he could handle playing what is essentially an older character. But then I realized that Robert's in his forties now and more than able to play an older type, so I went with him. He's playing a totally different character from Freddy. Blackie is a cynical, shyster-lawyer type. It will be interesting for people to see Robert playing a much more sophisticated person."

Craven's *Night Visions*, about a cop teamed with the psychic, played the tube last season. The director gives the telemovie, which starred James Remar and featured *Shocker*'s Mitch Pileggi, mixed notices. "From a filmmaking point of view, it was an interesting experience. The actors were fine, and overall, we got a good-looking picture for a television budget. I was a little disappointed that the network [NBC] did not get behind it; more what happened is they had a test screening, and one of the main characters tested weak. At that point, the network just kind of lost interest in getting behind the film."

Night Visions was not the first time Craven has had a disappointing excursion on the small screen. A series he created, *The People Next Door*, died a quick and merciful death a couple of seasons back.

"I've taken my lumps when it comes to TV," he laments, "but that's all right because I've pretty much known what I was up against. Television is much more restrictive when it comes to horror and dark fantasy, so you do have to be careful. But I am not too worried about *Nightmare Café*. It's not a blood and guts show. It's not *Freddy's Nightmares*."

Nor is it *Shocker*, a movie Craven hoped would sire a new film series he could have more control over than he did on the *Nightmare* movies. The 1989 release garnered mediocre box-office returns, not enough to warrant a return visit.

"Universal never felt it did the business they wanted it to," Craven confirms. "*Shocker* wasn't an expensive movie to make, and the studio probably felt they did not get the franchise character they were hoping for. I would love to do a sequel to *Shocker*, though. It's something that's prime to go off in a million different directions."

Craven turns philosophical when asked to ponder the recently released final demise of his most famous child. "Freddy's certainly had his run," he opines, "but the character will never really die. TV and video will see to that. As a business enterprise, Freddy won't pass away until the people who own the rights have squeezed every nickel out of him that they can."

The director turned his attention to the MPAA's recent adoption of the NC-17—a rating, given his seemingly endless battles with the dreaded organization, that seems tailor-made to end his gore battles. However, he claims the new category will only make his creative life even more challenging.

"Trying to reach a high intensity level with a picture and still get it past the sensors will always be a challenge," he affirms. "Every time I make a picture, the MPAA is a real presence. And now with the NC-17, it's going to be even harder to make an R-rated picture that passes. The ratings board is telling me, 'OK, you've got your rating, now stay out of our faces with this stuff.' But most studios, despite the new category, still want R-rated pictures. So in a big way, I'm still caught in the middle; my goal now is to make pictures that are very intense without being terribly graphic. It's going to be difficult."

But while the notion of how to create horror on film is changing, what is truly scary to the Cleveland-born filmmaker remains largely rooted in the home. "I try to find a basis for fear and heart in the world around me," he muses. "That idea has pretty much stayed the same. Ideas that come out of families which are fractured or disturbed in some way are the most profoundly terrifying things to me. I've always felt that I was on solid ground when I was making movies of our families. *A Nightmare on Elm Street, The Last House on the Left, The Hills Have Eyes*—they were all tied into the interworkings of families, and they scared the hell out of people."

Craven is a strong advocate of utilizing dreams while formulating cinematic thrill rides, and many of his greatest hits have their origins in subconscious mind trips. "I've probably got the most profitable dreams in the industry," he jokes. "It does not happen like that every time. But it does seem like whenever I get my subconscious working on something, it pops up in a dream. They're definitely a big part of my creative process."

This leads one to wonder if Craven has ever come up against a nightmare that was too frightening to put down on paper and ultimately commit to celluloid.

"That's never happened," he insists. "Sometimes you dream things that are so horrible that you have a hard time describing them. But I have no problem writing down the particulars of a truly horrifying dream. I found that making a movie out of a particularly vivid dream is a good way to exorcise personal demons."

Craven is already looking to the future. Upcoming plans, he hints, involve "large genre works," including a "*Jaws* kind of thing" (rumored to be the film adaptation of Peter Benchley's *Beast*, whose film rights have been picked up by Universal and Alive Films, the duo behind Craven's last two movies). He's also pursuing production and directorial duties on "some things out of the genre."

Craven's aiming for nonhorror work might seem, to those familiar with his history, the latest barrage of wishful thinking. While he insists that more mainstream projects, including at least one suspense thriller, are in the offing, he's also candid enough to admit that he may be hopelessly tied to the scream scene.

"I'm typecast as a horror filmmaker. I know it. But that's not necessarily bad," he avers. "I've got a lot of power within the genre that has not been afforded me outside of it. Look what I've got when I'm doing genre films. I've got my own production company, script and cast approval, and I don't have to show dailies to anybody.

I'm able to make films that are very unique and personal without any interference. I could not go outside horror and do that. But here I sit on a movie set, making *People Under the Stairs* and knowing that when it is all said and done, I will have exactly the film I set out to make."

Wes Craven's Parental Guidance

Fangoria / 1994

From *Wes Craven's New Nightmare: The Official Movie Magazine*, 1994. Reprinted by permission of Joseph A. Sonnier IV, CEO of *Cinestate* and *Fangoria*.

Wes Craven has heard it so many times before. Yes, he is the "Father of Freddy Krueger." Is he tired of the tag? Perhaps—but he's not above having a joke at the expense of his own notoriety as the creative force behind the *Nightmare on Elm Street* mythos.

"Yes, I'm Freddy's father," chuckles the fifty-five-year-old director in his trademark understated tones. "But boy, I wish they would speak to Freddy's mother about all this. I'd be curious to hear what she has to say, because we don't see each other anymore."

For Craven, 1994 is turning out to be a (blood)red-letter year. He, along with the legions of horror fans, is celebrating the ten-year anniversary of the release of his original *A Nightmare on Elm Street*, and his gift to Freddy's fans is his return to bad-dreamland as writer/director of the latest entry, *Wes Craven's New Nightmare*. Craven has gone into detail on the particulars of his reentry into the fold in *Fangoria* #137 and #138; now, with *New Nightmare* in the can and awaiting its October release, he is taking an occasional tongue-in-cheek and particularly reflective look back on a decade of *Nightmares*.

"I've always been comfortable with creating Freddy," says Craven, "and that has grown with the years and the films. I'm also comfortable with the fact that Freddy has come to epitomize a certain section of reality. He's very much here in our lives and appears to thrive in everything that goes on in our world today. He's there in the drive-by shootings in the United States and the horrible things that are going on in Bosnia and the rest of the world. There's a lot of Freddy out there in our lives, whether we like it or not."

It was with this real-world attitude in mind that Craven agreed in principle to come up with another *Nightmare*. "I knew it had to be something different," he says. "It wouldn't have worked for me to have *Freddy's Dead* simply be a dream and go on into another adventure. I've always liked the characters, I've always liked the concept," he continues, adding that an actual stalking incident in Nancy actress Heather Langenkamp's own life inspired much of the sequel's storyline. "I thought really hard about exactly what it would take to make a new and original *Nightmare on Elm Street* vision. Finally, I was reunited with Heather and heard about what was going on in her life. Those real-life terrors struck me as the perfect jumping-off point for a new look at what Freddy really means. Happily, New Line Cinema and [chairman] Bob Shaye were really excited about this new direction."

Craven recalls that *New Nightmare*, from its dream-inspired writing process to what he describes as "a fast-paced, documentary style of filmmaking," was a project that really got his juices flowing. "In many ways, I was feeling more free and creative than I did on the first *Nightmare*," he says. "I saw some real challenges in reprising themes and dealing with these same personalities ten years later. It was quite a unique experience to work with the same actors and approach the story from an entirely new direction. I knew from the outset that the approach would be risky, but I also knew that making this film would be intriguing and creatively very fruitful."

Not to mention the fact that he was able to make a movie more consistent with his groundbreaking earlier hit. "This film is much closer in tone to the first *Nightmare* than anything that has come since," he says.

"Obviously the reason is, to a large extent, that it was made by the same person. But this can only be considered a sequel in the sense that it looks at the people who made the first film. It is something totally new because it takes a very serious, multilayered look at the violence in our films and our culture and how it affects not only the audience but also the people who make the movies."

In Craven's realistic approach, his monstrous creation is a genuine ancient and unfathomably evil entity captured—then released—by the filmmaking process. "What we're finding out is that beyond the Freddy Krueger of the imaginary story, there is a spirit that has been around a long time," Craven says, "a spirit that has been given many different names through the years by many different storytellers. I gave that spirit the name of Freddy Krueger, but his spirit has probably been around since mankind has been on this planet.

"What this [latest] film is about," he continues, "is Freddy Krueger making his way into the real world. There are no jokes in this one. This is scary."

In this context, actor Robert Englund plays both himself and his fictional alter ego in the new thrill ride, while Craven, Langenkamp, and John Saxon portray themselves in the film. "Everybody came back because it's pretty much about our lives and our reactions to what is and has gone on in Heather's life," the director says.

Craven's thoughts turn to the days before Freddy, when he was first beginning to flex his creative muscles a few years after his disturbing classic *Last House on the*

Left in the mid-seventies. "It was a very exciting time in my life," he remembers. "I was feeling, creatively, very awake. I had just relocated to California to make *The Hills Have Eyes* and completed the television movie *Summer of Fear* (aka *Stranger in Our House*) with Linda Blair and appeared to have finally made the leap from 16mm to 35mm films. I was really feeling my oats as an independent filmmaker and felt that the next big step for me was to come up with something original."

According to the director, inspiration struck in 1978 at Lucky's Restaurant in Santa Monica, California. "I had been reading these articles about three people who died separately in their dreams," he recalls. "Those articles were fascinating to me, and, one day, I was talking to a friend of mine about them. Suddenly I just stopped and said, 'Jesus! A movie about somebody who attacks you in your dreams can be really frightening.' I wrote the initial outline of *A Nightmare on Elm Street* that same year, and the first draft of the script soon followed."

Craven's idea was rejected by every studio in town—some rejected it twice—before New Line took the bait. What followed was a pleasant filmmaking experience for the director. "It was different, and I think people who make movies can recognize the excitement and creative flow that we had on the set of that film," he says. "We had Heather Langenkamp and Johnny Depp, who were young and untried, veterans like Robert Englund, who had been acting a while but was still relatively unknown, and people like John Saxon, who had been around but were willing to try something different by doing *Nightmare on Elm Street*.

"We were working on a small budget and challenges popped up in almost every scene," he continues. "But everybody was very supportive and full of ideas on how to get the most out of the shoestring budget we were on."

One thing Craven is taking advantage of is the opportunity to make Freddy Krueger much more of a personification of evil than he's been in most of the sequels. And despite the never-ending debate on who's truly the greatest horror hero, the director says that there really is no contest.

"Freddy is the ideal character to represent evil," Craven maintains. "He's very much an articulate, sympathetic personification of horror. He's intelligent, he's able to speak, and, even though he doesn't talk much, when he does, it's right to the core of our fears. I've always felt that Freddy is more frightening than somebody in a hockey mask coming at you with a knife or a hatchet."

Craven's horror filmography has been all over the map and despite the occasional disappointment of a *Swamp Thing* or *Hills Have Eyes Part II*, the director has more often than not succeeded in delivering the horror goods. And he happily reports that he's recognized for more than just his forays on Elm Street.

"When my name comes up, people usually say that the first *Nightmare* really scared them," he says. "But then they'll usually mention *The Serpent and the Rainbow* and *The Hills Have Eyes*. Then there's the older audience who says *Last House on the Left* scared the shit out of them when they were growing up. Usually, those four films are the ones that always seem to nail people. I also love *The People Under the Stairs* and *Shocker* because they were done very independently. *People Under the Stairs* proved to be prophetic; it had a very political message that, a year later when the Los Angeles riots started, turned out to be very true. So, I guess, in a way, you'd have to include those two films too."

One potential film that would certainly bring Craven's name to mind is the oft-speculated and, apparently, now actively-being-developed *Freddy vs. Jason* film. Craven has previously reported (in *Fangoria* #138) what he knew of that team-up film and disclosed how a story idea changed hands between Jason creator Sean Cunningham and himself over dinner. He's still not sure, however, if he'll be involved.

"I'm not looking forward to doing anything with that film in the near future—but I don't rule it out," he says. "If it happens, it will be an idea that comes tumbling out of somebody's subconscious that will be made. For me, a *Freddy vs. Jason* movie would have to represent something meaningful in a much larger sense. That's how the latest *Nightmare* movie came about. It was a terrific idea and a concept that just worked. But *Freddy vs. Jason*? Who knows?"

What Craven is certain is that, over the years, the opinion of the world at large and the film industry in particular has changed regarding Freddy Krueger and the whole *Nightmare on Elm Street* phenomenon. "There's certainly a decent amount of respect, or grudging respect, directed toward the *Nightmare* films," says the director of the film series that has grossed over $200 million. "When the first film opened, nobody knew what the hell it was. Once the film was out there, people began to realize that it was scary, but I still don't think they understood how powerful the film and the message actually was. It wasn't until years later that people realized that maybe the whole Freddy thing ought to be taken a bit more seriously and that the films represented a feeling that was actually out there. It was something that just built up over the years. People began to understand that what was going on with Freddy and the *Nightmare* films was, in a way, very real."

Chase: You've had run-ins over the years with the MPAA and the ratings.
Craven: Yep.

Chase: What is your most memorable run-in, something that was like completely ridiculous where you didn't understand or just made you petulant?
Craven: I got petulant every time because you really feel very possessive about your film and also you know what things are effective and will make people jump or scream or love the film, and then you come to the very end to this group who are like protective parents. They are basically looking for those things that make your film really special, and they want you to take them out. And it's really hard. It started to creep up into the area where they would say, "We don't want to tell you exactly what to cut, but between footages such-and-such and such-and-such, reduce the intensity."

And I say, "What other art form do artists have to reduce intensity?" So it's very strange. It started to creep as the corporate takeover of film business started; films were talked about more and more in the halls of the studios as "products," and then products became subject to recall and lawsuits in their minds. They started thinking of them as chunks of widgets that they are pumping out of their machine. You have to try and fight and say, "This isn't a widget. This is something personal, and if it offends some people that means it's alive." Everything has offended everybody in the past . . . if you look at anything from Shakespeare; all the great novels we read at one time or another have probably been banned.

Chase: Intensity is so subjective, too. What one person would find intense and disturbing another person may not.
Craven: Yeah, it's like somebody who hates rollercoasters saying, "Take that hill and bring it down a hundred feet," and everybody else is waiting to get on it because they love it.

Chase: Do you just want to bang your head against the wall until it doesn't hurt anymore?
Craven: I want to bang my head against some censors! The great thing about the *Red Eye* is that it's PG-13. We thought they would be very upset by the way she gets off the airplane, which involves striking with a weapon, which you wouldn't expect, but they found the whole rest of the picture so uplifting and inspiring that they let us go. So it's great.

Chase: I'm very pleased to hear that, but it says a lot about the MPAA: just they were in a bad mood that day and they decided to take something out, or they were in a good mood that day and said, "Oh, this is uplifting."

of things. This isn't Eddie doing Axel Foley with a cape and fangs. This is Eddie doing a serious role, playing a romantic lead, and, basically, not being a very nice guy."

Scripted by Murphy's brother Charlie along with Michael Lucker and Chris Parker, *Vampire in Brooklyn* opens on an ominous, fog-shrouded night as a ghostly ship floats out of the mist and literally crashes in a New York City harbor. Dead bodies are found on board, but one very active undead type, the vampire Maximillian (Murphy), has escaped into the depths of Brooklyn. Aided by a lowlife-turned-ghoul named Julius (Kadeem Hardison), Max is on the hunt for a beautiful half-human/half-vampire Manhattan cop named Rita (Angela Bassett), who holds the key to repopulating a nearly extinct race of vampires. Racing against time and the coming of the full moon, Max must seduce Rita, convert her to a full-fledged vampire and, as the body count mounts, convince her to feed so that the children of the night can continue their reign. Fighting for the side of good are Rita's partner Warren (Allen Payne) and an old Van Helsing type with secrets and an agenda all his own.

Rounding out the cast are John Witherspoon, Joanna Cassidy, Jerry Hall and Craven alumni Zakes Mokae (*The Serpent and the Rainbow*), Nick Corri (*A Nightmare on Elm Street*), Mitch Pileggi (*Shocker*) and Wendy Robie (*The People Under the Stairs*). Handling the variety of vampire visages, transformations and occasional gore are the busy KNB team, while Peter Chesney took on the physical FX demands. The production only filmed for three of its 55 days on location in New York, spending the rest in Los Angeles—and 48 of those days were actually night shoots in cold and often damp conditions.

What ultimately makes *Vampire in Brooklyn* a potential diamond in the rough is that while Murphy obviously gets in his share of laughs, the character's humor is more subdued and subtle, tied in to an admirable attempt at playing straight. Barring any serious alterations in the final cut, this is the closest Murphy has come to serious business.

"This is not a real horrific film in the sense that it's incredibly hard-edged or difficult to watch if you're squeamish," warns Craven. "This does not set out to terrify an audience like I love to do. It has scares in it, but also a lot of laughs. It's more of a horror/comedy/romance. It's one of those hybrid films that is very difficult to pull off, but I think we did."

Craven's introduction to Murphy's world came a little more than a year ago when his agent was exchanging pleasantries with Murphy's manager, who mentioned that *Vampire in Brooklyn* was in need of a director. Craven's name was offered up, and Murphy's manager, who knew nothing about the director's horror track record, took the suggestion back to Murphy. According to Craven, the comedian was more than familiar with his work.

"Eddie's manager ran it by him and mentioned that I had done *Serpent and the Rainbow*, and Eddie immediately lit up," says Craven. "It turns out he's a big *Serpent* and *Hills Have Eyes* fan, and a real horror buff in general. He thought we would make the perfect combination. And it seemed the perfect opportunity for me as well. I've been saying for years that comedy was my first love, and I've been dying to do one for years."

Craven and Murphy subsequently met and discovered that they felt comfortable with each other and their respective takes on the film. "Those meetings were pretty entertaining," Craven recalls. "Eddie would recite whole chunks of dialogue from *Serpent and the Rainbow* and *Hills Have Eyes*. It was hilarious. He really had me rolling."

The discussions turned serious when both agreed that the screenplay, originally written by the Murphys and Vernon Lynch, needed some work. "The script had been around for a while, had been reworked many times and had a lot of problems," Craven reports. "It seemed to lack a center. Parts of it were too savage and parts of it were funny in ways that the audience would not have warmed up to. There was no romance. It was more of an action-buddy picture, the very thing that Eddie seemed to be trying to get away from."

Making the obstacle course that much tougher was the fact that Murphy was already committed to do his remake of *The Nutty Professor*, but a last-minute schedule shift opened up a small window of opportunity for *Vampire in Brooklyn*. "Suddenly, we had a very short time before Eddie was obligated to do that film." Craven recalls. "But if the script hadn't worked, this was going to have to be shot after *Nutty Professor* and probably never would have been done. Fortunately, Chris and Michael came up with a fresh concept and did a page-one rewrite in three-and-a-half weeks so that the movie could be made." (Originally, *Vampire* was to be held back until after *Professor*'s release, but Universal, the latter film's studio, relented and allowed *Vampire* to go first.)

According to Craven, the final screenplay plays fast and loose with a great deal of the accepted vampire lore. "Things like not having a reflection in a mirror and having an aversion to holy water and sunlight are there, but we've made the character of the vampire a little different," he says. "Max comes from the Caribbean; we figured it would be ridiculous to have a black vampire coming from Transylvania. We've also made him a lot less rigid and uptight than vampires are usually portrayed. He has a much more earthy, sly sense than vampires coming from Europe."

The casting process for *Vampire* proved to be a mixed bag. "I was able to get a number of people I've worked with before, like Zakes Mokae, Nick Corri, Mitch Pileggi, and Wendy Robie, for small roles, which was a lot of fun. But I knew finding the main players would be tough just by virtue of the fact that, once you cast Eddie Murphy, you need somebody strong to stand up to him."

This came into play particularly when searching for an actress to play Rita. "Originally, the idea was to cast a young starlet type," Craven reveals. "But we decided, 'Look, Rita is a very difficult role. She is somebody who literally has to be half human and half vampire.' So we pushed for somebody of a high acting caliber, and Angela Bassett immediately came to mind. Originally, we didn't know whether to go with an older or younger comic for the role of Julius, but we finally decided on Kadeem Hardison because he had this amazing combination of wit, warmth, and grace that just makes you like the character."

As filming on *Vampire in Brooklyn* began in earnest, it became evident that when Murphy wasn't commanding the spotlight, KNB's FX were. The closest thing to actual gore is an early sequence in which Max pulls the heart out of a victim, but the way Craven tells it, the FX team really shined in the scenes that did not require blood and guts.

"The basic looks and transmutations of the vampires are truly fantastic," the director raves. "We have Max going from being a handsome, dapper sort of fellow to being quite monstrous-looking toward the end. At one point in the story he morphs into the character of Guido, an Italian street hood who is obviously white, and the makeup was so good that when Eddie walked onto the set, nobody recognized him."

In typical Craven fashion, the director claims that "the entire film was one big challenge," but specifically cites the opening sequence in which the ghost ship lands in New York as a monstrous physical undertaking. "That called for some precision driving and crashing," he recalls. "It was done by having a pilot on the ship and a tugboat lashed to it on the side away from the camera, guiding it. The tug and ship captains were in constant contact. It was amazing how we were able to get that ship to hit its marks."

Craven gives Murphy, who plays multiple roles in the film, high marks not only for his performances, but also for his ability to make the physical sequences and especially the final fight scenes work. "He's tough. He wanted to do his own stunts whenever he could, and he did a real good job. I was also quite happy with Angela's work as Rita. She did the cop stuff well, and there's some real electricity between her and Eddie in the seduction scenes. I consider myself very lucky in this film. It was like, instinctively, everybody knew exactly what was required and what they had to do to make these characters come to life."

Craven's most vivid memories of making *Vampire in Brooklyn*, however, were of simply experiencing Murphy in action. "Watching him turn into the character of Preacher Pauly and then seeing him convince a whole congregation of people that evil is good was a real education for me in terms of comic timing," he marvels. "Eddie just took the script and ran with it. But that didn't detract from his take on the serious side of the role. In fact, Eddie turned out to be quite scary when he dropped the laughs and turned serious. It wasn't difficult to get that frightening side out of him, because doing something this different was what he really wanted to do."

The director himself was looking for a change of pace when he tackled *Wes Craven's New Nightmare*, the apparently final installment of the *Nightmare on Elm Street* series that received great reviews but only so-so box office. "Making that film was definitely a case of having a hard act to follow after they had killed off Freddy, said he's gone and suddenly we come back with another one. Especially one that was as cerebral as *New Nightmare* was.

"I did not want to do anything that was all Freddy," he says. "I thought it would be interesting to do a piece that had a lot of thought in it and focused more on Heather [Langenkamp]. I admit there was a certain risk in not featuring Robert [Englund] as much as some might have wanted. Frankly, I wasn't really sure about the ad campaign. I felt that around Los Angeles there were virtually no billboards or posters. A lot of people were not even aware of the movie until it came out on laserdisc. But I was happy that the film received some of the best reviews I've ever gotten."

He is, however, decidedly lukewarm on the upcoming *Freddy vs. Jason*, a film he reports he was given the option of writing. "But I frankly could not come up with an idea that I wanted to do," he says. "I feel like I drew my own personal closure to the series with *New Nightmare*, but New Line is going to do whatever they decide they want to do with it. There's a certain market inevitability that dictates they will squeeze every dime out of it that they can. I wish, in a sense, that they would let it have its dignity and end with *New Nightmare*. Now it's sort of like *Abbott and Costello Meet Frankenstein*. *Freddy vs. Jason* is taking something that had a lot of impact and dignity and dragging it down to another level. But who knows? Maybe they'll come up with a new direction that will make it work."

Taking a moment to play the proud papa, Craven praises his son Jonathan's initial production effort, *Mind Ripper*, which will make its debut on HBO in October. "It turned out pretty well for a first film on a limited budget shot in a hellish place," he says of the movie, which was directed by Joe Gayton. "I mean, you try and make Bulgaria look like the United States."

Craven is currently in negotiations on two non-genre projects: *Original Sin*, a sexual thriller with a Joe Eszterhas script, and *The Cage*, based on a novel about an expedition to photograph polar bears. But the big horror stop over the horizon is a remake of *The Haunting*, to be produced by Miramax with a script by Edithe Swensen, who contributed to TV's *Tales from the Darkside* and *Monsters*. "We're basically days away from getting a green light on the script," he reveals. "My take on this film is that we're doing something with the same sense of class but utilizing modern tools. Obviously, this will be a more contemporary view of what is scary—what the psychodynamics are between a mother and a daughter that would cause a house to resonate with its own haunting."

Craven admits that *Vampire in Brooklyn* may not break much new ground as a horror film per se but that there is a lot going on between the lines. "Eddie as a somewhat serious villain makes this different," he points out. "So does the way we attempt to mix horror and other elements. We've taken a lot of genre conventions and given them a slightly different twist. I know this will be something new for Eddie Murphy fans who have never seen him in a film like this before. To a lot of people, this might seem like a pretty conventional film. But there's more going on than meets the eye."

For Craven himself, who has long labored in horror heaven but mainstream hell, *Vampire in Brooklyn* marks another turning point. "I've really appreciated all the actors and actresses I've worked with in the past, and it's not like, 'Thank God! I'm finally getting to work with the big people.' But there's a strength in the marketplace that comes from working with actors with known names. It gives you more leverage and it gets your projects out there."

"And frankly," concludes Craven, "I'm sick of doing films that get released at weird times of the year. I would like a summer release or a Christmas release. You get an audience at those times of the year that's going to look for intelligence and a good story. Who knows? I may end up getting rediscovered."

Wes Craven: Early in my life, my father died and before that he left the family, so there was that whole set of the uproar of Dad leaving and, I think, the arguments before—I have vague memories—and then about a year later he had a heart attack at work and died. He was buried on my fourth birthday. So, you know, the early, those first early five years had a lot of disruptions and then, for the first time, we had to move. Thereafter was a series of different houses, different locations. Because of the fact that my mother's income went down, I had this one peculiarity to my upbringing that I should probably mention: just before my father died my mother—I think during the time with their troubles in their marriage—they were invited to a church and became converted to Fundamentalist Christianity, to a Baptist Church, and it's very hard to mention it in the general milieu of American thought without people thinking of it as something odd or, you know, extreme. But going back to what I said about everything seeming normal if you have nothing to compare it to, that was our church and that was very much a second family. So there was, in a sense about that church, a remarkable sense of stability and shelter; that was the positive side of it. The negative side, as far as being a filmmaker, is that they did not believe in movies with the exception of Walt Disney films, which were consistently kind of, you know, safe. Hollywood and its product were considered to be kind of the work of the devil, literally, so we simply did not go to movies. So my early influences were not filmic; like, they were—I think—I discovered the library very quickly, and so what I really grew up on was novels and stories, with the single exception of my kind of surrogate father. There was a family—the Biltens. Dorothy Bilten, my mother's closest friend when my father died, invited me into their household during the day when my mother was working and until my mother came back from work at night. And, one of Eddy's big hobbies was 8mm photography, and also he would rent a movie from the local camera shop, which was a custom in those days. And I was completely enthralled by film. Cut to, you know, many, many years later when I was teaching college, students who were really more aware—I think—of how films were made than I was came to me and said, "We would like to start a film club." So I said, "Fine." They said, "We have a couple movies we want to shoot." And so they had written a *Mission: Impossible* take off, and I became sort of their advisor/cameraman. We made it, spliced it together on a projector—using a projector as an editing machine—we knew nothing about the technical side of film really. We made our—the cost of our film, which I think was $300—back about ten times, about three grand, and at the end of that year my department chairman came to me. And he said, "You know, it's time for you to get serious. You're not working on your PhD, you haven't published anything, and you're running around with the stupid camera acting like an idiot. It's time you became a serious humanities professor." And, I quit.

that he saw and that was Sharon Stone, so it was her first speaking role. There was a scene where she had to have a spider—there was a lot of spider action in this particular film, and we had a spider-wrangler. There was a scene where she had to have a tarantula on her chest and it had to move. We needed a live tarantula, and I happen to have sort of a mild arachnophobia myself. So I said, "Listen, Sharon, I'm afraid of spiders, and I know you are. So I'll put a spider on me, and if I do it will you do it?" She said, "Yeah. Okay." So I put the spider on and actually it was—it was interesting because as soon as it was on my arm, like, I wasn't afraid. It was a very little gentle touch, so I said, "Okay, now—we'll put it on you." And she says, "What about those fangs?" The trainer says, "They don't bite you unless you push down on them, smash down on them." She says, "What if it did bite me?" He says, "It would be like a bee sting or a hornet." She says, "What if you cut the fangs off?" He says, "Well, we can cut them off, but they don't grow back. So the spider will just starve to death over a long time; it's actually quite a horrible death." She says, "Clip them!" (Craven laughs). That's my Sharon Stone story.

NARR: *Swamp Thing*, released in 1982, was based on the popular DC comic book character. Although plagued with production problems, this film has also gained cult status. The film starred Louis Jordan, Adrienne Barbeau, and Ray Wise.

WC: Well, the plot for *Swamp Thing* was devised. It was a very popular comic. It was one that I wasn't particularly familiar with, because it was another thing—it was forbidden by the church. You know, I read all the *Swamp Thing* comic books, just kind of made an amalgam of a story that was based on the major characters, and that's how that came about. It was sort of an adaptation, if you will. *Swamp Thing* was a film that, I think, was severely damaged by lack of funding. It was my first encounter with a guarantor—you know, an organization that would guarantee that the film would be made on budget—and it was underbudgeted from the get-go. And about halfway through the film they came in and were on the set all the time to the point that the producers literally were weeping and the second half of the film was basically shot in masters, so a lot of what was in the script was thrown out. It was made under incredible duress.

Adrienne Barbeau (actor, *Swamp Thing*): I remember when I got the script, which he wrote, I thought, "This can be just absolutely fantastic!" It was a very funny script. It was really delightful as well as being an action-adventure, which I hadn't done too much of, so I looked forward to it immensely.

Ray Wise (actor, *Swamp Thing*): We had a wonderful time doing it, but we did shoot in the swamps for about six weeks, the swamps outside of Charleston, South

Carolina. We were surrounded by alligators and water moccasins and deer flies and everything bit and stung.

WC: The tannic acid of the water itself ate through the costumes—the special effects costume of Swamp Thing—and everything was literally rotting off of the actor.

RW: They had to patch up the Swamp Thing costume with Elmer's glue.

WC: It was a plague of stinging caterpillars hanging in all the trees that were falling down our necks all the time. So it was like one of the most arduous shoots I've ever had.

AB: It ended up being difficult because we were under time constraints. I think we were a little underbudgeted. We were having weather problems, but my main impression of Wes throughout the entire time was an extremely calm, gentle, laid-back man who spent a lot of time getting the performances he wanted.

RW: I'm happy to see it on television every year, and here in Los Angeles, they sort of make it an annual thing to show *Swamp Thing*. It's become a real cult classic, and I'm happy to see that.

NARR: In 1984, Craven entered the mainstream with his portrayal of a group of teens struggling to define the line between their dreams and reality. With the release of *A Nightmare on Elm Street*, it brought to the screen the character of Freddy Krueger, a character audiences would come to love and hate in five sequels.

WC: The history of *A Nightmare on Elm Street* is kind of interesting. I read a newspaper article in the *LA Times* about an immigrant, a recent immigrant, to the United States. A young man who had complained to his parents about severe nightmares. I think they were from Cambodia, and he was assured that nightmares were not that unusual, he shouldn't be so afraid. He started staying up and refusing to sleep. The family became very concerned, and they sought the help of a doctor. The doctor prescribed sleeping pills. The young man apparently took them, and in the end it turned out he did not—he was taking them and putting them aside. He had a coffee pot in his room after a while to stay awake, and nobody knew quite what to do. At one point, he was downstairs watching television in the middle of the night and he fell asleep. And his family noticed, finally, that he was asleep, and they brought him up to his bed. The whole family went to bed themselves, thinking, "Thank God, finally he's sleeping." Then they heard screams an hour later, ran into his room, and he is thrashing in his bed. By the time they got to him, he was dead . . . and over the next nine months I found two more articles . . . so I wrote it and thought it was the best thing since sliced bread and then spent three years trying to fund it, and I have a wonderful drawer full of letters saying, "This is not scary. This is stupid. Nobody would ever like this," and I basically went broke in those three years. I couldn't get a job directing; both *Swamp Thing* and *Deadly Blessing* had not done that well. I couldn't get arrested, and kind of on my last gasp I had to borrow money to pay my taxes that year. I had made *The Hills Have Eyes II*, and it got me through a little bit. But basically, I was flat broke when that film was put into production. I've never forgotten those two times in my life—when you think you've made it and then suddenly you don't have work and how fickle the business can be and how difficult it is to write something that is a breakthrough because if you have a vision of something, that is kind of the next thing; there is no guarantee there will be another person out there that can recognize that. It's amazing how many people have read the script to *A Nightmare on Elm Street* and saw no potential in it whatsoever.

WC: You really look for actors who break through all of the nearest civilization in one way or the other, either as victim or as, you know, perpetrator. There's that sort of Kosovo factor of people who at one moment can be nurturing their children and the next moment slashing each other's throats. That is the appalling truth that's behind so much of what we like to think of civilization, so you look for that willingness in the part of an actor to expose that and to be cool or to be inventive in the cruelty. And a lot of people just don't want to bring that out or say they don't have it. You know, whatever you want to think about it, but you have to find people that can do that. Quite often, it's the person that's the most gentle or the most civilized.

Robert Englund (actor, *Nightmare on Elm Street* series): I'm sort of —to put it politely—a conversationalist. I'm a jabber mouth, but I forced myself to shut up and let Wes do all the talking at that particular interview because I was not really correct for the part. I think they wanted a 6' 4" stuntman or something originally, and I—for once—just sat there. I was going to force myself to listen to Wes and not say anything and just sort of stare and let him look at the potential my face had for makeup or for being scary or whatever. And it was so easy because Wes is such a raconteur, and he was telling me this great, kind of strange concept he had for the original *Nightmare* film. It was all that I could to do to kind of go, "Oh, tell me more, Uncle Wes." It was like this great story that he was telling; that was my first meeting with him. Wes sort of set the blueprint and the bible for the entire *Elm Street* series, and whenever we have strayed from that, I think the films have suffered somewhat. When we have broken Wes's rules, I think the films—or at least sequences of the films—have suffered. With Wes, I feel a little more beholden to protecting Freddy. Wes sort of knows there's a fine line with Freddy's dark sense of humor and kind of a cruel clown as they would have it in the sort of Roman theater sense. But Wes, I don't have to protect it with Wes. He understands where that line is. With other directors, there's a tendency to allow me to either improvise too much or to end a sequence on something jokey or humorous, even if it's black humor and the dark humor of Freddy and not to have that alternative take that might be just cruel and downright mean, which in postproduction I really think it's necessary because you don't really know where that balance is going to fall until you get in there—in editorial. Wes has that instinct right on the set and when he's steering on the set. You kind of know which way to err in the direction of—you know, whether to go for the dark or whether to bring in that kind of dark sense of humor that Wes sort of blueprinted for Freddy.

WC: At that time, it was *Halloween*. In those, you know, several other films that feature the unusual instruments, and I was thinking, "Well, okay. What will it be? A chainsaw or sickle or Scythe or whatever." And I said, "Well, take yourself—you know from my academic background—take yourself back to the earliest phenomenon that you can." And I thought, "Take yourself back to primal man, to mankind when he was not equipped with shields or weapons. What did he confront?" And, it was tooth and claw, so I literally thought. I had read an article about how the cave bears would reach around through the crevices that early man would be hiding in and hook them out with these claws, and I said, "Well, that's got to be buried deeply in the subconscious, that whole idea of the claw." So I simply put that on to what I thought was the most human instrument—which was the hand. You know, the reality of real life is that you have a huge spectrum of organisms, all trying to rend each other open to get at their protein. Somebody said, "We are a series of tubes trying to put the other tube in one end and excrete it out the other." And that's the darkest view of life itself. One of the deepest fears of any critter and certainly of human beings is being opened up. That skin is so, so thin, and it takes so very little to—you know—spill us out into the world. Deal with that reality, and our existence literally ceases. It's important, in a way, in a horror film to deal with that reality, and I think that's why horror films so often go down to a slash instrument. It is because that is the primal fear.

NARR: After the release of *A Nightmare on Elm Street*, Craven directed some television before directing the 1986 release of *Deadly Friend*, starring Kristy Swanson and Matthew Labyorteaux. The film did not advance Craven's reputation, nor did it do much business—a fact he blames on what was happening in his personal life at the time.

WC: I'll tell you what happened in the year of making *Deadly Friend*. I discovered, to put it discreetly, that my marriage was no longer anything but a sham. I was supposed to be directing the next *Beetlejuice* and about two months in the preparation for that I was yanked from it. I was supposed to direct *Superman IV*. I had an interview with Christopher Reeve, and he said, "Wes Craven will never direct my film." I was being sued for about $30 million by somebody who thought that I had copied a script that was so different from *Nightmare on Elm Street* that you can't believe, but I was being sued. I was not at that time covered by the errors and omission policy, and New Line was letting me float and dangle in the wind. All that was going on at the time when I was directing that film.

Kristy Swanson (actor, *Deadly Friend*): This is going to sound sick. My most favorite scene in the movie was—we had an actress by the name of Anne Ramsey, and she was the nasty old lady across the street. I had come back to kill her and basically throw a basketball at her head, and her head explodes. It's pretty gruesome. Her body walks around headless, and it's just sick.

WC: It was also my first big studio film, and there were about twenty producers on it. They all had different opinions, so it was like—I am amazed that anything that came out of that film is watchable whatsoever.

NARR: In 1988, Craven released *The Serpent and the Rainbow*, starring Bill Pullman, Cathy Tyson, and Paul Winfield. The film was an ambitious examination of black magic, zombies, and Voodoo practices in Haiti.

WC: *The Serpent and the Rainbow* is a fascinating film. In many ways, it's one of the few treatments of voodoo that treats voodoo as a religion and as a factual thing.

Bill Pullman (actor, *The Serpent and the Rainbow*): . . .and Wes, I think, was really curious about not just thinking of it is a fiction, but also as an experiment into, kind of like, "What is the envelope to be pushed about rational thought and the occult and especially magic-based religions, trance-based religion?"

WC: It was the examination of the origin of zombies, which is an actual phenomenon. For many, many years, people just thought they were a fictional thing. They actually are the creation—chemically—of people that have had their brains virtually erased and have been put into a state of apparent death, which is the medical term for where you appear to be dead and your pulse is so faint that it's not recognizable, unless you're really, really carefully looking for it. They are buried and then, you know, revive in the grave and are dug up by the people who poisoned them, processed further until their brains are virtually erased, and then they are released, so the local people who are at the funeral they think their loved ones are now back as the living dead.

BP: In the movie there was a scene that was meant to reflect what was really going on in Haiti in that they had to do things that they often do in voodoo ceremonies where they take long needles and push them through the skin of their cheeks and then make them come out the other end.

And my wife was there, we just got married, and she was an extra in that. Wes had said, "You know . . ."—this is the type of present Wes will give you from time to time—he said, "Why don't we have your wife go up and push the needle through the guy's cheek?" And my wife thought that this was somehow going to be simulated, this is a prop guy thing, or something; and before you know it, she's up there. And she's pushing on the cheek, but the cheek wasn't—it wasn't going through the cheek, you know, and Wes said, "Push harder! Push harder!" And she pushes this needle right through the guy's cheek. Unbelievable. And the irony is that, you know, most people who see that scene just assume that it was some prop guy who had figured out something, and it was an illusion of film. But that stuff really happened.

WC: Personally, it was one of our most fascinating and enjoyable and terrifying films. I think, as a film itself, it suffered probably from many different visions; some of the producers wanted a love story and someone, a history or religious story, the history of voodoo. The studio wanted a horror film, so if it suffers, it suffers from that kind of diffusion of purpose, I think.

BP: You know, he has good friendships that he's maintained through his career—the ups and downs and ins and outs—and he's remained a very steady guy. You know it was the only movie I did with him—was the only movie I ever did—where we had a reunion of the crew, and this was like seven years after we made the movie! So it was a testimony to a thing that we all did together and his sense of loyalty and friendship. You know, that really was kind of a lasting thing that you bring away from pictures you make with him.

NARR: The 1989 release of *Shocker*—starring Mitch Pileggi, Peter Berg, and Heather Langenkamp—was Craven's attempt to create another Freddy Krueger character. After being sent to the electric chair, a serial killer played by Pileggi uses electricity to come back from the dead and carry out his vengeance on the football player who turned him into the police.

WC: We tried to create another franchisable character for Alive Films and for Universal. Obviously, we didn't succeed, but I think we made a film that was interesting and fascinating. You know, it was kind of the beginning of my exploration of in-and-out of the reality of media itself, with characters that were diving into television sets and onto programs that were already in progress and then back out into somebody else's living room, continued through, I think, *Nightmare 7* with behind the scenes of making a film and on to *Scream*. In that sense, it was an interesting film. And we scored above the level that we had to, so we had final cut on it too.

Mitch Pileggi (actor, *Shocker*): Wes has always been great with just letting me do what I do. And if there is anything that needs to be tweaked, he'll come up and then let me know, but he's great about that . . . If it's going right, he just lets you go. When I worked with him on *Shocker* there were times when he wanted more from the character, and the character was just way out there—it was—and he'd say, "Okay, give me more in this, give me more," and I'd say, "Oh Wes, man, it's so far out there, and I don't know if I can." And he went, "Yeah. You can." Sometimes I'm a little gullible, and I don't know when I'm being—I don't know when my leg is being pulled, so sometimes there were times when I was like, "What?" And then I realized he was joking with me; you know, he's very, very focused, and yet he keeps things light. And it's always a lot of fun.

NARR: Before bringing to the screen the 1994 release of *Wes Craven's New Nightmare*, Craven directed *The People Under the Stairs* in 1992. A social parable about the exploitation of the "Have Nots" by the "Haves," the film was awarded the Pegasus Audience Award at the Brussels International Festival of Fantasy Film. *Wes Craven's New Nightmare* brought back Robert Englund as Freddy Krueger, along with original cast members Heather Langenkamp and John Saxon. Craven played himself in the film and playfully poked a little fun at Hollywood.

WC: My return to the *Nightmare* films was based on two things: One, Bob Shaye and I had had a series of disagreements and sorts of things in the press, and we had a meeting in his office and kind of decided we really, really should be grownups and put this all behind us. He said, "You know," so we went over the things that I thought were, you know, hadn't been fair about our deal and that was actually ironed out. And the second thing was that he said, "You know, we killed off Freddy in the last film, but we thought there might be a chance for one more.

We thought it'd be great if maybe you came back and did it." I said, "The only way I would do it is if I could feel like it was a step-up, because I think the films had been stepping down recently." I looked at all the films, and I couldn't see any pattern, anything that lead to anything really. But what suddenly struck me was fascinating: when I had lunch with Robert and I had lunch with Heather Langen-kamp—who played Nancy—we talked about how the film had kind of changed our lives and we were known for it so much, and I said to my partner, Marianne, [Maddalena, Craven's producing partner] the interesting thing here would be to make a film *about* the making of the film and how the film has become a thing on its own, and couple that with how important it is to make scary films—in a sense, how important scary stories are and what might happen if there were suddenly no scary stories. So working with this idea that Freddy as himself encompasses something as a character that is more real than the character itself and that, if the character were not there, then that thing might be free to be more powerful than it is if it's able to be caught in a character.

Robert Englund (actor, *Wes Craven's New Nightmare*): The Wes Craven of the *New Nightmare* was just much more relaxed, and I think there was a bit of a—I don't want to say; payback's a little harsh—but he was getting some stuff off his chest in that. And it's interesting because the *New Nightmare* was what we would call a success, but I don't know if you'd call it a hit or a blockbuster in terms of when it was released. Now, because of the success of *Scream 1* and *2*, a lot of fans have rediscovered *Wes Craven's New Nightmare* at the video stores, so I'm getting a lot of attention on the street from that. A lot of fans come up to me, many more now than when it first came out back in '94/'95 because they have rented or bought it since *Scream 1* and *Scream 2*, and they like it. They really think it's a smart film and a really nice little lampoon at Hollywood.

WC: I think it did exactly what I wanted to do, which was it took it to almost like a fairytale area, and I wanted to show that the set of agelessness of scary stories was part of that whole tradition of fairytales and stories of hell, even, and religions. And that was an element to the whole spectrum of human storytelling that was natural and apt and deserved to be there.

NARR: Eddie Murphy both starred in and co-wrote the 1995 release of *Vampire in Brooklyn*. Angela Bassett costarred. It proved to be an uneven blend of horror and comedy that did not quite hit the mark.

WC: *Vampire in Brooklyn* came to me, I think, from a call from my agent saying that Eddie Murphy, who had been a big fan, apparently—yeah, especially of *Hills Have*

Eyes—wanted to make a vampire movie and would I like to be the director? It was interesting because in *Vampire*, Eddie wanted to do—he wanted to play a really dark character and a bad character. He didn't want to do comedy necessarily, and the studio very much wanted him to do comedy. I think they sensed that they were just one *Nutty Professor* away from a lot of money, but Eddie did and didn't want to go that way. So he kind of played the comedy, but he also played the character as quite dark, not completely insanely funny and not vulnerable, which is a way that we had suggested to him. He simply did not want to take that course, so it played kind of as a—you know—straight character with funny ancillary characters that would kind of spice up and show his comic chops. One of the interesting things to realize about a star of that magnitude is that their area of privacy is very constricted, and it was the first time I really felt that so extremely, and that when he would get into the complete makeup of some of these secondary characters that he did, he seemed most relaxed. Sometimes, he would even go out—off the lot—because he could move through culture, through society unrecognized, and could just be himself. I heard a report from *Nutty Professor* that once in the complete fat get-up, he went to a play yard and just played with the children and was completely, innocently free. It's a very interesting thing. Someone like that, who when he is himself has to move surrounded by people in dark vehicles, and anytime that's he is out among the public he is just, you know, people just go for him. It was a fascinating thing to watch.

NARR: Craven hit the cinema jackpot with the 1996 release of *Scream*. The irrelevant, genre-bending film went on to spawn *Scream 2* and *3*. *Scream* received the 1996 MTV Best Movie Award and once and for all placed Craven at the forefront of horror filmmakers.

WC: *Scream* came to me first with a director of development that was working for me at that time, Lisa Harrison . . . sent it to me and said, "You have to read this over the weekend. There's going to be a bidding war on Monday, and we'd like to get Miramax to buy it for us." I read it and—this is ironic—but I said, "I don't want to go there." The opening scene with Drew Barrymore, at that time of course was not Drew Barrymore, but I felt it was so violent and so much back at where I had started, I thought, "I'm going to screw up my Karma if I do this." So I passed, and it was bought by Miramax—and we were developing something with them for almost a year, actually *The Haunting*. At a certain point, they didn't want to do *The Haunting*. The scripts were not to their satisfaction. It went into turnaround. They said, "We have another picture we want you do—*Scream*." I said, "Seen it." They said, "We think you should do it," and I passed and then I sat. I thought—you know, a lot of the interviews I do with kids, they say, "*Last House* was your best film because you really kicked ass." And I thought, "Am I getting soft? Or what is it? You know, so okay, I'm going to do one more 'to-the-wall' horror film." And I called up Bob—Bob Weinstein—and I said, "Okay, I'll do it."

Courteney Cox (actor, _Scream_ franchise): I really had to do some persuading to get the part because they didn't really think—most people think of me as the studious type or I play a doctor, which is so odd or vulnerable—they didn't really see me as a bitch, so I had to try really hard to get this part.

Neve Campbell (actor, _Scream_ franchise): I had actually just done _The Craft_ the year before and then was doing _Party of Five_, and it was my second hiatus. I wasn't necessarily sure whether I wanted to do another scary type of movie, so I wasn't very certain about the choice. But I knew that I wanted to work with Wes, and I went in and auditioned for him. He gave great directions. It was actually a fun process. I like auditioning.

David Arquette (actor, _Scream_ franchise): I had a meeting to come in—sort of a meet—for the role of Billy, I think in the first one, the role Skeet [Ulrich] ended up playing, and when I came in I said, "I don't . . . I really don't think that's the part I'd like to play . . . I sort of like, like the role of Dewey." Everyone sort of, like, stopped. Well, they didn't picture it that way. It was written as this sort of big hunky guy, so I guess it was a little forward of me—but then they sort of went, "Oh well." I guess Wes sort of liked the idea, and it just kind of worked out. And it was heaven sent for me.

WC: You always ask yourself, "Why do you want to scare people?" And you can make an intellectual argument that people are scared already from real life and that they need to vent these things. I think, indeed, that is the process that takes place in scary films, but still you wonder, "Why the hell have you done this with your life as opposed to making people laugh or feel good or whatever?"

DA: Yeah, I do think they are scary. There is a lot of stuff that's shot that we don't see. Even the stuff that we do see, if what the music—music just adds so much to these movies. Yeah, they become very frightening.

CC: I know what's going to happen and I know, but it doesn't matter; the timing of things changes everything. Just knowing what's going to happen, I get scared and don't know when to exactly close my eyes. And I still do that.

NC: I never get to a place where I'm terrified because I've got sixty people standing around me and they say, "Cut!" And all of a sudden the guy takes off his mask, and it's not a scary guy; he's not a killer. But it's very important as an actor to get yourself into that state or get to something that will seem that way, whether that's the high amount of fear or whatever. I mean, it's still reality; it's still just making movies.

WC: There's a sense of pleasure to know that you've gotten to that place where people don't like to talk about, but have done it in a way that hasn't—hasn't bruised them so much—has allowed them somehow to come out of the film happy, and that's the majority experience coming out of a good scary film: the audience is bubbling. Something has been released in a way that scared the bejesus out of them but also lifted something off them.

NC: I don't think there will be a [*Scream*] 4. I think that this is kind of the part. I think we are really happy with the fact that this will sort of be the finish and trying not to be make it one of these films that we have go on forever.

NARR: The success of *Scream* gave Craven the freedom to pursue a career-long dream. Miramax Films offered him a three-picture deal, which included the green-light for a non-genre film. The former teacher and longtime lover of classical music chose to make *Music of the Heart*, based on the real-life story of Roberta Guaspari and her violin students in East Harlem. The film was released to enthusiastic notices in 1999.

WC: Sort of the combination of almost thirty years of trying to do something out of this genre, not because I don't like this genre a bit, but because I'm a person—I think as any artist wants to do a lot of different things. Just never before has that opportunity been presented, and it was presented very dramatically to me by Harvey and Bob Weinstein. Following the first and only test screening of *Scream 1*, which went through the roof in Secaucus, they found us. Marianne and myself and our crew, cinematographer, you know, were out having a celebratory dinner in the Village, and somehow they found us and literally walked in the restaurant, pushed people away, sat down, and said, "We want to make a deal with you. We want to make a three-picture deal, and you're going to be a Miramax/Dimension guy. And we understand that you want to make"—this is Harvey speaking now—"we know that you want to make a 'petticoat movie.'" And I said, "What's a 'petticoat movie'?" He said, "Well, you know, the kind I make. You know, costume dramas, whatever. So we want you to make a couple of Dimension films for us, and you can make one of my films." They started rattling off the properties that they owned and, one of the things they mentioned was this documentary called *Small Wonders*. I'm a member of the Academy, and I had been on one of the prejudging committees for documentaries and had seen that documentary of Roberta Guaspari's work as a violin teacher. And I said, "I want to do that one." It was just like instantaneous love. I had been a teacher myself. I love music, love classical music. It seemed perfect, so off we went.

Meryl Streep (actor, *Music of the Heart*): It is a true story of a single mother from upstate New York with two small children, husband leaves her, she has sort of no resources, except the ability to teach violin, and she takes that ability and a dream she has into East Harlem and starts the East Harlem Violin Program, sort of against the odds without much backing from the board of education. But she gets a toehold in and starts teaching kids that other people feel won't be—their lives won't be enhanced by violin playing, classical music, and she works a little miracle there. They had sent me the script, which was terrific, but they sent it to me at a point where I would only have had a month to get ready to play a violin teacher. And I thought I would probably have to learn to play the violin, and I didn't think I could do it in four weeks. But not taking "No" for an answer is sort of Wes Craven's specialty, and I didn't know anything about him. I—honestly—I'd never seen any of those scary movies because I don't get them. I am a total wimp, you know. But my son had seen a lot of them, I trust him, he's almost twenty, and he said, "He's a really good storyteller, Mom." And I feel like anybody, and I knew that he was wildly successful in that genre, anybody that can spin a yarn, keep people interested, doesn't really matter what the story is, it's the skill of pulling you along. And I knew he'd been very, very successful in that way. So it could only help in this story.

WC: So she came into a film—which had originally been with Madonna—at a rather late date that we had to shoot by fall and went from never having picked up the violin to playing the Bach Double Cantata on the stage of Carnegie Hall with Isaac Stern and Itzhak Perlman so well that their mouths dropped open.

MS: If you practice, you do get better, where you can't really practice acting. You know, it's sort of this ephemeral thing, it either happens or it doesn't, and you can get ready before you come in, but it's not the same thing. It just happens, or it doesn't in a moment, and so there was something uniquely satisfying in encountering and playing an instrument in a way that was a different type of artistic satisfaction for me.

WC: If you put an isolated mic on her, it wouldn't have sounded great, but her form, her fingering—everything was perfect.

MS: Wes sees reality in a different way than other people do. He has a very clear understanding of the darkness in life, and I think that he waited twenty years to explore the flipside of the dark side. And I think he got a chance to do that.

WC: It was just a great pleasure, and she took me as an equal and as a collaborator. It was a huge honor and affirmation of my own, you know, skills as a director. You never know at what point in your career you get to be put with somebody and they look at you and say, "You are a fraud—get out!" and I'm off this picture.

MS: A lot of our shots were intricately orchestrated with kids and music, and if one part of the shot was not good, but the part that he needed was okay, we'd know he'd say, "The first part was great, but I'm going to use that in the master . . . for what we needed it for, when we come in close that was great." I mean, I quickly saw he was really, really smart and really sentient about what was coming through the performance, and he was on me—he knew what I was doing, what I was trying to achieve in different takes.

NC: On the first *Scream* there was this really neat moment where Wes and I were sitting, and I think the sun was—the sun was coming out because we were shooting nights that whole time and we were very tired and the whole crew was sort of working very hard and they were all lighting up the last shot. Wes was just sitting on a bench, I went and sat next to him, we watched the sunrise, and it was really cool because a lot of people think, "Wes Craven, he makes all these horror films; he's going to be really sick and really twisted." And they always ask me that, and he's actually nice, very Zen in a lot of ways. . . . is a very calm spirit. He keeps it a very cool atmosphere on set, and he's very warm and deep in a lot of ways. So it's kind of interesting.

CC: Wes just has a really special place in my heart besides being an amazing director and a friend, I think he was also really instrumental in David and I getting married. David really respects Wes as well, and I know that kind of after we had been dating for a long time, Wes really kind of put it to us in the right way and made us realize how lucky we were and what we had and—he's just a really caring, sweet man.

RE: Wes takes very seriously certain things in his life; certain images are recurring images or images or memories that either stay with him or perhaps even haunt him a little bit, and he does purge those in his work somehow, I think he's very true to that belief or that trust that's a source of inspiration and perhaps even art.

WC: Am I the Stephen King of movies? Nobody likes to be called—are you the "somebody else"? No, I'm just the Wes Craven of movies. I think there's a lot of really fine directors that have come out of this genre. I mean John Carpenter has done wonderful work, and I really admire the work of Cronenberg. And Tobe Hooper did a really seminal film with *The Texas Chainsaw Massacre* that has not been equaled in many ways. There are many others that I'm forgetting now—forgive me. It's attracted, I think, a lot of very intelligent and very innovative film-makers. I would cite a recent film, *The Blair Witch Project*, which I think is such a wonderful, wonderful example of the sort of vitality of film itself and, especially, with the new technologies of video and digital technology, that it is there for the opening. You do not have to depend on anybody but your own imagination to make something wonderful happen. *Sex, Lies and Videotape* was another example of a very low-budget film based in sort of that video technology or semidocumentary technology. It's not necessary do a huge expensive film in order to make a powerful film. I would say to them, "Just be aware that it's going to be incredibly difficult, but it is possible, and that the technology is there for you to work on a shoestring and have your visions and dreams come true and just be prepared for a lot of hard work and try to keep your sense of humor and your sense of positivity about the human species." Because there's a lot of darkness and chicanery and banality in the film business, there just is a lot of things that you just as soon not know about human people, but there's also a lot of wonderful care and love, especially among, I think, cast and crew that is there and will sustain you through a lot of very, very dark moments.

Interview with Wes Craven

J.M. and Randy Lofficier / 1999

From www.lofficier.com, 1999. © 1999 Randy Lofficier. Reprinted by permission of J.M. and Randy Lofficier.

Q: How did you get started in films?

Wes Craven: I wasn't allowed to see movies when I was a child. It was against the religion I was raised in, Fundamentalist Baptist. I didn't go into a commercial movie house until I was a senior in college, and that was on the sly. It wasn't until I was in graduate school that I immersed myself in films. Then, I went to see all the films by Bergman, Fellini, etc.

The first film I made was when I was teaching. Some students came to me and said, "We see you have a camera; would you be our faculty advisor on a movie we want to make? You can shoot it." I said, "Sure," and got all of these free rolls of film from the drama department, and we went out and made a forty-five-minute *Mission: Impossible* spoof. We taught ourselves how to edit just by doing it. We didn't have any sort of editing machine, so we did it on a school projector. Splices were scotch-taped and then glued for the final version. We couldn't figure out how to put sound with the movie. We knew that there was some film that had sound stripes along one side, but then we couldn't figure out how to do any sound overlap or put music on there. So we did all our sound on a 1/4-inch tape and then ran it at the same time with the projector, and we had a rheostat so we could slow it down a little bit or speed it up to keep it roughly at the same place.

We showed the picture at the local school auditorium. Well, we were smart enough to put everybody at the school, and everybody in the town that was of any significance, in the movie. So we had this huge turnout, and we made more than the cost of the movie in the first night! The next weekend, we showed it at the college that shared the town and had another sellout crowd. Then we showed it at another college that was fifteen miles down, and they all came to see it. So we made a lot of money. We had this great cast and crew party afterwards, and we spent it all on that!

From this, I got the bug. I wasn't happy teaching. I was enjoying the teaching, but not the grades. The students that would come and say, "I'm going to be drafted if you don't give me an A." The department chairman wanted me to get a PhD on Elizabethan lutes in the time of Chaucer, or something that obscure. So I quit my job, I went to New York, and I looked that summer for a job in film. But I wasn't able to find anything.

I went back to upstate New York, and I taught a year of high school at a terrible school. At the end of that summer, I was talking to a student friend of mine, and he said he had a brother who was a film editor. That was Harry Chapin, who had once won an Oscar for, I believe, the editing of *Legendary Champions*, a short film on the great champion boxers.

So I sat down with Harry, and he was very kind. He was working on a Steenbeck. He showed me how a film was put together. I sat with him for about a week, just watching him cut. He explained to me why he was cutting, pacing, and a great deal of things which stuck with me to this day. At about the end of that week, a man whose offices we were renting the room in fired his messenger and said, "If you know anyone who wants a job as a messenger, I'm looking for one." I was thirty years old, had a master's degree in philosophy, two kids, and took the job as a messenger! That's how I got into film!

It was a film postproduction house, and within ten months I was assistant manager! Then I quit that job for an assistant editing job. During that time, I crammed myself on film. I would work at night, synching up rushes or documentaries all over town, and got to know the young documentary film crowd in New York.

After that job, I drove a cab in New York for about three months, looking for a job in actually making a film. I finally got a chance on this small film that was being done by a twenty-seven-year-old named Sean Cunningham. It was a small, homemade film, and I got the job of syncing up rushes determined on the system editing. And it turned into a full-time editing job, and even some directing because he was having a falling out with the filmmaker that was working with him. We ended up finishing this film together.

The film came out and made around $7 million. It had costed about $70,000. It was called *Together*, and very few people have heard of it. But it played all over the country for a summer. It was sort of like a sensitivity-training course for couples. It had a little nudity here and there. We all called it *Reader's Digest Sex*. It was Marilyn Chambers's first film. She did a nude diving scene in it. But it had nothing beyond that. It talked about how to be more attuned to your husband's or wife's needs.

The releasers of this film, a small company called Vanguard, offered us $50,000 to make a horror film. Sean said to me, "Why don't you write it, direct it, and cut it, and I'll produce it. We'll do it for $40,000 and pocket the $10,000. We'll do it in three weeks." So I went out and wrote the script for *Last House on the Left*, and the reaction to it was so strong because it was just a crazy, wild script! Our agreement was that we would just hold nothing back. We would do the most outrageous things we could think of. So I wrote this crazy sort of ribald comedy, horror thing, and we couldn't get it out of the mimeograph place! That was the first sign that we had something special: they were all passing around the mimeographs to read!

We went out, and we made the film. We went over budget. Vanguard had to give us another $40,000, so we ended up doing it for $90,000 after all. When it came out, it was immediately a big hit, and it's still playing. It was a sort of phenomenon, and I've been directing ever since—or trying to direct. (laughter)

Q: Why was it also called *Krug & Co* on some prints?
WC: It's an interesting story about how an advertising campaign and a title can influence a film. Originally, the working title of *Last House on the Left* was *The Night of Vengeance*. When it came out, we didn't like that, so we did a big contest among all the friends and relatives. We came up with three titles: *Sex Crime of the Century*, which is part of the conversation Sadie and Krug have in the car at the beginning when Sadie concludes that the greatest sex criminal of the century was Freud because he made everybody self-conscious about sex. We also came up with *Krug & Co* because Krug was the main villain. Finally, *Last House on the Left* was a title suggested by an ad man, whom we all thought was terribly off the wall for suggesting such a title, which had nothing much to do with the film.

They opened it up in three towns simultaneously, all with the same demographic profiles, but using different ad campaigns. What an ad campaign determines is who comes out those first, crucial two nights to get the word-of-mouth going. The first two nights in the towns with *Sex Crime* and *Krug*, nobody came. And in the town where they had the *Last House* title, and the ad campaign that said, "Keep repeating, 'It's only a movie!'" a crowd came out. And the next night, there was double the crowd, and it just took off. So it was a very dramatic example of how a title change and an ad campaign can work. To this day, there are people who still remember the ad campaign. You can hear the audience repeating, "It's only a movie!"

Q: Had you had any ideas for scripts before?
WC: As I said, they gave us money specifically to do a crazy horror film. Before that time when I graduated from college with a bachelor's in English, I was sort of undetermined between a musical career—I was playing guitar in some of the cabarets in Chicago—and I also had been writing short stories and poetry. I received a full scholarship to John Hopkins' writing seminars under a poet named Coleman,

so I decided to do that. So I studied writing and philosophy at Hopkins and got my master's degree.

Then, when I got out, I didn't know what I could do for a living. So after someone suggested I teach, I did just that. I was very fortunate. I put in an application at a place. And there were no openings, so I started a job selling rare coins in Baltimore. But then, some English professor in Pennsylvania dropped dead of a heart attack the day before the classes started! I got this telephone call, and they said, "If you come out right away, you can have this job!" It's the story of my life! So I jumped in an airplane and ended up in Pennsylvania teaching college.

Q: Other than for the fact that it got you in films, do you feel that *Last House* was a worthwhile experience?

WC: Absolutely! It's funny because I would never have thought of going out and doing a horror film, but now, I can see through whatever set of circumstances and luck that I was well-suited to doing that. The horror film is a typical way for a young film-maker to gain entree into the film-making world. It is a kind of film that can be made on a low budget, and that can make a great deal of money.

As I look back over my entire life, I can see that I always enjoyed spooky stories, and I always enjoyed doing outrageous things. So I was indeed suited to doing that kind of film, although it would have never occurred to me, at that time, to actually do a horror movie on my own. I was trying to write very artistic stories and poetry. I was going in totally different directions, and not getting very far, and all of a sudden somebody gave me a chance to do something that I never would have allowed myself to think about doing. Because I was totally anonymous at the time—I was living in New York on a shoestring—I figured I would do this picture and nobody would ever know I did it or even go see it! So I just went crazy and did this really bizarre movie. And then, everybody knew that I had done it, and I became notorious for doing that kind of movie. It's kind of ironic how it all happened!

Q: Did you have fun making *Last House*?

WC: Yes, we had a *lot* of fun making it! It was all friends that did it. Sean Cunningham and I were friends by that time, and we shot most of it in the homes of either his mother or his own backyard. We used friends of ours as actors, so it was a very homemade fun family movie, in a weird sort of way. Compared to some other shoots that I've had since, it was relatively trouble-free. I believe the original was shot in three weeks, then we went back for a fourth.

At the time, I didn't know about storyboards. I was sort of feeling my way as a director. So I did weird things like drawing lines in the script, like "this shot is sort of similar to that shot on this page," and I would draw lines until it was such

a mess I couldn't follow any of it! I really didn't know what the established proce-
dures were for organizing a film. We had it budgeted, and we knew we had a certain
amount for props and costumes. Beyond that, there was very little organization.

I didn't have much of an idea about what a director actually did, beyond shout-
ing "Action!" and "Cut!" My orientation was more in documentaries, because that
was the type of film I had worked on during that first year in New York. So I covered a lot of *Last House* as a documentary filmmaker would cover an event. The
scene in the woods, for example, where the girls are first taken in the woods, I covered three times continuously, never stopping the action. Just played the entire
scene as an event, and I had the camera stand in three separate places in general
and follow the action and then planned to cut it together later. That scene had
a real spontaneous feel, so we would rehearse it beforehand and then just do it.

As a result, the editing of *Last House* took nine months because it was such a
mess. I didn't know what a master was. I didn't know how a master and reading a
close-up could be used together. All of these things, I learned by either shooting a
lot of material and then finding out later that I should have done something else
or by finding from experience what worked and what didn't. But somehow, in the
end, it all turned out okay.

Q: Did you have to do a lot of trimming down on *Last House* because of the
violence?
WC: We had requests from sub-distributors, people in other sections of the country, who said that this film was too wild to play. They were getting audiences,
but the audiences were tearing up the theaters! We had reports of people fainting, threats of lawsuits, fist fights, and near-riots. We had a case of people trying
to get in the projection booth, and the projectionist had to barricade himself in
(laughter)! Wait! We had a case of half an audience leaving and cowering in the
lobby (laughter)!

We had lots of cases of projectionists and theater managers editing the prints
themselves with scissors. We would get the prints back in pieces in the cans. So we
voluntarily took out several scenes, two of which I don't really miss because they
were so outrageously painful to watch and one of which I think really hurt the film.

In the murder of Phyllis, the first of the girls to die, my whole intention was to
show murder in a film that was as I would imagine it to be, rather than as it was
depicted in films normally at that time. That is, the person delivered the killing
blow, and the victim died, maybe with a few gasps, but not always. They would
never fight a protracted fight and would suffer clearly in front of the camera. So I
did that with Phyllis. I carried it through all the way, and the people that were killing her then went into a sort of psychosexual frenzy, where clearly they were going

beyond what they even thought they were going to do. And it ended with them realizing that they had partially disemboweled her and reaching down and pulling out a loop of her intestine. That was the point where a lot of people fainted . . .

But that, to me, was the *reality* of murder because at that point their whole character changed, and they were suddenly sober and horrified by what they had done. And we had to cut that out. To me, now, that murder, as it stands, loses the whole climactic rhythm of that sudden realization. I think it gave the film a truth that was very painful to watch, but also very real.

Q: Was there anything about *Last House* that you didn't like?
WC: Oh, yes! The comedy scenes. I think the clichés of the stupid rural sheriff and his assistant did not work. All of us, for years, were under the influence of *In the Heat of Night* and the stupid southern sheriff. Some of the sound is also terrible: the scene in the old Cadillac where Krug and the others are riding along and do the bit about the sex crime of the century was one of my favorite scenes in the script, but you can't hear it because we didn't know how to mike people and how to make any postproduction dubbing either!
Q: Did you feel able, after *Last House*, to go out and be a director?
WC: Yes, but the phone never rang! (laughter) It was quite a period of time. Because *Last House* was so upsetting to the establishment, I think I had only one call in two years, even though commercially the film was a big hit. That was from the producers of *Let's Scare Jessica to Death*, a horror film of about the same period. But Sean and I went out and wrote scripts for quite a while after that. We wrote comedies, we wrote a script on Vietnam, we tried to get serious, but nobody would take us seriously. So I ended up accepting an offer from a friend of mine to do *The Hills Have Eyes*. By the time *The Hills* was out, people saw that there was not only this wildman, but somebody who knew how to sit and direct. From that, I got on a television show and from there to some more wide acceptance.

Q: How did *Hills* happen?
WC: Someone came to me and said, "Let's do another *Last House*." He'd waited and watched me for years, and he knew that I wasn't having any success getting out of the genre. So he said to me, "So it might not be what you want to do, but you need some money to live on." At that time, I was virtually broke.

The idea of the specific story was my own. I researched quite a while in the New York Public Library on murder and mayhem in general and ran across a story of a weird family that lived in Scotland in the seventeenth century. They were cannibals living in a cave overlooking the ocean, and they would waylay travelers between London and some other town. The whole countryside got the reputation of being haunted because those that went in didn't tend to come out. Finally, a husband and wife were attacked on their way home, and the wife was grabbed. But the man escaped and saw the people. He went back to London and brought back help. They discovered a cave with this inbred family of about twenty-five people and vats of human bodies pickled in seawater. This wild and crazy family was captured and dragged back to London and executed in a most bizarre and uncivilized way. That was my inspiration for the family in *Hills*, who lived on the Nevada gun range.

Q: Did you have a much bigger budget to shoot *Hills*?
WC: Yes, but with inflation, it ended up being just about the same. We spent about $230,000, and we shot for five weeks. We still shot in 16mm, but we had special effects, like we blew up a big trailer, which was very exciting to us. We had animals; we did some stunts, which we had an actual stuntman do. We actually did some fun things!

Last Housemates

David A. Szulkin / 2001

From *Fangoria* 200, March 2001. Reprinted by permission of Joseph A. Sonnier IV, CEO of *Cinestate* and *Fangoria*.

It's hard to imagine where the modern horror film would be without Wes Craven and Sean Cunningham. From their collaboration on the classic 1972 shocker *Last House on the Left* to the enormously influential '80s successes of Cunningham's *Friday the 13th* and Craven's *A Nightmare on Elm Street*, these two filmmakers have done more to change the face of the genre than they ever could have imagined or intended. Then, with the *Scream* trilogy, Craven hit the biggest box-office score of his career by directing a script that commented on *Friday* and *Elm Street*, which spawned yet another craze of sequels and imitations.

Although they haven't made a movie together since *Last House* (which some still consider their best), Craven and Cunningham have remained loyal friends and colleagues through it all. And while they've both expressed a desire to break away from horror, neither one is about to abandon their fans. Cunningham recently produced the tenth installment in the *Friday* series, *Jason X* (which launches the masked madman into outer space) and has returned to the director's chair for the reality-TV thriller *Extreme Close-Up*. Craven attached his name to the recent *Dracula 2000* as executive producer and plans to direct the movie adaptations of his sci-fi-themed novel *The Fountain Society* and the horrific video game *Alice*. In honor of this two hundredth issue of *Fangoria*, the diabolical duo reunited in Craven's office for a look back at thirty years of movie madness.

FANGO: How did the two of you originally meet?

WES CRAVEN: I had been in New York for just a short time. After working my way up in a postproduction house for about a year and a half, I was fired. I drove a cab for a while, then I heard about this job at an office in the same building where I had been working before. It turned out to be Sean's office. He and a guy named

Roger Murphy were making a small feature called *Together*, and they hired me to sync up dailies. Sean and I were really the same age, we had kids the same age, and there were a lot of similarities in our backgrounds. So during the course of that picture, Sean and I became friends.

FANGO: What did you learn from each other in your early days?

CRAVEN: When we were making *Together*, there was a lot of contention between Sean and Roger. At a certain point, Roger dropped out of the picture, which put me in a position to move up to much bigger things than one would ordinarily get a chance to learn. I went from being the schmuck syncing up dailies to doing some editing and writing. Actually, I learned a lot from Roger; he came back once after leaving and tore apart everything I'd done. Roger left for good just before the mix, and Sean and I finished the picture together.

SEAN CUNNINGHAM: When Wes and I met, I didn't know anything about movies. I knew a lot about theater, having been a stage manager. I think what we were doing with *Together* was discovering the difference between theater and movies. I had to learn that movies work in a visceral way. It's not what you say; it's what you show. When Roger became unavailable, Wes and I were left with this 16mm footage that made no sense, and we were trying to make something out of it. I never could have finished the film without him, and we became very close friends. So when the opportunity came to make a more conventionally structured film, I said, "Great, let's give it a shot." I didn't know if Wes could really write or not, but I knew he could type like crazy!

CRAVEN: I remember Sean telling me, "Write something! Pull out the stops; pull all the skeletons out of the closet!" It was absolutely the most genius call on his part because I never would have thought I was capable of that. In his usual trenchant manner, Sean saw something floating around in my subconscious! So I went off and wrote *Last House*. Sean offered me the chance to be the director, writer, editor, or all of the above and gave me a 50/50 deal on it. It was an incredible gesture of friendship and generosity. We made the picture on a shoestring—though at the time, we thought we had a lot of money!

CUNNINGHAM: That's right; we had $40,000! Neither one of us quite knew what we were doing or how to do it. If someone came to me today with the same plan Wes and I had for *Last House*, I would say, "Don't do it; it's impossible; it's crazy." But because we didn't know any better and nobody was telling us we couldn't do it, we went ahead and somehow finished the film. It was a crazy, heady time.

FANGO: Did either of you have an interest in horror before making *Last House*?

CRAVEN: I remember going to see *Night of the Living Dead* when I first got to New York and being amazed by the wildness and the energy in the audience; the crowd was all university students. But I had no awareness of the genre. Did you?

CUNNINGHAM: No. I saw *The Wolf Man* and things like that as a kid growing up, but I didn't particularly have a fascination with it. Wes and I didn't have the luxury of entering the film business to follow a muse. I was trying to make a living and support my family and so was Wes. So the judgments that we made for many years had to do with the question, "That's very nice, but will somebody pay me to do this?"

FANGO: Are you surprised *Last House* still has a following?

CRAVEN: I've always been amazed by that. I didn't think anybody would ever see it. We were a couple of guys in a small office on West 45th Street, making this little movie. It was during a time when there were a lot of underground/guerrilla movements going on, and that's reflected in the film. A big part of its staying power is due to the fact that it's so incredibly raw.

FANGO: Will we ever see a completely uncut version of *Last House* on DVD?

CUNNINGHAM: We've tried very hard to get the [unedited] film released, but the rights have been tangled up in the Orion Pictures bankruptcy. We'd be happy to see it come out again.

CRAVEN: I'm not against the idea. There is still a fair amount of material around. I have a lot of photographs that have never been released. But I don't think there's any chance of seeing a completely reconstituted version of the original cut. As I understand it, that stuff is gone forever—unless a print turns up in some projectionist's garage! It's a hard film, but it deserves to be preserved. It would be fun to do a commentary track for that!

CUNNINGHAM: [Laughs] "What were we thinking?!"

FANGO: How has the business changed since your early days?

CUNNINGHAM: The studio system, as it exists today, is our only system. It's naïve to think you can go out and raise money from your family, your dentist, your doctor, and expect to make a successful film. It happens, but it's not a very good idea. If you want to make movies, you need money. You can do *Blair Witch*, but you can't do *Sixth Sense* without a budget; you can't do *Jason X* without a budget. So you need to understand that these people who are putting up tens of millions of dollars to support you are in business. You have to behave in a responsible, businesslike way, or you're of no use to them. And they won't give you the money to make movies.

FANGO: Have you consulted each other on film projects over the years?

CUNNINGHAM: Wes and I talked about things between ourselves all the time.

CRAVEN: Yes, all the time. I spent a day in the cutting room on *Friday the 13th* discussing things with Sean. And Sean directed the second unit on *A Nightmare on Elm Street*. We were having trouble toward the end of the shoot, and he came in and directed some shots of Nancy running around in one of her nightmares.

FANGO: Wes, what did you think of *Friday the 13th*?

CRAVEN: I always think of *Friday the 13th* as one of the strongest lessons I've ever had on the power of music and sound effects in film. There was a point before the movie was completed when Sean was worried about it. I came into the cutting room to look at it before the sound had been mixed. We watched it together, and there were things like somebody looking down a hallway, where it seemed to go on forever with nothing happening. At the end, I wished Sean good luck, but I felt my friend had made a film that was kind of slow and uninteresting. Then I went to see it when it was released, and it was like that theater where I saw *Night of the Living Dead* times ten! That haunting music worked so powerfully; it literally felt like electrical jolts were hitting people, including me. I remember going to the restroom at one point, and there were kids cringing out in the lobby; they were darting into the theater for two seconds and then running back out. When I left the theater with the rest of the audience, everybody was passing the line of people coming in and saying, "You're gonna love it! You're gonna love it!" It was a realization of the power this kind of film can have and of how difficult it is to know how a film is going to do before it's finished. The film we saw in the cutting room wasn't working without music, but suddenly, when all the elements were combined, it worked magically. One of the great things about *Friday the 13th* was its tremendous use of suspense, along with Sean's completely outrageous sense of humor. Sean's sort of the John Lennon of our partnership! I think he just had fun with the idea of interesting ways to kill teenagers, so there was this raucousness to it—"Oh my

God, I can't believe it; there's an arrow going through this guy's head!" I think I worry much more about social and psychological themes, but I really appreciated the dark sense of humor in that movie.

CUNNINGHAM: *Friday the 13th* was so stripped down and so low-rent; there was nothing in it except what I thought it really needed. I was trying to make a horror film, and I didn't want to spend a lot of time and money on production values that did not feed into the core experience. Nobody thought it would be as successful as it turned out to be. I'm not sure it would have been as successful if that epilogue I had hadn't worked so well. Up until that point, it was more like watching a car wreck than an entertaining night at the movies!

FANGO: What did you think of *A Nightmare on Elm Street*?

CUNNINGHAM: I had exactly the same experience watching *A Nightmare on Elm Street* as Wes had seeing *Friday the 13th*. I was really concerned about the script for *Nightmare*—I just didn't know if anybody would believe that dreams could interact with real life. I was like, "That doesn't happen! How are you going to sell that?" But Wes was convinced—maybe not 100 percent—but he believed it could work. I said, "I don't know. Maybe! I hope so!" And in the same way that I was having trouble when I got through *Friday the 13th*, Wes was having difficulties getting his movie made. He had his vision, and he absolutely stuck to it. But other people didn't quite get it, and it was like that all the way to the end. Then I got to see it early in its run, and the theater just lit up with excitement. People loved that movie! They had so much fun. I was so happy to be wrong!

FANGO: Sean, why did you decide not to direct the *Friday* sequels?

CUNNINGHAM: There were a whole bunch of personal and professional reasons. I thought of *Friday the 13th* as a kind of sample reel; it was just something that showed what I could do. I was so naive. I was living in Connecticut imagining how the movie business should be, rather than understanding what it was. I thought, "Now I've got a successful film. I can go out to Hollywood, and they'll give me good movies to make."

CRAVEN: Like *Rain Man*!

CUNNINGHAM: Yeah! And I did go out there. Talk about getting your fifteen minutes of fame; I was courted by every studio head in town! And they'd all say, "What do you want to do next? *Friday the 13th Part 2*, or something else?" At that point, I could have said anything I wanted—and I certainly would have been supported. But I didn't know that it was really up to me to develop or find something else I wanted to do! I was hoping they'd give me something good, and I'd make it—and after thirty years, I still can't get hold of that script, whatever it is! [Laughs]

FANGO: What's your new movie *Extreme Close-Up* about?

CUNNINGHAM: It's a thriller set in the world of reality TV. The assumption is that there are various reality television shows, and there is a serial killer out there some-place. And a few people come up dead. I was fascinated by the potential of using different storytelling techniques than we ordinarily use. It's very exciting that you can take a dramatic situation and have any one of the characters turn and talk to the audience. *The Real World* and *Survivor* use that technique often—cutting to inter-views where characters give the audience information about what they're thinking. It's a way of creating a dense story that I hope will keep the audience interested and off balance. I'm shooting it on a *Last House* kind of budget and trying to do things that haven't been done before. I may fall flat on my face, but I think it'll work.

CRAVEN: Are you shooting film or tape, or a combination?

CUNNINGHAM: I'm initially shooting it on tape. I'm not sure what resolution, probably digital Beta. Because it's meant to be a television show, there is plenty of artistic justification for having something that looks that way.

FANGO: What's the status of *Jason X* and *Freddy vs. Jason*?

CUNNINGHAM: *Jason X* is finished. It will be released in August, though that's still not definite. I think people are going to have a lot of fun with it; that's the underly-ing attitude. *Freddy vs. Jason* is still in development hell.

CRAVEN: That's the longest development hell I've ever heard of!

CUNNINGHAM: Well, *A Chorus Line* took longer, but I think we're about to break the record. *Freddy vs. Jason* has major structural issues that make it difficult for us to agree on what the movie should be. Everybody says they think they know what *Freddy vs. Jason* is: Simple, you take Freddy and Jason, and they fight. And I say, "OK—about what? And who wins?" If you start a fight, your movie's on hold until the fight is over. Even the best fight sequences, say from a *Rocky* film or *Raging Bull*, can only sustain your interest for a few minutes. So there has to be another story living inside this commercial idea of Freddy versus Jason. And it has to be a story that services both of these kind of negative pop icons. Neither Freddy nor Jason can turn out to be a nice guy who just did some bad things. They're not that way; they're meant to be the dark side of our natures given license to do things. There was a point when I felt it was put together pretty well structurally, but I couldn't persuade the people at New Line to go down a different road. We have tried several more roads, and I'd like to think we're getting closer. It's one of those things where when the script finally works everybody will finally sign on.

FANGO: Is there a chance that the two of you could reunite for *Freddy vs. Jason*?

CRAVEN: Sean and I always felt we should do another film together, but I couldn't work on *Freddy vs. Jason* because of the deal I have now with Miramax, which is an exclusive deal.

FANGO: Is it true that Miramax approached you to make *Scream 4*?

CRAVEN: No. It was always conceived as a trilogy.

CUNNINGHAM: They did approach me, and I said I'd do it cheap!

FANGO: Wes, when you attach your name to a project as executive producer, how much involvement do you have?

CRAVEN: It varies. I've done it a few times. *Dracula 2000* was much more of an in-house production than the others because it was directed by my ex-editor Patrick Lussier. So we were part of it from beginning to end. But I didn't go to the set to look over his shoulder. I visited the set twice to basically establish a mood and give whatever support I could. As an executive producer, getting a distributor to not make it look like I directed the movie is the tricky part. Everybody tries to make it look like "Wes Craven's" whatever.

FANGO: Where do you see horror movies going in the future?

CRAVEN: I don't know how to answer that question. I've always found that you go through periods of time without an idea in your head—that could amount to years—and then suddenly, you get an idea for a script. And I don't come up with those ideas based on where I think the genre is going. In my case, it's whatever idea interests me. In retrospect, you can say that *Scream* was a continuation of the deconstruction *New Nightmare*— it was taking account of the audience knowing that they're watching a horror film. What do you think, Sean?

CUNNINGHAM: I think the horror film is going to stay where it is. In its own way, it functions like a fairy tale. Most fairy tales aren't really good stories, but they address some underlying fear that maybe, depending on what kind of pop psychology you subscribe to, lives in your subconscious. Essentially, you take something you're afraid of and look at it in the safety of a story or movie theater, usually dressed in some kind of costume so it doesn't look like a part of your real life. At the end, it's put back in the closet of your subconscious, and you go out feeling a little stronger because you have just dealt with something that's a little scary to you. That's the way fairy tales work, and all successful horror films will have that element across the board. Why any particular one will work, where others seem hackneyed, that's just a function of the storyteller.

CRAVEN: Let me ask a question I've heard several times in the past year and a half: Do you think *The Blair Witch Project* and *The Sixth Sense* represent a new kind of horror film, where things are suggested rather than seen?

CUNNINGHAM: No. I don't think *Sixth Sense* is a horror film at all; maybe I just have a self-serving definition of horror! *Blair Witch* is a wonderful story; it's like *Last House* revisited, only on a huge level. It seemed like these kids didn't know what they were doing, but they grabbed the gold ring. And that was great. It showed that you don't need Hollywood or anything fancy, and audiences supported that spirit. Most people loved the success story behind *Blair Witch* more than the movie itself.

CRAVEN: I was bored by it. I wasn't aware of all the internet hype beforehand, so I just saw it cold. I was annoyed by the girl [Heather Donahue]. I found her shrill, and after a while, I was thinking, "How many times can you say the word 'f**k' in a film?" But I was intrigued by the idea of someone making a film that works for ten cents. It's always smart to latch onto something that's a part of the audience's lives. There was a turn in the last ten years with video cameras becoming ubiquitous. For a while, they were kind of exotic, and they were sort of controlled by Dad and Mom. But then they became so cheap that kids had 'em. And that aspect of *Blair Witch* was very canny because there hadn't been that recognition in a film before. It was like what *Scream* did with cell phones; the idea that a person calling you could be anywhere hadn't quite been recognized in a film before. That sort of acceptance of new technology into the film was very astute; it was tailor-made for the audience who saw it. I thought the rest of it was derivative. The kids lost in the woods. I watched it with my girlfriend, and she said, "Why don't they follow a stream or something?"

FANGO: Do you feel that you lose creative freedom doing big-budget films?

CUNNINGHAM: Not really. It's all about what you're setting out to do. If you're going out to make a James Bond film, you shouldn't be having a serious conversation about creative freedom. If you really want creative freedom, you can go out and buy a camera and editing package for $15,000 and make anything you want.

CRAVEN: I believe you go through a period where you have enormous freedom when you start, and then you sort of have your entree. If you're lucky, you get a chance to do something on a bigger budget, and there are usually a lot more producers involved who want to show you how it's done. With *Deadly Friend*, which is one of my worst films, my agent was very excited because it was a Warner Bros. production. There were four full-time producers on that film, along with a couple of associate producers, plus studio people. That was an incredible confusion of input, suggestions, or dictates. At a certain point, if you make enough money with something, then you might get in a position where you can more or less get back in control. I've had a situation for years where if a picture scores above a certain level in test screenings, I get my own cut. So I've been able to earn final cut on my films. Recently, I looked back at the films of mine that have made the most money and the ones I felt were the best, and I realized that they were all done for people with roots on the East Coast. Sean Cunningham and Peter Locke are both East Coast guys, and then New Line Cinema, Miramax and Dimension are all very much New York people. So there's been a little bit different take on how to make movies; it tends to be made more with a very tight, sometimes contentious but respectful relation between the director and the distributor. The distributor can say yes or no, which is very important. Sometimes with the studios, people are afraid to say yes or no, and there's a lot of confusion. I've stuck with the East Coast model for most of the things I do, and I've been fortunate enough to get in at Miramax/Dimension in a way that's been an incredible boost to my career. It's taken thirty years to get somebody to offer me a non-genre film.

FANGO: What are your thoughts on *Fangoria* and its readers?

CUNNINGHAM: *Fangoria* readers have been very supportive and kind to me over the years, and they are the core audience. I respect them, and I always try to give them the entertainment they deserve.

CRAVEN: God bless 'em. I'm always impressed by the amount of detail and seriousness that *Fangoria* has brought to the genre.

The *Cursed* Is Over?

Marc Shapiro / 2005

From *Fangoria* 241, March 2005. Reprinted by permission of Joseph A. Sonnier IV, CEO of *Cinestate* and *Fangoria*.

So you think the much-troubled werewolf epic *Cursed* is finally complete, now that it's set for a February 25 release? Even Wes Craven is not that sure.

"I hope it's over," says the director with a laugh more sadly ironic than humorous. "I talked to [Dimension chairman] Bob Weinstein recently, and he's talking about making it a PG-13 movie. I can't win at this point, so I'm just going to walk away. I'm way past what my contractual obligations are to this film. If Bob wants to spend the rest of his life making this movie, that's fine. But I'm going to go on and do other things."

Cursed's final rating had yet to be determined at press time, but Craven has, in fact, moved on. He's talking candidly about the troubled lycanthro-picture during a break on the DreamWorks thriller *Red Eye*. And he's having the time of his life on this film. "It's nice to be at a fresh studio with a completed script that's ready to shoot," Craven says. "Nobody is telling me, 'This is how we have to cast, and this has to be rewritten.' I'm just being treated with more respect."

Craven has always been a good soldier, and he's not about to poison wells by taking a cleaver to Dimension and a film that has consumed him for two years. "I did the final day of mixing on *Cursed* the other day, and it looks terrific. It's a solid little film. And Dimension is still a great place to get released from. It's a good movie, but it took a long, long way around to get to that point."

The sixty-five-year-old director is obviously torn: He wants to put the best possible face on *Cursed* and makes no bones about wanting it to do well, but there's an air of frustration and candor in his voice as he takes *Fango* down the film's long and bumpy path.

Things weren't always so bleak in the world of *Cursed*. When this writer visited the initial shoot back in 2002, *Cursed* was an upbeat, potentially envelope-pushing project. The vibe on the set was good. Craven stopped filming to talk up the project to *Fango* and seemed legitimately excited at the prospect of adding new teeth to the werewolf genre. Scripter Kevin Williamson, who at the time was cramming to finish the final episode of *Dawson's Creek*, stopped by the set to chat about his latest collaboration with Craven, following their success with the *Scream* films. On set, some taut, emotionally draining moments were unfolding. But what was seen then is moot at this point—because, over two years later, that scene and a whole lot of others are nowhere to be found in the finished movie.

Cursed tells the story of two teens and a young adult who are bitten by a lycan-thrope in Los Angeles. The trio return to their normal lives but find themselves changed by the experience. It was with this premise that Dimension chairman Weinstein boasted, in an October 2002 *Variety* interview, that "Wes Craven and Kevin Williamson will reinvent the werewolf genre," with Christina Ricci, Jesse Eisenberg, and Skeet Ulrich (*Scream*) starring. Craven, in hindsight, felt he had a clear vision of what *Cursed* would be.

"I definitely went into it thinking we were going to make a movie about were-wolves in Hollywood," he recalls. "That was kind of interesting to me. By the time we got to the second version of the film, *Cursed* was definitely about two rather ordinary people, a sister and a brother, who have been mildly bitten and are turn-ing into werewolves. How it would impact their lives, how it would make them feel and the complications that would come from it—that was an intriguing idea. That's what we set out to do, and while it took a while for us to get there, I still believe the premise is funny, likable, and warm."

Cursed was originally announced as an August 2003 release (with Weinstein tell-ing *Entertainment Weekly* that "nothing is going to move us" off the date), but by February 2003 the media was abuzz with stories that the debut had been bumped to summer 2004. By June 2003, news began to leak out that *Cursed*, eleven weeks into filming, had suddenly ground to a halt and the production was on a reported four-week hiatus. The problem was reportedly with the screenplay—in particu-lar, a perceived weak third act that Dimension executives picked up on once they began to review dailies.

"We had a completed script going in," Craven notes. "But it was a script that we all felt needed a lot of work and wasn't ready to shoot. And it was not the first time this has happened. From *Scream 2* on, there has always been script development while we've been filming, due to the fact that Dimension always insisted on going forward before the scripts were ready. Part of the hallmark of dealing with this studio is that you're always having to be desperately writing while you're shooting. I don't think that's the best way to make a film at all."

But as Craven gritted his teeth and waited, Williamson not only rewrote the much-maligned third act but, ultimately, pretty much the entire script, which re-sulted in changes to the feel of the film as well as much of the old storyline. "In many ways, the tone did change," Craven says. "In the first version of the story, three strangers met after being infected by the werewolf. They were all individuals. It was very difficult to do because while we were trying to develop a love story between Skeet and Christina's characters, Jesse's character was moving totally separately from them. It was kind of like he was in another movie. So when we changed things around and went with the idea of Christina and Jesse being brother and sister, it all just kind of flowed together."

By September 2003, the four-week hiatus had turned into an eleven-week vacation. Once Craven and company began to deal with the script problems, other stumbling blocks surfaced, centering largely on the creation of the lead creature. "It was a crazy shoot from beginning to end," he says. "Rick Baker designed the werewolf and built the early forms of it. But then, about the time the production shut down, Rick just stepped back and decided not to work for a while (amid rumors of job burnout brought on by the accelerated preproduction schedule and largely resulting from the undeveloped screenplay). At that point, KNB jumped in and took over. All I can say is that any film based around a monster is going to be tricky, because monsters are hard to do."

Well into September and October 2003, the ripples from the reworked script were spreading like an oil slick. At that time. Craven indicated during interviews that many scenes were being reshot and numerous roles were being recast or written out. In a story on the *Cursed* website, the director finally admitted that "90 percent of the existing footage had been thrown out." "It just wasn't working," Ricci stated on the same site during this period. "We're almost reshooting the entire film."

Part and parcel of the *Cursed* screenplay changes and shooting delays was the juggling of actors in and out of the film. In no particular order, and by no means complete: out—Ulrich, Omar Epps, and Corey Feldman; in—*Scream 2*'s Joshua Jackson, Portia de Rossi, and Freddie Prinze Jr.; remaining—Ricci, Eisenberg, and Shannon Elizabeth.

For Craven, the departure of past collaborator Ulrich was a particularly bitter pill. "The character Skeet played in the film's first version was changed so much in the rewrite that Skeet really didn't want to come back and do it again," he says. "And it's sad because he gave a beautiful performance in that first version of the film."

Cursed finally began lensing once more in November 2003 with yet another promised release date: October 2004. Craven recalls that the already dizzying experience of making this werewolf epic had been made all the more complicated by the fact that, shortly before *Cursed* began production, Dimension had pulled the plug on a project he had been especially excited about: a remake of Kurosawa's Japanese chiller *Pulse*.

"It was all a cumulative effect on everybody's head," says Craven. "We were already kind of dislocated and not confident in the script the whole time we were doing the first shoot. Then everything shut down for five months, and we went back to film a totally different version. We were able to salvage a few scenes of Jesse from the first round, but the nature of Christina as a single person was different from Christina as a sister—and so, in many cases, everybody had to make these adjustments to footage that already existed. We ended up with four major shoots on the film, and each time we were trying to accommodate continuities that had already been established. The entire process was extremely difficult."

As the reshoots and release dates continued to change, Craven's frustration grew. "I swear I've got gray hair from this film," he says. "I've got to tell you, the idea of shooting for eleven weeks, getting great performances and ending up having ten weeks of that just thrown away is really hard. It's like a death in the family. It's wrenching. There's so much I could have done with my time. There were so many other offers. After a while, I just felt that the film was eating up my life."

Cursed ultimately wrapped in early 2004. Months of postproduction and reportedly positive test screenings scattered throughout the concluding days of last year seemed to indicate that the prolonged hard work may just have resulted in a decent film. But by this time, websites and genre mags were standing in line to tag *Cursed* as a movie in trouble. Craven, who finished up his final day of mixing on the film in December, is happy with the completed product, but concedes that his ego is taking a bit of a beating with all of the negative press that has been dropped on the movie. As a result, it's painful for him to discuss *Cursed* on any level.

"You just don't want to be a part of a movie that is being talked about so badly," he says. "It's very difficult to discuss because there were personalities involved that contributed to these things happening. I'm not the kind of person who goes around poisoning wells, but it has been frustrating.

"I was very excited about doing *Pulse*," he continues, "and we could have done that film and at least two others in the time it took us to make *Cursed*. Bob and Dimension would have been fabulously wealthy. With *Pulse*, we were prepared to make a film two and a half years ago that would have been the equivalent of *The Grudge*. But to have to go through two years of constantly changing and going back and doing it again—I mean, I've got maybe ten more films left in me before they take me off to the old person's home. To spend two years on something that is still struggling seems obscenely wasteful of my time, everybody's talent, and Dimension's money." Those final *Cursed* costs are rumored to be in the $75–80 million range.

Craven says that in a perfect world, *Cursed* would have been in script development for at least a year, which would have avoided turning the first eleven weeks of lensing into just a dress rehearsal. But despite the debacle that *Cursed* may or may not ultimately turn out to be, Craven has not let the situation drive a permanent wedge between himself and Dimension.

"I don't think this is the end of my relationship with them," he says. "But I do know that I would not do another film there unless I had final cut and a definite budget, and the studio went away and let me make my film. After I turned in a cut of *Cursed* that he really liked, Bob sat down and told me that he had made a really big mistake on the film and that if I still wanted to do *Pulse* he would give me a budget and just go away. If I have a project and I wouldn't be interfered with, Dimension would still be a great place to work. The big problem with the studio is a lack of trust in the filmmakers to make the right film. With Dimension, the ideas and concepts change rapidly, and that's just not the way I like to work."

The current production of *Red Eye* is definitely an example of the way Craven enjoys doing his thing. No relation to the airborne zombie movie of the same name that George Romero was once attached to, this one's a thriller about a young woman (*Mean Girls'* Rachel McAdams) held captive on a plane by a stranger (*28 Days Later*'s Cillian Murphy) who attempts to blackmail her into arranging a murder. Craven describes the film, scripted by Carl Ellsworth and tentatively scheduled for release this summer or fall, as more of a psychological drama than a straight-out horror film.

"There's not going to be a lot of gore and it's not going to be as high-concept as *Scream*," he explains. "It's real people in a real situation. The acting will definitely be a little more restrained."

A more explicit horror project on which Craven served as an executive producer is the third *Project Greenlight* movie and its first horror entry: *Feast*. The initial two films in this ongoing series, in which first-time directors and screenwriters are given a chance to make a feature (with their efforts documented in a six-part TV show; the third edition airs in March on Bravo), were failures at the box office. On their third try, the powers that be (including producers Matt Damon and Ben Affleck) figured that a genre feature stood a better chance of breaking even, and Craven seemed a logical choice to be brought in to consult. "It was a canny move to do a horror film this time," Craven says. "To get a first-time director to do a horror film is not as long a longshot. It was a smart move."

Over four thousand screenplays were submitted, in horror and other genres, with a multi-tiered selection process narrowing the field down. The winners were Patrick Melton and Marcus Dunston, whose *Feast* script deals with a group of people in an isolated diner plagued by a flock of flying, flesh-eating creatures. At the same time, aspiring directors submitted short scenes on VHS, with their work also judged by different groups. The process involved interviews and internal discussions among the *Greenlight* team about which filmmaker was right for the script. Ultimately, John Gulager (son of *Return of the Living Dead* actor Clu) won the job helming *Feast*, which lensed in late 2004 for release this spring or summer.

"I went out to dinner with John," Craven says, "and told him some things I thought would help him—things I had learned from mistakes I had made." One can only guess how many of those life lessons were gleaned in the course of making *Cursed*, yet Craven still holds out high hopes for its success. Barring the potential slashing for a less restrictive rating, he feels strongly that the end product is a worthy film. Should *Cursed* go on to defy the bad vibes and become a hit, would the director be willing to let himself run the gauntlet of a *Cursed 2*? "If *Cursed* is a smash and they wanted a sequel," he concludes, "I would just tell them good luck. But at this point, I would not be involved."

Fangoria Screamography: Wes Craven

Tony Timpone / 2005

From *Fangoria*, March 2005. Reprinted by permission of Joseph A. Sonnier IV, CEO of *Cinestate* and *Fangoria*. Transcribed by the editor.

Wes Craven: Horror films in general are about the terror event entering the adulthood because you think adulthood is actually evil.

Narrator: He has written, directed, and produced some of the most disturbing movie images of all time. For over three decades he has challenged, manipulated, and entertained his audiences. This is Wes Craven in his words told to *Fangoria*'s Tony Timpone. This is his *Screamography*. A product of a strict Baptist upbringing, Craven had a difficult childhood, but one that shaped him into the icon he is today.
WC: My father died when I was a kid, and I was raised by this other family during the day, while my mother was working. And that guy, his name was Eddie Biltin, had an 8mm camera and was always taking 8mm films. He also would rent them from the camera shops. In those days we—to rent little 8mm features like, you know, *Daredevils* and all that stuff, so I was really fascinated by it. But I never thought of making them. As you said I—we were forbidden to see films, with the exception of Walt Disney films, and I think it all just hit me at once after I got out of graduate school. I had seen *To Kill a Mockingbird*. I actually snuck out of the college that I was going to, that would have expelled me for going to the movies and it all sounds insane now, but—I thought the film was so fantastic, you know; it just was like, "Well this can't be simple; this is stupid," you know?

Narrator: That forbidden trip to the theater made an impact on Craven which would stay with him to this day.
WC: I don't know, I think—I always think—that being raised the way I was raised gave me more, certainly gave me a great love of film because they were forbidden and that always—you know, if you forbid anybody to do anything, then it's like that becomes really a great thing to do, but also it made me literate rather than

steeped in films. So I kind of have a very—I think—a deep story sense because I just read books up until the time I was in my mid-twenties. But I'm sure I have a bit of rage in me, probably a good deal of it, just of what was taken from me by being raised in the group that said, "The world is sinful; you don't want to be part of it. Sex is bad; you can't dance; you can't smoke," that kind of stuff. When you look back at it, you realize that that kind of fundamentalistic way of looking at the world really isolates people from life itself. I totally understand why fundamentalist Islamists can do what they do because it's crazy-making, you know? It makes you feel like you're not where you actually are.

Narrator: It took some time for Craven to figure out where he wanted to be.

WC: After I got out of grad school, I was teaching, and they had an art house in the town. It was right in the middle of the European New Wave, so all those films by Fellini and Buñuel and Truffaut and, you know, that incredible, incredible outburst of fantastic creativity. I just fell in love with it. I decided, "I want to make films," and I didn't really have an idea of what kind of films to make at all. I think I still have my head up my butt as far as what reality was or anything because I had come from this very kind of tight, narrow, little background, so there was a lot of just taking big leaps of faith, quitting my job and even going to graduate school. I didn't have money to go to graduate school, but I just hitchhiked there and got a couple of scholarships within three days. So I'd had about four or five key moments in my life where I've been just kind of like, "Here we go!" Because there just—it felt like nothing's going to happen if I'm still teaching up in upstate New York. Nothing's going to happen if I don't quit my job teaching, and it worked out. So I think sort of a passion and kind of, you know, bold moves like that are very, very important.

Narrator: It was not only his risky moves that got him on his way, but the friendships he made that would turn out to have a great impact on his career.

WC: I had a lucky break. There was a guy who was a big brother of a student of mine, Harry Chapin, who later went on to write "Taxi" and become a very famous kind of urban folk singer, but at that time he was in film. So through his brother I got linked up with him, and he taught me just the basics of how to cut so that was really invaluable. I wasn't making any money, but I learned how to basically edit on a flatbed. Then somebody in that facility where he was cutting fired their messenger, a sixteen-year-old kid, and asked if he—Harry—had a cousin or nephew or something, and I said, "I'll do it." So that was my first job after college professor, as a messenger for a postproduction house. But I very quickly worked my way up, it was a very small company, and I was assistant manager in a year. And then I quit because I didn't want to become the businessman-side, you know.

Narrator: Craven's passion was to be the creative type, so yet again, he made another bold move to get him on his way.

WC: I started looking for jobs. I was driving a cab in New York and thinking maybe I'd blown my career, my life, everything else, completely in debt, selling everything, and I got a job on a small film syncing up dailies and met this guy Sean Cunningham. It turned out to be a lifelong friendship. I worked for him, and I just kept moving up the ladder because it was only Sean and one other guy. At the end of that particular film, Sean and I were friends, and he said, "I've got some guys with $90,000. They want to make a scary movie. You want to write a scary movie? If they like it, you can direct it!" and that is how it happened. I knew nothing about making scary films; I don't think I'd even seen a horror film. It was just one of those weird things where you look back and say, "Well, how the hell did that happen?" It's just the way life goes sometimes.

Narrator: This is when Craven's life began to change, and he would soon realize all his bold moves were about to pay off.

WC: I tell kids, you know, take any job you can to get in the door of a film, of a place where people are working on movies, in post or making movies, whatever, or even work for nothing, because it's all about context. It's all about meeting people, and in that case, it was just meeting Sean Cunningham. The guy was willing to say, "You know, we'll be partners on this," and he'd only known me for a year and started off hiring just me . . .

Narrator: Their first collaboration was 1972's infamous *Last House on the Left*.

WC: Yeah, Bergman's *The Virgin Spring* was, you know, obviously the basis of *The Last House on the Left*. I always say that *Virgin Spring* was based on a medieval . . . they were called lays—not what they sound like—but they were songs with stories, so it's a pretty ancient kind of metaphor for getting the experience of life the hard way. Two girls on a pilgrimage and one is the one who's murdered and one gets away for a while, kind of the wilder girl, and the shepherds who kill them, which happens kind of accidentally. They really raped them, and then they end up killing them almost out of shame or whatever it is. It's very unclear, all the moralities and—anyway, they take shelter in the parents' house of the girls they've just killed, without even knowing it. And the parents, in the middle of the night, discover the bloody clothes of one of the girls and realize what's happened and, through the course of the night, prepare to kill these men and then do kill them in the house. So I just thought that was a fantastic story.

Narrator: A story that was considered one of the most disturbing movies of its time.

WC: Well, I wasn't comfortable with the viciousness in the real world, so, I think, doing the story with viciousness in it—was like this is what I'm talking about. So it was kind of a subversive thing in the sense of rather than doing violence that's entertaining, we'll do violence that's appalling. It was happening to real people and being done by people who, even a few moments after they do it, are nauseated at what they've done themselves and then try to clean up and wash the blood away. But they can't and they have nightmares about it even as they're sleeping in the house of the parents of the girls they killed, so it's like all of this kind of . . . there are no black and whites here, all gray. You know the parents, respectable couple, but they plan, really, murder within a very short time and carry it out so it wasn't "be comfortable with it." In fact, it was just the opposite; it was doing violence that you weren't comfortable with. I remember at the scene where Phyllis dies and they are stabbing her so many times they disembowel her without even realizing, then stop, and that's kind of where they're just revolted by what they've done. We shot that in one morning, and there had been sort of a tone on the set of—as Sean used to say, "Laughing and scratching," which is often when you're making a horror film and doing the bloodiest stuff. Everybody's kind of giggling because there's this exuberance from playing in mud and doing the forbidden and everything else; but after that scene we broke for lunch and nobody touched the food. Everybody just went off by themselves, including myself. It was very interesting because it was just the first time we realized that we were doing stuff just as real, in a strange way. It just felt chillingly real and repulsive and, that's what it was.

Narrator: Cunningham and Craven's next effort was to get *Last House* that elusive R-rating, but with the story so violent and so intense, this would not be easy.
WC: You know, it's funny because Sean and I delivered *Last House* to the boys in Boston, as we call them—we thought they might be mafia, but they were theater owners in Boston; they had outdoor theaters, about a hundred of them, and they're the guys that financed the film—and, you know, we shipped it off. We thought, "Well, it will show up in Boston, and we'll never hear from it again. And we'll go on with our lives." Then we got this call saying, "You know, you won't fucking believe this: they're lined up around the block, and we've got riots. And somebody had a heart attack, and they're attacking the projection booth!" It went on and on and caused this huge sensation, but we had no idea that that was going to happen. And then Sam Arkoff heard about it and bought it and put it out nationally. It was funny because it was something that we just kind of tossed off and thought none of our friends would see. Suddenly, we were completely identified with it, and all of our friends started keeping their children away from us and stuff like that. It was funny, but it's interesting because I didn't know anything. I didn't know the MPAA existed when I made that film, and Sean knew it. He said,

"We have to send it off now to get it censored," and I said, "What are you talking about?" He said, "No, there's this place in California we have to send a film in order for it to be released." I said, "I can't believe this!" So we sent it off, and we got this appalled letter back saying, "You have to cut the entire ending; you have to cut this scene and that scene." And we started cutting it down and sending it back, and each time they said, "You have to cut more and more, more!" Finally it was just to a point where we'd have to cut the whole film in half, and Sean said, basically, "Screw it." So he said, "Put it all back; put it all back!" And we went across the street where we were having a blow-up done and said, "Do you have the negative for an R-rating? You know, the blue screen with the R on it?" And he said, "Yeah!" "Put it on the front of ours!" And that's how it got an R-rating. I mean, it was totally illegal. We're past the statute of limitations now, but it was put out as an R-rated film but it was completely X-rated really. There was a point, I think about two weeks into its running, when there were so many riots and so many people cutting it up and, you know, trying to get at the projection at booth and everything that we did some cuts. I actually did it just by telephone because I was at that time in California, and Sean had somebody snip away some of the stuff that was out for twenty to twenty-five years until we finally—I had kept the stuff, and we put it back in for the uncut version.

Narrator: Craven was now making a name for himself in Hollywood, even if many had the wrong idea of him.

WC: I don't know; you walk into an office and everybody goes, "Oh, you're Wes Craven? I expected, like, Charles Manson." Yeah, kinda it's like everybody thinks that anybody that just does this kind of film is really bent out of shape, is really weird, has horrible thoughts all the time, and so they would never ever think of using that person to do anything but that kind of horrible film. So after *Last House*, both Sean and I tried to do other kinds of things. And I wrote comedies and everything else, which is stuff I had been writing all the way from junior high school. I had written much more comic material than anything else, and nobody wanted to know about it. It was always, "But if you want to do a horror film, we'll give you money." So we held out, both of us held out for about four years, and then we were broke. Another friend of mine, Peter Locke, said, "I've got money if you want to do a scary film." So I wrote *The Hills Have Eyes*, and I went off and did that. Sean just maxed out all his credit cards and, you know, wrote or had somebody write *Friday the 13th* for him and went from being in debt to everybody to being a millionaire. It's all those weird reversals that happen that you just can't predict, but many times in my career I've tried to get away from horror. It just keeps dragging me back. I suddenly realized horror films are great, and I have real talent for it—so stop complaining, just make really good ones.

Narrator: Craven finally embraced his talent and continued to make films that made his fans face their fears.

WC: Well, the inspiration for *The Hills Have Eyes* was Peter Locke, who called me up, and he was always after me to write a film. He said, "Listen, I'm out here in Vegas"—his wife at that time was a singer/dancer/comedian, Liz Torres—"She's playing Vegas, and there's all this desert out there. Nobody cares where you go, so why don't you write something for the desert?" Okay, fine, and I went to the New York Public Library, went through their sociology division, just looking at crime books, and I found the story of the Sawney Bean family from the 1600s in Scotland. It was a family that had gone wild, ran around naked, and attacked wayfarers, people going between Glasgow—I believe—and London and pulling them off their horses and eating them and their horses. So people would go on this particular route and just be vanished, you know.

Narrator: One character from *The Hills Have Eyes* will forever stay with Craven.

WC: Yeah, I certainly—just years and years of people saying, "Oh, who was that bald guy?" That was just a key stroke of luck in casting. Michael [Berryman] walked into the office, we were in a little tiny room off Sunset Boulevard, off a parking lot, and Peter and I just looked at each other and said, "Oh, you're hired. You'll be a Pluto." So yeah, because he was—just no prosthetics, he was just scary-looking, you know? Michael said, "I've got twenty-four birth defects. I don't have any sweat glands, I don't have much hair, I don't have fingernails, I . . ." He had practically no body fat, he had a misshapen head, and we just put him out there—no makeup— and he was just so scary. He was the first one of them that you saw—I mean—everybody was just chilled and that carried me through the rest of film.

Narrator: The film really put Craven and his crew to the test.

WC: It was only my second, and I think Peter's second—he had done some tiny film, and neither one of us knew diddly-squat about shooting in a desert or even being west of the Mississippi. We were both New Yorkers, basically, and the first time we went out on location scouting with Bob Burns, our production designer, we rented a car in something like Barstow, a nice air-conditioned car rental place, and got in the car, turned the air conditioner on, and started following these Bureau of Land Management maps that cut off into the dirt roads. And the guy said, "Don't get off the main road; you know, people die out there all time." We were like, "Yeah sure," so we found these dirt roads and drove, just drove, and like two hours out in the middle, we're like, "I can't believe there's a place like this in the United States!" There's nothing you can see for miles, and we said, "Well, let's get out." So we stopped the car and—you turn off the engine and get out and it was like stepping out into a furnace. It was just incredible, so we're walking around, drinking all of our water and everything else, and we finished the last water and got back in the car. The car, which was now 200 degrees inside, wouldn't start, and we just look at each other said, "We've done exactly what they told us not to do, and now we're gonna die!" Fortunately, after we let the car cool down, it started, but the whole thing was just kind of an experience of learning what it was like to shoot there by just doing it. It was up to 120 degrees during the day and down into the 40s at night. We were miserable all the time, you know, physically, but it's exhilarating to be doing the shooting. There were rattlesnakes, and there were scorpions and tarantulas, all that stuff. Like the tarantula scene, we just had it—a tarantula walking through the set—we just grabbed it, and I said, "Put it out on his coat!" So when Lynn goes to get her husband's coat there's the spider, and it was just like stuff we were discovering ourselves.

Narrator: The heat of the desert could not compare to the stink of the *Swamp Thing*.
WC: I got to see Adrienne Barbeau topless; I guess that was the high point. It was a very difficult shoot. We had a completion bond company that was on the set all the time and were really nasty. You would constantly be told to "Wrap it up, wrap it up," you know, so very little coverage, and the whole last two weeks was just— we shot basically masters, and they said, "Okay, move it along or we're shutting you down," so that was horrible. We were working in swamps that were full of alligators, usually up to our bibs—you know, coveralls. We had these waders, and there were just crocs or alligators going by like they're commuting. But nothing happened, there were so many of us I think the alligators were like, "I wish they'd go away so I could have my swamp back again." But it was—it was very uncomfortable, and it was extremely hot and muggy. There was some sort of plague of black caterpillars, so they were constantly falling out of trees and going down your neck and stinging you. There were deer flies all the time, and there were a lot of water moccasins. We had to watch out. All that stuff was really, it was really—it was a pretty damn difficult shoot, actually.

Narrator: Finally leaving the swamp, Craven moved to suburbia and began his greatest film achievement.
WC: Yeah, *Nightmare on Elm Street* was inspired by, I think, three articles in the *LA Times* over a period of about a year and a half. The first one was kind of sketchy: it was the story of a young man dying after having a severe nightmare, and they couldn't figure out how it happened medically. Then there was a second story about nine months later, and nobody—the newspaper didn't seem to correlate it. They didn't seem to remember the other story, and then the third story—and the one that really made me feel I have to write a script about this—was this kid—all

these kids were Asian from all over Southeast Asia—all came out of kind of war zones from Vietnam and Pol Pot, the killing fields—and their families had gone through location camps and then ended up in the United States. This kid was having nightmares, and he said, "Somebody's after me in my nightmares. If I sleep I know I'm going to die." And as his father was a physician, he said, "I'll give you sleeping pills; you'll be all right. We've come through a horrible time; now we're in America. You're safe." And the father started giving the kid sleeping pills. The kid supposedly was taking them, but he stayed up and he stayed up—for something like five days, it was like an amazing—just, you know, himself, awake, almost by putting matchsticks in his eyes. Then finally he fell asleep while the family was watching television, and they took him upstairs and put him in bed. The parents later said, "We were all convinced the crisis was over," and in the middle of night they heard screaming and thrashing and ran into his room. And he was like kicking and screaming, and they got to him. And he just fell dead. He was dead. And there were three things that really just made me think this is a movie. One was they did an autopsy on him, and nothing was wrong. There was no physical reason for it. The second was that they found, the family said—they found all the sleeping pills that he supposedly had taken hidden, so he'd obviously put them in his mouth and when [his] dad wasn't looking, it was right back out because he didn't want to sleep. And the third thing was this incredible thing: this kid had run an extension cord behind his bedroom curtains and into the closet. He had a Mr. Coffee in there with black coffee. So he had a source of keeping awake even when he was in his room supposedly sleeping. It was just so . . . it was heart-rending because this kid . . . he was right, you know? He died as soon as he fell asleep.

Narrator: Craven once said, "Horror films don't create fear; they release it," and Freddy released a lot of fear with his fans.

WC: Freddy was based on—I think he was based on—a man who scared me when I was a little kid. You know, again, my father was dead, it was always a sense that I had—like nobody's around to really protect us because Dad's gone, and I just was lying in my bed. We had—we're in a second-story apartment—I heard this guy sort of mumbling, grumbling, and shambling along, and it was this guy kind of dressed like Freddy—you know, dark jacket, the sort of brimmed hat that they wore in those days—and he stopped and somehow just looked straight up at me. I was so scared, you know, just like jump back, and I was back in the shadows waiting for the sound of him going away and waited, waited—it seemed like I waited forever and finally, "Well, he must have gone." So I went back to the window, and he was there and he just went [Craven stares menacingly]. Then he started walking down the sidewalk, looking over his shoulder at me like [glances threateningly], and he went into our building. I don't know who that guy was, but he became

Freddy. My brother went down with a baseball bat, and the guy ran away. So my big brother saved my life. Who knows? He might have just thought, "I'll scare this kid for the hell of it," you know so that became the basis of Freddy, that sort of adult that took delight in terrifying a child was the basis of it, and then the rest was actually a quite intellectual process of, "What will he wear?" and I thought, you know, like an overcoat would be good. Then I thought of the idea of a janitor. Because I'd taught Greek mythology and the descent into Hades was always going down in fire, I made his job basically being in Hades, you know. The sweater, the striped sweater was a *Scientific American* article on the two colors that are the most difficult for the human retina to see side-by-side. That was those colors, and there were a lot of films being made with villains that had masks but I wanted him to be able to talk. So I said, "Instead of a hockey mask or whatever, I'll give him a mask of scar tissue, and that'll be the way the parents killed him." And the final thing, with the claws, we went through the usual thing of "Shall it be a hunting knife? Should it be a scythe? Should it be, you know, all this crap?" I said, "We'll go back to the most primal weapon you can think of," and I thought, "Well, it would be tooth and claw; you know, what men faced before they had real weapons." Then I thought, "Well, cave bears, you know, that claw comes in and grabs you." And then, combining that with the human hand, you had kind of the elements of both the ancient—a highly-evolved, dexterous thing that makes humans so incredibly unique is our hands. So putting those two things together just made something that was pretty powerful.

Narrator: Freddy is still one of the most feared movie characters of all time.
WC: It's funny. Freddy—originally I was thinking, "It should be a guy in his seventies." We looked at a lot of, you know, older gentlemen, and they— I think if you get to be seventy you're kind of like mellow, you've seen it all, you're just grateful to be alive, and life has a lot more preciousness to it. And then Robert Englund came in, and it was like, "Not this guy, you know, he's too young." And he just had such an enthusiasm for it, and I found that when we looked at a lot of big stuntmen—and I found stuntmen—who were very, also very gentle people in general—they were so in control of their body and physicality. They didn't have these issues; you know, people that are a little bit more normal and were beat up as kids or whatever. Robert Englund just had no hesitation to play something really evil, and I realized that that was what it took. It didn't take an old guy, didn't take a big guy; it took somebody who was comfortable, you know, looking inside and saying, "What would I be like if I was utterly evil?" A lot of people can't do that, you know. They don't want to go there, so they play kind of bold to, you know—kind of too big or kind of do it jokey. But Robert was willing—at least on the first one—to be serious, and that's what worked.

Narrator: It worked so well that *Nightmare on Elm Street* has grossed over $25 million to date.

WC: Horror films are, in general, about the terror-event entering the adulthood because you think adulthood is actually evil or, at best, incompetent, and in almost every horror film the adults are either, you know, in league to kill you or they are incompetent like the sheriff, the bumbling cop, the person that tells you, "Go to bed!" when you know if you go to bed, you're going to die. So it's about that transition into adulthood and leaving childhood behind, so you know that's an important thing for horror films, is that kind of the adults in some way have sold their souls or are incompetent to deal with what you know. And I think as a child, a child-adult, if you can put yourself in that sort of twelve- to seventeen-, eighteen-year-old period, you don't—you're not sure you are going to be able to hack it as an adult, you don't want to be a child anymore, but you've got all those memories of vulnerability and the family struggles, you know, mom not being able to come with you and your dreams, all those sorts of things. And then there's sex starting to become an issue, and you don't know what the hell all that's about and how you're going to do. So there's a lot of real primal things that are going on in that five year, six year, you know, sort of pre- and postpuberty/teen period there. That's really powerful, and there's no real guidelines that you can take from adults and, increasingly so, because each generation is so remarkably different from the previous ones. So adults are just kind of like—it's a period where you kind of have to kill the adults almost, you know. My theory is that when you do a horror film it's almost like you construct a very complex character that has all sorts of things hanging off of him or her: the past and what mom thought, what their friends think you should do, and everything else, and list, one by one, you kill, and it sounds like you're just a butcher. But what really, if you look at it in a mystical sense, you're actually stripping away parts of a personality or persona that don't work. You know, the parental attitude, "Oh, just follow the rules." Get rid of that—you know, you get rid of it until you end up with this core persona—the hero or the heroine that knows exactly what's going on, still has goodness, but is able to kick ass and take names and stays awake, you know. And that's what it's all about, and I think that is the template that kids unconsciously are looking for: "How do I get through the worst hell I can imagine?" or "the worst hell that I think the world might throw at me after watching the evening news?" You know, "What would I do if I was tortured?" "What would I do if somebody threatened to cut off my head?" I mean, just open the *New York Times*; it's there all the time. So I think kids are always wondering like, "How do I survive in this world of adults that seems to be quite maniacal and crazy and full of duplicity?" And we're really nice people at the same time we're killing people. You know, that's . . . that's pretty heady stuff for a kid to figure out.

Narrator: After *Nightmare on Elm Street* Craven created some more notable films to his credit: *The Serpent and the Rainbow, The People Under the Stairs,* and *Shocker,* but *Shocker* didn't cause too much of a jolt at the box office.

WC: It's humbling that you do something really fantastic like *Nightmare on Elm Street* that goes on and on and on, and you say, "Okay, I'll just do another one." And it doesn't always happen, you know, for a hundred reasons. I mean sometimes it's casting, sometimes in the case of that one, the guy who was in charge of special effects went crazy in the middle of the shoot, and he kept saying, "The special effects are coming! They're coming! I'm going to give them to you all at once!" And then he finally came to me in tears and said, "I don't know what's happening. I can't think and I haven't done any of them and it doesn't work and I'm so sorry," and started sobbing. I sent my son to get the negative from him, and he didn't know where it was. And then we had like a three-week search for negatives. We were finding it under benches in the labs with, no labeling. We found some in the trunk of his car. It was insane, so all that was going on while we're trying to make a movie. So yeah, it's like you never know what's going to happen in the course of any given film, whether the gods are going to be with you or not, so all—a lot of the special effects of Pinker, Horace Pinker, going into the electrical field and so forth were severely compromised by the fact that one major part of the infrastructure of the filmmakers just fell apart. That's the way it is, you know; it's like it's a big crapshoot every time you make a movie, and you never know what's going to happen. That's what makes it so much fun, though.

Narrator: Then in 1995 Craven did the movie *Vampire in Brooklyn* with one of Hollywood's A-list stars, but Eddie Murphy had his own ideas for the film.

WC: Yeah, it was—you know, I don't want to get in trouble with Eddie; he didn't want to be really evil, which I think hampered it because it really needed somebody who could be evil. He kind of wanted to do a horror film, but he didn't want to be a bad guy. And he wanted to look kind of buff all the time. At that time he was just kind of into being a leading man. It was funny because the very next film, he let all of—you know—let his hair down completely and played the Klumps or whoever that family was and was brilliant, so—but it was very difficult. There were a lot of members of his family involved— some talented, some not—and so we're fighting that all the time. And there were a lot of other things that I won't talk about, but there were just—there was just kind of personality and psychological stuff going on that didn't help. And the studio wanted us to do it in the backlot, so that was kind of limiting, too. I thought it was good, a fun little film, and it was nice to get a chance to do comedy. But I think the script really hampered it.

Narrator: Then in 1996 Craven reinvented the teen horror genre with a huge commercial success of *Scream*.

WC: I read the opening to *Scream*, and it was just brutal and—"I can't kill another poor girl you know?" Geez, you know you do—we have to go into a dark place in your mind when you do these films, and it always seems like it's got to be a lot worse than it is because, actually, when you do it, it's just as I was saying earlier: it's a strange experience of quite often it being fun. Not that you're killing people but you're dealing with these horrible things in a way that you're in control, and everybody gets very close on a horror set for some reason, so I thought it was— maybe I shouldn't go back there, and then at a certain point I think there was a little kid at a convention at an appearance I made. He says—I swear he was like fourteen years old—"I've seen all your films, but in *Last House* you really kicked ass. You should kick ass again." He walked off, and I thought of that kid: "Oh damn—okay. I'll kick ass one more time," and that's literally how I decided to do it, thank God.

Narrator: And he did it in a way that brought horror and humor brilliantly together.

WC: I think horror films are—or at least the kind I make—are kind of black, black humor. It's kind of making jokes about the graveyard and disease. I mean all jokes are about things that we're profoundly uneasy with. They're about religion and mothers-in-law and doctors telling you have six days to live, race—you know, they are always about things that are really disturbing. They build up a lot of tension, and the sudden release is explosive laughter. A horror film is kind of the same timing, same release, only it's a scream. So I always felt like—I used to write comedy for Liz Torres. I wrote her comic acts. I was like—that was second nature to me; making people laugh is much more second nature to me than making people scared, afraid—I never thought I would be doing that, but the skill set is very similar. So no, I didn't find any difficulty doing it. And I must say, it was an excellent script, and I also just found some really great actors, especially Jamie Kennedy, who I could just kind of let go, you know. Almost every scene we did one take where he just went, and I just kind of went with it. But also Matthew Lillard was quite brilliant in improvisation. There was a famous moment when Neve has escaped and she calls up, and he's totally bloody bleeding to death because their stupid way of getting out of being suspected was completely backfiring. They were bleeding to death, and he says, "Did you really—you know—did you really call the police?" and she said, "Yes." And he just says, "My mom and dad are going to kill me!" That was just his line, and it's trying not to laugh, you know, and stuff like that just comes from actors. It just comes from everybody kind of like putting their best ideas into things.

Narrator: But the studio heads did not think everyone was putting their best ideas to work.

WC: The first week of shooting was the Drew Barrymore sequence, and I think it's been a while since I had directed. I was thinking, "Am I too much of an old fart? Can I do this anymore? Who knows?" Yeah, you never know. So it was a week of shooting, and we did a lot of steadicam moves and everything else. But you never, you know, you think you're doing your thing, you think it's going to work, but you don't know. And on the Monday of the second week I get a call from—let's say the studio and the studio person said—Bob Weinstein pretty well knew they did this—"Nobody's got to tell you, except me. I looked at your dailies, and they're just workmen, like at best phoning-it-in. I'm not hiring you to phone-it-in." I just felt my blood run cold, you know: "Oh God, is it that bad?" So it's like Bob Shaye turning around saying, "Do we have a film here at all?" And what I should have thought of—but you know, no matter how many times you experience it—is that people that don't make movies, they can't look at dailies. It's impossible for them to know what you have in your mind as far as how it's going to be cut together, so the second week of shooting was this frantic behind the scenes, you know? Cutting it together by my brilliant editor Patrick Lussier and, we had special music made and sound effects, a whole mix, sent it to Bob at the end of the second week of shooting—total exhaustion—and figure, "I'm gonna get fired." I get the call from Bob, and he says, "I saw your footage. It's brilliant; it's fucking brilliant. What do I know about looking at dailies? I'm taking it to Ken, thank you very much." And that's Bob, you know, as he can totally make you nuts, or he can support you and throw in tons of money and make it even better once he has faith in it. So my experiences with that guy were all over the planet. I mean, from some of the worst experiences I've had to some of the best, and it seems to be the way he makes movies. But it was pretty horrible, you know, at the end of the first week.

Narrator: But when Weinstein was finally on board, he fought for this film.

WC: The first *Scream*, for instance: two guys who are the murderers and their idea is they will stab each other, so "We'll look like victims, and they'll never suspect us." Then they start bleeding to death because they're two jerks that don't really know what it is to get hurt, and they're covered with blood and bleeding out for a fifteen-minute scene. The censor said, "Basically, you just have to remove it. I don't know—we don't know how you're going to make your story make sense, but you can't have it end your movie." And I wrote also—you know—"This is a First Amendment issue!" And finally, Bob Weinstein called them up and said, "It's a spoof! It's a spoof! We're just making fun of it all!" I swear to God, the next day we got an R, and we had to cut one little thing. There was a shot of Matthew Lillard's hand, and it was blood dripping off the end. And at that particular time it was you can't show flowing blood, so trim that like ten frames. We got an hour, so it's like the whole censorship thing is so incredibly arbitrary and unpredictable. You can never cite precedent. You're lucky if you get the same group of people to look at the film twice.

Narrator: The box-office success of the first *Scream* led to a very successful trilogy but not without some apprehension.

WC: There was a sort of encroaching craziness on the way it was put into motion by the studio. With the second one, no the third one, Columbine happened just before we were to start work on it, and understandably, the Weinsteins called us up and said, "We're not sure we should do this." There was this horrible, you know, whole controversy all over again: horror films make kids do these things. And I mean, two years later, they find out the kids had horrible parents and all these other things, but people immediately point to horror films so. . . . Kevin's outline was, you know, set in the high school. And the plot was that this girl and a group of friends were killing people, and she was the principal's daughter. I was like, "That's not gonna happen." So I just said, "You know, I think the third one should take her to Hollywood and just complete the sort of referential look at film itself." And so we put that in motion, but it was already late; and it was a lot of writing while we were shooting—actually, on both the second and third.

The second one was our first experience with, sort of, the threat of the internet and spoilers—I had never heard the term before. I think it was pretty much when they were emerging—but Kevin sent his forty-two pages of a really brilliant opening for the second film. And the next night it was on the internet, you know, in format, the whole damn thing, which just killed us, just killed us. So all you little spoilers out there [mock scolding]! So we had to go back; we had to reconceive the whole damn film as we were shooting and fighting to make some alternate ending as good as the original ending was going to be. Suddenly the scripts are all numbered. They had a purple stripe down the middle so if you Xeroxed them, it came out black. And we had little—we changed a word in each script so we would know whose script it was and all that stuff. It's to try to safeguard ourselves against somebody publishing on the internet, and I have to say it's—I have to be very careful with what I say these days compared to what I used to say. You should be able to say to somebody, kind of in confidence, "This happened to that happened." But now it's like on the internet right away, and this kind of—I don't know—this kind of feeling like it's okay to just kind of try to get something out there that was told in confidence or something. It makes it really a pain in the ass, to be frank, or hard to talk in private about certain things. So you find yourself censoring yourself much more and being much more careful about what you say because it's just going to end up on the internet—not that this will but you know what I mean, especially during press tours when you're talking to a lot of reporters.

Narrator: Craven won't let anyone spoil his creative genius. He continues to make brutally honest horror films, which put his audiences through an emotional wringer. His vision cannot be matched, and his passion remains his greatest inspiration.

WC: Again, the business is, like, it tests you, it really tests you, and you just have to say, "I don't give a damn what happens. I got to do my best to make one more film," and that's all. That's what I do. I'm just an animal that makes films, and maybe they won't let me do it after a while. But as long as I can, I'm going to keep making films.

Narrator: The dog that has a flashback [in *The Hills Have Eyes Part II*]. What were you thinking?

WC: The reason is, you can't do that—look stupid—and I guess it was, but it's still the only dog flashback that I know of in cinema! We didn't have money to shoot enough to fill ninety minutes of film, so that would give me another five minutes by showing that sequence for the first film. Okay, so I just thought, "Let's do it. Screw it." Sometimes it—that—works, sometimes people end up just thinking you're stupid for the next thirty years.

Red Eye—Wes Craven Interview

Andrea Chase / 2005

From *Behind the Scenes* on PRX, August 8, 2005. Reprinted by permission of Andrea Chase. Transcribed by the editor.

This is Andrea Chase, and I am talking with Wes Craven who brought nightmares to Elm Street and taught us all to scream. His latest film is an old-fashioned thriller at least as scary anything Freddy dreamed up and all the more effective for staying squarely, mostly in reality.

It is the story of an innocent victim played by Rachel McAdams who falls prey to a ruthless hitman played by Cillian Murphy who is bent on forcing her to help him with his latest target, and he is not shy about using any weapon at his disposal. I am going to start with a technical question. Forty minutes of this film takes place in an airplane. Talk about the pleasures and the perils of advancing the story and maintaining a level of terror on a small set like that.

Craven: I once had an old filmmaker tell me that there are two places that you should never agree to do a film in. One is a boat, a small boat and the other is an airplane. We built a set of a complete 767 on a soundstage so that part was under control, but it was very, very claustrophobic. And we didn't break it open; we didn't like have half an airplane that we were shooting into and behind us were open spaces. It was always in that closed space, you know. It was very important because the plot is basically all about this young woman who is entrapped by this guy to make a phone call that will result in somebody's death, and she is never able to get away from him because if she says anything to anybody this guy is going to get on the phone and tell his cohorts to kill her father. So that kind of puts the casing around the psychological drama that takes place. As you said, he will use any weapon he can; all the weapons he uses at the beginning are psychological. And they're very deeply, profoundly disturbing things he does—not creepy, but just scary.

Chase: I wanted to ask you about the difference in creating a mood of terror when you have the supernatural to work with as you did in, say, the *Nightmare on Elm Street* series, and here you have to stay in reality. Is there a difference in the approach you take, or is it all basically the same thing?

Craven: It is somewhat different. I would say in a horror film you're dealing with things that are almost oceanic, these kind of primal fears that we have as human beings, as bodies. I always tell film students you know it is about that fact that there's 1/8 of an inch of skin between you and bleeding to death, and so the edged weapon, knives are just iterations of the claws of animals that chased us around as we were first emerging. That's what horror films are about. Human beings have other bodies, the kind of invisible bodies of your mind and your soul and heart, and that's where the arena is for this picture. And it is much more complex and subtle, and it demands more of the audience.

Chase: Is it more fun or more challenging or both?

Craven: It is all of those things. It is challenging because it is my first thriller, and frankly, I've been scaring kids with broader strokes although I must say I have made films that have made people think too, but this is really about those little details between human beings not only when they are traveling but when they are trying to get something from each other or trying to run from somebody or from the past. So it was fun because I found myself drawing upon experiences of myself as an adult rather than as myself as a child, which I often do in a horror film.

Chase: Do you like to fly?

Craven: I don't mind it at all. I think the actual act of flying is one of the great miracles of modern life. I always get the window seat, and I try to look out and just watch as we fly over this vast continent that is endlessly fascinating. People are always saying, "For the courtesy of your fellow passengers, please lower your blinds." And I'm saying, "Why? It's a billion-dollar view." And sometimes it is achingly beautiful. I mean, flying into San Francisco last night with this layer of fog coming out of this beautiful sunset and down into this very mysterious fog. I love it, but a lot of people have problems with airplanes. They are very confined, and you are trapped there. It doesn't bother me. I do a crossword puzzle.

Chase: I have to ask: the name of the airline is Fresh Air—is that an homage to Terry Gross of some kind?

Craven: I once did her show. It wasn't intentionally; we were trying to think of a name because none of the airlines would let us—I don't know why!

Chase: I can't imagine!

Craven: They wouldn't let us use their names, so we had this list. It got narrower and narrower and more and more narrow, and I didn't like any of them. So I thought of the idea of Fresh Airlines, and their logo was basically Fresh Air.

Chase: You were brought up in a family where films were considered sinful. Was it a fire-and-brimstone sort of religion?

Craven: You know it wasn't like Southern Baptist where people were screaming at you—I don't want to offend Southern Baptists—but it definitely was about basically "come to Jesus," or you will unfortunately burn in hell forever. So they were pretty high stakes right from the beginning, but that whole group of people, group of churches don't believe movies are a good thing. So none of us kids went to movies except for Disney movies; we were allowed to see those. You know it's funny when I talk to a lot of other fellow filmmakers. They say, "So did you like all of these films?" And they list all these films that were made in the times when I was young, and I hadn't seen any of them. I think it's kept my stuff original because I'm not basing it on old horror films that I saw as a kid.

Chase: Did any of the religious imagery—do you think—seep in there?

Craven: It comes in a little bit. I did a film *Deadly Blessing*, which was about a religious sect, and *Nightmare on Elm Street* when there was a cross on the wall that when Freddy presses at it the cross falls off. So little subtle things like that, but I've never gone into a strictly religious film.

Chase: Is it something you'd like to do one day?

Craven: If I did I would do it realistically, and probably just growing up that way— I don't know what it's like to be in a church like that these days. I'm sure that they are not quite as strict or as phobic of film. But it was a pretty amazing way to grow up, in a way, and our religion is so powerful it calls to the mind so deeply. Unfortunately, a lot of the trouble we are in right now, just historically, has to do with the God part of religion, but people are taking it and making it their own, for their own purposes. And it does influence us right down to our DNA. It's hard not to be astonished and humbled by life and the universe. Just what comes out of the Hubble telescope is enough to make you realize whatever it is, you could just fall on your knees and say that this is just so much more vast than I am [and I am amazed by it].

Chase: Or flying into San Francisco at sunset.

Craven: Yeah.

Chase: I want to talk a little about the character of Lisa that Rachel McAdams plays. One of the things I love about this film, besides being terrified the whole time and finding new and fascinating ways to use pens, is that there is a wonderful subtext of female empowerment in this film. I was wondering if that is what drew you to the script, or is it just a little serendipitous thing that came up?

Craven: Actually, if you look at my films, it'd be hard to find one that wasn't a female empowerment film of some sort or another. Sidney Prescott in the *Scream* series was a central character, Nancy in *A Nightmare on Elm Street*, *Music of the Heart* my "out-of-the-genre" film with Meryl Streep. You know, I think it goes back to—first of all, I think that the course of women in the twentieth and the beginning of the twenty-first century has been one of the most dramatic and striking passages in the history of humankind as we know it. Traditionally, women were kept under the thumb of men and the fact that they have emerged as equals and are able to divulge their incredible power without any worries of repercussions—in most cases or, at least, in the best of cases—is a great thing because of that. A woman in that type of fix becomes equally—or even more—evocative of overcoming terrible power.

Chase: Even [the character] Cynthia in this film . . . she got several lines in the review because she was perfect.

Craven: She was perfect.

Chase: That actresses is amazing.

Craven: Yeah, and this is her first film.

Chase: . . . and had like maybe two dozen lines and yet indelible.

Craven: It started with one dozen lines, and she was so great we kept writing new things for her to do.

Chase: Very wise. That's why you're a master filmmaker! I have to ask this—Brian Cox plays Lisa's father in this film. Did you deliberately dye his hair and dress him up to look a little like James Lipton from *Inside the Actors Studio*?

Craven: Oh, that never occurred to me. You know, the last time I had seen him was in *The Bourne Supremacy* where he was hefty, let's say . . . and silver-haired, and that's what I was expecting to walk through the door. As it turned out he was doing a play in Scotland, which involved him having a beard, kind of dyed this weird kind of henna. And he had just been through this very rigid diet by some diet guru, and he lost like sixty pounds. I didn't recognize him when he walked to the door. I was like, "Oh. Hi." That was kind of fun. But once he started acting it was like, "Oh." He does it so deftly and so quickly. He shot for two days total, and it feels like he is there throughout the whole film.

Chase: You filmed in an actual airport, the Ontario Airport in Southern California.
Craven: Actually three. We did LAX and also Miami.

Chase: How do you get clearance in these times when there is so much security—or there should be so much security, maybe I should say.
Craven: Let me tell you; there is because by getting into those airports you realize the layer upon layer of security that are in places like this. We heard one airport had decided not let anymore film crews in although they stipulated very clearly that they loved having us and we hadn't caused any security risk. Just the amount of work that they had to do to make sure it was safe was beyond what they wanted to do ever again. But they were great, and they were completely aware that this was pushing the limits. They wanted to help filmmakers especially. They read the script, and they really liked the script.

Chase: What were some of the limitations that were put on you?
Craven: Limitations imposed by the airport were—it wasn't bad. We all had to go through security—that's the one part of flying I hate—everyday. But not just me walking in in a shirt and pants, but crewmembers with big tool belts and containers of tools and all that stuff had to be checked every single day. And, you know, there were limitations on where we could shine the lights, so we didn't blind people in the tower. No scenes with guns and all guns had to be plastic guns and all that sort of stuff for the security people, and we were restricted to very specific areas of the airport that were not used.

Chase: There is a certain angst today associated with flying that there wasn't before 2001. Does that inform anything that you did in this film?
Craven: Yeah, when I read the script and went to the studio, and they wanted to know what my take was I said, "Post-9/11 has created kind of a texture of tension and unresolved angst and also the war in Iraq or whatever they're calling it this week. Our kids are fighting in places where they are so at a disadvantage because the people they're fighting were born and bred there, so I build a lot of the third act from the way it was originally written, playing around with the fact that she was chased into the house where she was born and raised and knew every nook and cranny. So this guy, inadvertently, is enraged to catch her and kill her, unlike being on the airplane where he has it all planned out, he stumbles into the fact that he is fighting his enemy on her turf, and that is how and when everything turns.

Wes Craven Q&A

Bilge Ebiri / 2007

From *Nerve.com*, 2007. Reprinted by permission of Bilge Ebiri.

No, you heard that right: Wes Craven is indeed one of the directors on the romantic omnibus film *Paris je t'aime*, which tackles love in the City of Light through brief vignettes, each set in one of the city's twenty neighborhoods (or *arrondissements*). True, his film is set in the infamous Pere Lachaise cemetery—home to the final resting places of, among many others, Jim Morrison, Edith Piaf, Yves Montand, Marcel Proust, Maria Callas, and, the focus of this short, Oscar Wilde. Leave it to the auteur of *A Nightmare on Elm Street* and *Scream* to milk romance out of such a funereal setting: Here, a couple (played by Emily Mortimer and Rufus Sewell) begins to bicker when a visit to Wilde's grave inspires the woman to chastise her fiancée for not having any sense of wit. Needless to say, it's all happily resolved— all in all, a bit of a departure for this director. And it may be a welcome one, as far as he's concerned. *Nerve* spoke to Craven recently about his fondness for other genres and his lifelong desire to make a romance. We also made sure to speak to him about the particular cultural relevance of horror during periods of social upheaval; the man is, after all, a former humanities professor.

Bilge Ebiri: How did you, of all people, wind up making this movie?
Wes Craven: Well, the producers were kind enough to call me and ask. One of their directors had fallen through, and they needed a replacement. Once I heard who else was participating in the project, it was a real no-brainer for me. They did say it had to be in that particular *arrondissement*, and they told me there was a great cemetery there. So at first I thought they were gonna want something weird, where a guy jumps out from behind a gravestone or something. But that wasn't the case, which was a relief. They told me it didn't need to be scary, that it just needed to be about love in Paris. That felt like a great opportunity—not having to scare people.

Wes Craven Q&A

Bilge Ebiri / 2007

From *Nerve.com*, 2007. Reprinted by permission of Bilge Ebiri.

No, you heard that right: Wes Craven is indeed one of the directors on the romantic omnibus film *Paris je t'aime*, which tackles love in the City of Light through brief vignettes, each set in one of the city's twenty neighborhoods (or *arrondissements*). True, his film is set in the infamous Pere Lachaise cemetery—home to the final resting places of, among many others, Jim Morrison, Edith Piaf, Yves Montand, Marcel Proust, Maria Callas, and, the focus of this short, Oscar Wilde. Leave it to the auteur of *A Nightmare on Elm Street* and *Scream* to milk romance out of such a funereal setting: Here, a couple (played by Emily Mortimer and Rufus Sewell) begins to bicker when a visit to Wilde's grave inspires the woman to chastise her fiancée for not having any sense of wit. Needless to say, it's all happily resolved—all in all, a bit of a departure for this director. And it may be a welcome one, as far as he's concerned. *Nerve* spoke to Craven recently about his fondness for other genres and his lifelong desire to make a romance. We also made sure to speak to him about the particular cultural relevance of horror during periods of social upheaval; the man is, after all, a former humanities professor.

Bilge Ebiri: How did you, of all people, wind up making this movie?
Wes Craven: Well, the producers were kind enough to call me and ask. One of their directors had fallen through, and they needed a replacement. Once I heard who else was participating in the project, it was a real no-brainer for me. They did say it had to be in that particular *arrondissement*, and they told me there was a great cemetery there. So at first I thought they were gonna want something weird, where a guy jumps out from behind a gravestone or something. But that wasn't the case, which was a relief. They told me it didn't need to be scary, that it just needed to be about love in Paris. That felt like a great opportunity—not having to scare people.

Craven: You know the thing about the MPAA is that it is set up in a way . . . that they have a pool of people that are volunteered to do this and on any given screening on any given film it's a different group of people. So let's say that group of people looks at your film, and it says it should be changed this way and that way. And you go and change it, but when you come back you show it to a new group of people. So you don't even have continuity between the people who objected to your film and the people who look at it the next time; it is quite maddening.

Chase: You could actually show them the same piece of film.
Craven: I hadn't thought of that.

Chase: Wes Craven, thank you so much for talking with us.
Craven: My pleasure.

BE: You noted that it was a relief to not have to scare people this time around. Have you thought about branching out of the horror genre more? *Red Eye* was more of a thriller, and you also did *Music of the Heart* a few years ago.

WC: It's really a matter of what kinds of movies you can get people to pay you to do. I had a good opportunity on *Music of the Heart*—it was a sweetheart deal with the Weinsteins, where they gave me a three-picture deal and told me one of the pictures could be out of genre. I did a few episodes of *The Twilight Zone*, and a couple of them could be called romances. But really, it's about the opportunities you're presented with. I've tried to wedge romance into some of my films. *The Hills Have Eyes* had it, and I had the ongoing romance between Dwight Riley (David Arquette) and Gale Weathers (Courteney Cox) in the *Scream* series. That was a fun little romance to carry out over three pictures. So you can get away with romance if you put it in a genre pic, as long as you can make it scary. Of course, that's another reason why I leapt at the chance to do *Paris je t'aime*.

BE: Do you hope to continue going in other directions?

WC: I've been trying to go in other directions from the first time I started making films. Sean S. Cunningham and I worked in an office for years generating scripts that were not horror, that were in other genres. We wanted to do different things, but nobody was interested. Everybody was offering us money to make scary films. We held out for as long as we could—and then we gave up. I went and did *The Hills Have Eyes*, and Sean went and made *Friday the 13th*.

BE: You're also credited as a producer on the remakes of some of your work, such as the recent *Hills Have Eyes* films. How closely involved are you with those?

WC: They're being made under the aegis of myself and my producers. The whole point was that we thought it'd be nice to find people who would put their own mark on these films, who will come back with a great film, without us interfering or micromanaging them. These are really their own work. And while I'm certainly not phoning it in, I'm giving the filmmakers the freedom to do what they want.

BE: Do you think horror is a more pigeonholing genre than others? It seems like people who make horror films are always thought of as horror directors.

WC: Absolutely. When you start out making horror films, you're trapped. I guess if you're really successful at comedy, something similar happens: Woody Allen tried to branch out into serious films, and people said, "Why don't you make us laugh again?"

When you make a horror film, people think you're crazy, cruel, nuts. They don't think you have the ability to make a comedy. So you try to educate the audience to accept you in other genres. But you're kind of stuck, as a director. Horror reflects things about ourselves that are ugly, and people need to deny that, to assume that it's just coming from whoever made the film and not reflecting human nature. They have to think, "This is coming from that person," so that they don't confront certain things about themselves. They don't look around them. But seeing the world around you in a clear way is the beginning of wisdom.

BE: It seems like we had a real boom in horror during the Vietnam years, and now we seem to be undergoing another one, in the Iraq years. Do you think horror's popularity coincides with this sort of social anxiety, or is that just something sociologists and film professors like to think up?

WC: None of us can tell for sure, but it seems likely that horror has a kind of relation to what's happening in society. There is definitely a sense in the air today that things are not right. The stuff you see in horror films is not *sui generis*. It doesn't just come from the minds of twisted filmmakers. I mean, we had a group of people strike a severe blow right at the heart of America on September 11. And then we have a government that has broken its own laws and has really put us in a bad place. Our government has actually admitted to torture, tapping wires, getting rid of habeas corpus. This is scary stuff.

People talk a lot about the torture that we see in films today. But that's specifically why these films have connected: This is a unique time in American history, where the government has admitted to torturing people. I mean, it's like Chile in the '70s or Argentina under the time of the generals. We've got people who've been imprisoned for five years without being charged or tried. It's in the air. The culture cannot help but reflect that atmosphere.

Just the other day, I was reading the blog of a soldier who is in Iraq. He said at the end of one of his posts, "I used to wonder how good people can do evil things. Now I wonder how good people can *avoid* doing evil things." I think that maybe films can help us in some way take an honest look at ourselves.

A Chat with Wes Craven

Jason Zingale / 2007

From *Bullz-Eye.com*, November 28, 2007. Reprinted by permission of Jason Zingale.

Arguably one of the most influential horror directors of his time, Wes Craven is perhaps best known for crafting some of the most original slasher films in the history of the genre. It goes without saying, then, that the man is directly responsible for a good majority of my nightmares as a kid, and while the 2005 thriller *Red Eye* was a minor departure for the director, it doesn't even come close to his latest project: *Paris je t'aime*, a collection of films by eighteen of the industry's best directors all examining the City of Light and its magical allure. While out promoting the film's DVD release, the master of horror sat down to chat with *Bullz-Eye* about his love for romantic comedies, the future of the horror genre, and why he would never direct a remake of his own film.

Wes Craven: Hello?

Bullz-Eye: Hello, Wes?
WC: Yes.

BE: Hi, how are you doing?
WC: I'm doing well, thank you. How are you?

BE: Very well. Thanks for taking the time out to talk to me. I know I'm on a bit of a short leash, so I'll go ahead and get started. I was wondering how a man best known for his horror films gets involved in a French movie about love.
WC: Well . . . I guess I've been doing horror films for a long, long time—with the exception of *Music of the Heart*—so it was an opportunity to use my craft or chops or whatever you want to call it in a different set of genre. And, you know, it's a part of me that I usually don't get to address very directly in a film, obviously, but

it's a part of me. I'm romantic, I have a sense of humor, and it's always been a bit of a frustration. So in this case, it was pleasant to be able to go out and do that.

BE: You wrote the segment as well. Did you find it difficult being confined to only five minutes for, really, one of the more complicated relationships in the film?
WC: (laughs) Well thank you. They actually gave me five minutes and thirty seconds, I believe, and it would have been hard to get it down below that. It was pretty tough, but I knew writing it that it had to be roughly five pages. So it wasn't terribly difficult.

BE: I noticed (director) Alexander Payne showed up as the ghost of Oscar Wilde. Was that a casting decision on your part, or was it a matter of Payne's own involvement with directing a segment for the movie?
WC: He actually put a pitch in for it, and I just heard through all these people that Alexander Payne wanted to play Oscar Wilde. I had a meeting with him—I'd never met him (I didn't even know what he looked like, frankly), but I'd seen his work—and he said, "You can dub me." (laughs) That was kind of a dealmaker because I knew that his voice was nothing like Oscar Wilde, who was really Irish. And it worked out beautifully.

BE: Was there a specific reason you chose Wilde as the ghost of the story?
WC: It was strange. It kind of snuck up on me. I originally wrote something for Jim Morrison, and it was a very different kind of story—they were all stories about getting married and one or the other having second thoughts—but we couldn't get anywhere near getting the rights to use even his name, let alone the gravesite. And that took about a month, or a month and a half, early on of legal efforts on the part of the people who were mounting all this, and then rather later, when I was finishing *Red Eye* and doing a press tour, I wrote one for Edith Piaf. And much more quickly we realized we weren't going to get the rights to use her name either in time. And so literally in two hours, about two days before we were going to shoot, I wrote the one that we shot, and I think it turned out to be the nicest and the freshest one of the three.

BE: I'm assuming you've seen the completed film the whole way through . . .
WC: Yes, I have . . .

BE: . . . and I was wondering, when you saw Vincenzo Natali's segment with Elijah Wood and the vampires, if you said to yourself, "Why didn't I think of that?"
WC: No, I thought it was very nice and original and quite beautiful. I was struck by just how gorgeous it was and how moving in a very minimalist kind of

way—because there's very little dialogue and it's very cinematic—so I was quite pleased. It was a very magical piece.

BE: I agree. It caught me completely off guard.
WC: Yeah.

BE: You mentioned *Music of the Heart* earlier, and really, with the exception of that and *Red Eye*, you've rarely strayed from the horror genre. Is that something you'd like to do more in the future, and do you currently have any plans to?
WC: Lemme see. I think my next film, if it gets off the ground, will be a little bit more *Red Eye* and little bit less of . . . it's certainly not a slasher film, but it does involve murders and so forth. So it will be something of a hybrid, I think. If I had my choice, I would go out and do all different sorts of films, but I'm also a realist. I like to work, so the fact that I've been able to work extensively in the genre—and it's a genre I enjoy—it ended up with me doing mostly those kinds of films. But I saw with *Music of the Heart*, frankly, how difficult it was to sell a film once it was directed by somebody who was so well known for horror. We kept my name in the background and sold it on Meryl Streep's name, so I can understand that it might be a long curve that I would have to make to establish myself. But I also feel like I could get there.

BE: I think we'd all like to see you branch out, but I also understand the hindrances of trying to do so. With movies like *Saw* and *Hostel* pushing the envelope further every year, do you ever worry about the direction the horror genre's going in?
WC: No, because wherever it goes, it has its side trips and it has its excesses . . . but, you know, I had a hard time getting myself to go see *Saw*. I don't like watching somebody suffer like that, but the funny thing was that when I saw it, I thought it was very entertaining and well done. And I haven't had time to see the sequels (mostly because I've just been working a lot), but I think to a certain extent that they just sort of become inhuman and maybe they're missing something that they could be doing. But it's pretty difficult to judge that sort of thing because it's coming from a very uncharted territory of the creative mind in general. I mean, with *Last House on the Left*, people thought that I was just sort of gutter slime for making that film for years and years, and so sometimes these films have a very long half-life before they're seen as legitimate at all. I try not to judge.

BE: You've been credited for more or less reviving the genre in the mid-'80s with *A Nightmare on Elm Street*, and then twelve years later, you did it again with *Scream*. Next year marks that film's twelve-year anniversary. Do you have any projects lined up that you expect will have a similar effect?

WC: Maybe. (laughs) Who knows, you know? I think it's very dangerous to say, "This one's going to do this," because then you just begin to fall all over yourself trying to be special or profound, so I try to just do them as well as I can but not think too much about their importance. I remember when I did *Shocker*, I was like, "Okay, I'm going to invent the next Freddy Krueger," and that didn't happen at all. (laughs) I think the important thing is to just keep making films.

BE: There are rumors floating around that an updated *Shocker* is in the works. Is that true, or is that just paper talk?
WC: They're not rumors, but it's just very early on. We have interest from Universal to remake *Shocker* and *The People Under the Stairs*, but it's nothing we're going to be doing this coming year. But it is something that could conceivably happen soon.

BE: If you were to direct that movie, would you be the first director to remake his own film?
WC: Nope. I'm going to try to not be that director. (laughs) That's where I draw the line. You know, if some other guy wants to go out there and do a new version, like Alexander Aja did . . . but I don't want to go out and try to redo my film.

Publicist: Jason, you have one minute left.

BE: Okay, I'll make this my last question. With so many comic books and graphic novels being retooled for the big screen, have you had any desire to get involved in a remake of *Swamp Thing*?
WC: No. (laughs)

BE: You're done with that?
WC: You know, I don't think it's what I'm best at, frankly, and I didn't grow up on comic books like a lot of those guys have, so I don't have the knowledge and everything else. I think I'm just better off doing things from my own mind.

BE: Thanks again for your time, and good luck with your next film.
WC: Okay, say nice things about *Paris je t'aime*.

BE: Will do, goodbye.
WC: Thanks, bye.

Wes Craven Talks to Capone

Steven Prokopy (writing as "Capone") / 2009

Originally published March 1, 2009 at www.aintitcoolnews.com. Reprinted by permission of by Steven Prokopy.

Hey, everyone. Capone in Chicago here. How much do we have to say about Wes Craven? Do we need to say anything? The man has creeped and freaked us out for more than thirty-five years, beginning in 1972 with *The Last House on the Left* and continuing as the writer and/or director on such iconic works as *The Hills Have Eyes*, *A Nightmare on Elm Street*, *Swamp Thing*, *The Serpent and the Rainbow*, *The People Under the Stairs*, *New Nightmare*, *Scream 1–3*, and 2005's *Red Eye*, which marked a suspenseful return to form for Craven, who realized that the most terrifying monsters are the ones that are 100 percent human. His upcoming film, *25/8* [*My Soul to Take*], has recently wrapped shooting and has a scheduled release of sometime next year. Craven returns to the themes of the offspring carrying on the sins of the father and of dead teenagers being the source of spectacular amounts of entertainment. At Comic-Con, Craven premiered a two-minute clip from *25/8* that showed off his masterful use of suspense as one young man is stalked and chased down by a strange figure on a bridge. Now, I've heard Craven explain the plot of *25/8* three times (once during the panel, once during a roundtable interview just before I spoke with him, and once to me), and I'm still not totally sure what the plot of this movie is. I'm sure it will all make sense when I see it, but all I care about is that *25/8* marks Craven's first original screenplay since his last turn behind the camera on an *Elm Street* film, *New Nightmare*, nearly fifteen years ago. During the aforementioned roundtable, about fifteen journalists bombarded him with the same tired questions about what it would take to get him to return to the *Elm Street* franchise or what he thought of all of his older films getting remade. (During the *Friday the 13th* relaunch panel just before Craven's, the production team stated in no uncertain terms that they were doing a *Nightmare on Elm Street* remake at some point in the near future.) Craven is a master storyteller, and so hearing variations of the same inquiries was a huge disappointment. I was determined to ask him during our one-on-one interview a bit more about the new film and dig a bit deeper into his state of mind about moviemaking in general. I hope you dig it. I've never met the man before, so this was a real treat for me. And he was a genuine pleasure to talk to. Oh, and consider this interview one big spoiler for the plot of 25/8. I'm not sure how much he's actually revealing here, but I'm not taking any chances. Consider yourself warned. Enjoy . . .

Capone: You said during the panel that 25/8 is your best work to date, or among your best. How so?

Wes Craven: Among my best, yes. It feels fresh and original, and we've got a great cast. It looks fabulous; we got a great DP, Petra Korner, who has *The Wackness* coming out soon.

Capone: Actually, it's out already. It's funny you say that because when I spoke to the director of *The Wackness*, I made sure to mention to him how gorgeous the look of the film was, almost contrary to the harsh story being told. I couldn't believe how beautiful the film looked, almost other worldly.

WC: Yeah, we saw her reel, and just fell in love with it. So she was our shooter.

Capone: Are there reasons story-wise why you think this is one of your best films? You haven't written a script in fourteen years. Can you still read something you've just completed and say, "Wow, I've still got it"?

WC: [laughs] I thought I had written something like that, and then people read it and got really, really excited. You know, I didn't know if I could write dialogue for kids, but everybody said to me that they loved the writing. "How did you do it? How do you know how kids talk?" And I said, "I just have them talk like me." I don't try to make them speak in any kid dialect, which I always think is so phony.

Capone: And doing that dates the film almost immediately.

WC: Yeah, in one year, it's dated.

Capone: I know you explained the story during the panel. We're talking about different timeframes here and various chronologies. What's going on in this film?

WC: The first act is the night of this man's discovery and a confrontation with the police. He murders his wife, and she's virtually about to give birth to their son. And the son is rescued by the medics who come onto the scene. The second act starts on the sixteenth birthday of seven kids born that night. And this kid is kind of . . . well, his sister calls him a retard; he seems to be slow, totally innocent, doesn't know anything about the events. His [adopted] mother has kept him from it entirely. As the seven kids start to be targeted and attacked and everyone dies, he gets their attributes. So he kind of matures and turns into a man in the course of absorbing both the male and female elements of his closest friends. He starts off a bit like Candide and ends up like Voltaire. [laughs] Everybody will know what I'm talking about now!

Capone: Wow, it's a good thing you didn't bring that up during the panel.
WC: So that's the concept, and I find it very interesting. And the actor, Max Thieriot, was just fabulous. He literally had to take on all the different qualities and change his character continuously depending on who had just died.

Capone: You said male and female victims?
WC: Yeah. I mean, he doesn't start to mince around. The two female characters have individual personality traits, and he gets them as they die.

Capone: So, it's not a mystery who his identity is? Or is the mystery whether the boy's father is still alive?
WC: The mystery is whether the father is alive or died that night because he was shot and killed, but he was revived. But shortly after this, on the way to the hospital, some events happen. The ambulance crashes right next to the river that runs through town, and the guy's body was never found. So they don't know whether he's alive or dead. Everybody assumes he's dead because he was practically comatose. But he could be alive or he could be the evil persona in this man who has multiple personalities or he could have gone into one of the seven children or he could be the central character.

Capone: So this sounds much more based in the psychological world than anything you've done before. You could make a case that *A Nightmare on Elm Street* tackles that a bit, but dealing with someone with six or seven personalities—that's pretty loaded.
WC: No, I think you're right. I think it is. One of the MTs [medical technicians] in the story is first-generation American from a Haitian family, and she tells the story of her grandmother saying, "You Americans talk about people with multiple personalities, but it's really people with multiple souls." And the cop says, "What's the difference really?" And she says, "Because when a man dies, the personality dies with him, but the soul goes on." So it does have that spiritual level to it in dealing with things that happened before people were born that they come into this life without knowing it. The only people who really know what was in the previous life are people seeking revenge, which is the killer, so they carry it over.

It's their curse; they're captured by their hatred. We don't know where we came from, but there are things we bring with us. That's the concept, and that's really more a psychological thing than a spiritual one.

Capone: Is it easier for us to believe that a father who has these issues could somehow, even to a son he's never met, pass these qualities on?

WC: It's nature/nurture. No one has figured that one out, and it's been studied a lot. Some things seem to be passed on. Identical twins separated at birth, they have very similar qualities in certain areas. They do things that seem to be passed on from the parents just because we got half of their DNA.

Capone: You also mentioned during the panel that you produced a remake of *The Last House on the Left* and that you've discovered some unknown director to make it. Tell me about that.

WC: Dennis Iliadis is his name. What we do with these remakes is we go exclusively to European directors because, well I hate to say it, but it's because we can't afford a DGA [Directors Guild of America] director and pay the DGA rates. I'm a member of DGA and very grateful for what being a member guarantees me, but at our budgets we can't afford it. Dennis had done one film [*Hardcore*]—and it was kind of an art film—but it showed a talent for the dark side. It was about street prostitutes in Athens in their mid-teens. And it was really beautifully done, so Mary, who's the lead, is played by Sara Paxton, her father is Tony Goldwyn, and the mother is Monica Potter. And her best friend is Martha MacIsaac. Krug is played by Garret Dillahunt, and his son is Spencer Treat Clark, a kid who's about fifteen. His brother, who is the Weasel character, is Aaron Paul, and Sadie is played by Riki Lindhome.

Capone: With *25/8*, you've gone with a young, largely unknown—with a couple of exceptions—cast that most people won't be familiar with. Do you find it's easier to work with lesser-known actors than you did maybe with *Red Eye* where you've got some known actors?

WC: It's a fairly big cast, so the fact was that Bug, Max's character, is by far the lead. But I didn't want to have somebody that people would know really well. And we couldn't afford to hire a lot of kids that had a high price tag. Plus, I've found that if you can find a talent and recognize it, like a Johnny Depp or someone like that, the audience has no associations with that actor, there's no baggage that comes along with that person. So it's like, "Holy shit, this isn't an actor; this is this character." So in some ways it has much more of an authenticity to it. Denzel Whitaker's [from *The Great Debaters*] sister is Shareeka Epps, she was in *Half Nelson*, and she's great. There's a detective character who's in both time periods played by Frank Grillo, his mother is played by Jessica Hecht [*Dan in Real Life*], who's been in a lot of films. The Haitian-American MT is played by Danai Jekesai Gurira; she was in a film recently called *The Visitor* about a guy who has an apartment in New York City . . .

Capone: Oh sure.

WC: She's the woman in the apartment. Who else? Zena Grey has been in a lot of Disney films when she was twelve and thirteen. Dr. Blake is Harris Yulin, who you probably know.

Capone: Yep.

WC: And then there are all these kids. Denzel you know. John Magaro you probably don't know. Nick Lashaway hasn't done many films, and he's just incredible. Paulina Olszynski is practically right off the boat with her Eastern European mother. She's incredibly smart and funny, great comic timing. And this girl Emily Meade, who plays his sister, although it's not revealed that she's his sister until halfway through the second act, she's just incredibly beautiful. Oh my God. Every time people see her on film, they just gasp. Really. So we ended up with a really good cast.

Capone: You mentioned that part of making this film was putting yourself in an experimental situation of working with a crew that you've never worked with before. Why was that important?

WC: Totally new to me. For one thing, there was the practicality of it. I would have had to have waited because *Last House* got going sooner than we did. They had most of the people that we usually work with, or other people that we usually work with were working on other films. So I always think of Eric Clapton leaving the Yardbirds. Maybe there's something beyond that. I don't know. Almost everybody I'd been working with was someone I'd been working with for a long, long time. A lot of them—like my editor Patrick Lussier was seriously going into directing, so he wasn't available. We were going to have to shoot it in Connecticut, and in order to do that everybody had to basically come out of the New York–Connecticut area. So I was like, "I think this is going to be creatively really healthy to just go meet new people." My wife, this is the first time she's produced a picture, but she worked at Disney for years with people like M. Night and a lot of great directors. So I knew she could do it. We also had this guy [producer] Anthony Katagas, who has made five films in Connecticut, so it was like I knew we would be on solid ground. We might have been uncomfortable the first week or so, but within a week we were all great.

Capone: I heard the big roundtable group inside asking you about whether you'd want to be involved in this remake or that remake, or whether you'd be interested in getting back into some of your franchises again. But it makes me wonder, are there certain films of yours that you look at and say, "Maybe not that one. Maybe you should leave that one alone"? Like the panel right before you, the producer and director said they were signed on to do the *Nightmare on Elm Street* remake with Michael Bay.

WC: Well yeah, *Nightmare on Elm Street* very early on kind of went off, and the tenth anniversary one [*New Nightmare*] was kind of [executive producer] Bob Shaye saying, "I'm sorry. We'd like one more, and we don't know how to do it and make it original. We know we've kind of ignored you, so why don't you come and do it." And that was great. Then they don't call you again for anything for years and years, so you just kind of have to write that one off and say you made a good film, you made a studio get on its feet and prosper. But since you don't have creative control over it really, there isn't much reason to be going back or trying to go back to that well. As opposed to something like doing a remake of *Hills* or *Last House*, which my two partners did. Those contracts were that we owned those films after thirty years, and the joke is that we're still alive and now we own them. For the first time, if you make a film and make some money, you actually make some money. That's kind of nice when you reach my age. [laughs] It pays to live long. There's been some initial contacts about *Scream 4*, but again, the *Cursed* experience was so screwed up. I mean, that went on for two-and-a-half years of my life for a film that wasn't anything close to what it should have been. And another film that I was about to shoot having the plug pulled, *Pulse*, so it was like . . . I did learn from the *Cursed* experience not to do something for money. They said, "We know you want to do another film; we'll pay you double." We were ten days from shooting, and I said fine. But I ended up working two-and-a-half years for double my fine. I could have done two-and-a-half movies and done movies that were out there making money. In general, I think it's not worth it, and part of the reason my phone hasn't rung is that that story is pretty well-known. If they can do something with Michael Bay, they'll knock something off and make a lot of money and won't have to put up with me. [laughs]

Capone: And you can go do things like your *Paris, je t'aime* short, which I loved, and it's so funny and tragic. And the fact that you got Alexander Payne to play Oscar Wilde . . .

WC: He came after me. I'd never met him. I didn't even know what he looked like, but he was great. He said, "I'd love to do it, and you can dub me. I know I can't sound Irish." So we did. [laughs]

Capone: Well, thank you so much for talking to us.

WC: Yeah, this was good. [To the publicist] Capone can come back.

Interview: Wes Craven

Scott Tobias / 2009

This interview originally ran in *The A.V. Club* (www.avclub.com), March 11, 2009. Reprinted by permission.

Raised in a strict Baptist family in Cleveland, Ohio, and ensconced in academia as a young adult, Wes Craven doesn't seem to fit the profile of a master of horror. But when he and producer Sean S. Cunningham (who went on to direct *Friday the 13th*) got the opportunity to make a drive-in movie on the cheap, Craven responded with 1972's *The Last House on the Left*, a crude but hugely resonant horror landmark that brought a new level of unvarnished realism to the genre. The film follows two teenage girls who are abducted and terrorized by an escaped convict and his three associates, and one desperate set of parents who take revenge when the perpetrators wind up on their property. From there, Craven become one of a generation of filmmakers—George Romero and John Carpenter among them—who used the genre both to scare audiences and to smuggle in political ideas. Among the highlights of a career well into its third decade: *The Hills Have Eyes* and *The Hills Have Eyes II*, *Swamp Thing*, *A Nightmare on Elm Street*, *The People Under the Stairs*, *Scream* and its sequels, *Music of The Heart*, and *Red Eye*.

After giving his approval to retoolings of the *Hills Have Eyes* movies—he even co-wrote the second film with his son Jonathan—Craven returns to the producer's role in the new *Last House on the Left* remake. Directed by Dennis Iliadis, a relative unknown from Greece, the film follows the basic outlines of Craven's original but deviates substantially in style and substance. In a recent conversation with *The A.V. Club*, Craven talked about those differences and shared thoughts on his first feature and his subsequent career in horror.

The A.V. Club: Lately, there have been many remakes of classic—and nonclassic—horror films from the '70s and '80s, but few involving the original filmmakers. With the *Hills Have Eyes* movies and *Last House on the Left*, you're the exception. Why is that?

Wes Craven: Good luck, I guess. The original contracts for both *The Hills Have Eyes* and *Last House* gave us possession of the film rights after a certain amount of years. Thirty years, I believe, was the time period. And there was just a moment where we looked at the contracts and realized that the rights to these films, which we long-assumed belonged to other people, actually belonged to us. The discussion of whether we should do a remake of *Last House* came up, and it just seemed like there was a market for it, there was an interest in it. And with *The Hills Have Eyes*, we had already done it once or twice and had had good luck and found it an interesting experience. So we started looking for a director and writers. You know, it took several years, but finally we found a director that we were very excited about. And that's how *Last House* started its way to being remade and reimagined, which I found to be the way to go about these things, finding someone who is passionate about the original but wants to make his own picture. Give some guidance at the beginning but then kind of turn them loose.

AVC: What guidance do you give them at the beginning?

WC: The original *Last House* is based on an Ingmar Bergman film [*The Virgin Spring*]. I had seen it years before I wrote the script for *Last House*, and I don't think I even went back to it. But I remembered the core of the story, and then I knew Bergman had based it on a medieval folk tale from his region of the world. I said [to the new filmmakers], "Think about it more as a fantastic story that has a very, very strong spine. We'd like to have it recognizable to the audience, but we'd like you to make it your own." And we developed several scripts and found the one we liked best and sort of guided it. Then with [director] Dennis [Iliadis's] notes, we made it into a script that we felt comfortable with. And that seemed wise. Once we had that script and figured out what to keep from the original and what to take out from the original or alter, Dennis was given a modest budget and all the support we could give him and told to be brilliant. [laughs.]

AVC: So in your capacity as producer, how much influence did you ultimately wield over how your film got reinterpreted? And at what point did you have to just stand back and let other people do their work?

WC: I think in the original processes of laying out the deal, it was solid that we had final cut, and a budget that was realistic enough for us to feel like someone could go out and make this film in today's day and age. The guidance and going over the story and script notes and meetings with writers—all that was very, very intense. And the search for the filmmaker . . . With the help of a young man named Cody Zwieg in our office who just pored over all the emerging films and emerging filmmakers, we found [Dennis Iliadis's] *Hardcore*. We watched that and thought, "This is really a wonderful filmmaker." The material was very dark, very edgy, and yet at the core of it were magnificent performances and totally believable characters. And about that time, you start to back away and say, "What do you see here?" You want to give the person as much freedom as you can within the boundaries of being a responsible producer with a contract to a studio. It's about giving as much freedom as you can, and the more the filmmaker proves he or she is on the track that you feel good about, then you just kind of watch dailies.

By that point, I was writing and in preproduction on 25/8, the film that I wrote and directed last year, and we're in post right now. I had my hands full, too, but I still watched dailies every day and would email him if I had notes. And not very frequently, frankly; more it was moments of encouragement or that we were behind him or that I thought he was doing terrific work. Things like that. Or if he wanted a piece of music that he was having a hard time having people get behind, I would step in and say, "Let the guy have this piece of music." It had to be within an overall budget that the three producers agreed upon. Especially, I think, myself and Sean Cunningham, but Marianne Maddalena as well.

AVC: The original *Last House on the Left* has a very crude, home-movie quality that the new one decidedly does not. Is something lost as a result of that?
WC: Crudity, I suppose. You know, the first film, not only did it have a modest budget, but even at the time, it was pretty miniscule. I think it was about $90,000 total. But I had never done a feature film before; I had never directed before; I had never cut before; I had never written a script before. So for me, who had just kind of left academia the year before and was just learning the rhythms of how to cut film, it was a matter of discovering how to make a movie. And we had very limited resources as to actors. We used almost all people who had not acted before at all, so there were limitations imposed on us just by the reality of the thing. Given that, I think we did a very powerful film, and obviously it's lasted and been influential for a long time. But with Dennis, we had a man who had done a great movie already; he had other works behind him and had done commercials, too. So he had a great skill set and familiarity with cinematic techniques that I was just beginning to discover.

AVC: The original has a very famous tagline ["To avoid fainting, keep repeating 'It's only a movie . . . it's only a movie.'"] that spoke to its raw style. But that tagline doesn't really apply to the remake, which seems more like a movie.
WC: I think that's fair, but they were made under very different circumstances. When you look at the making of the original, it was basically me working for [producer] Sean Cunningham. It was a matter of Sean having an offer from some backers in Boston who owned outdoor theaters to make them a scary movie so they could use it as a second bill and not have to pay for two movies to distributors

and suppliers. And so Sean came to me and said, "I have some guys who are willing to give us a budget to make a scary movie. Do you want to write a scary movie? If they like it, you can direct it, and you could even cut it." And Sean owned a Steenbeck flatbed editing machine that was, back then, very, very new. It was like, "Okay, I don't know anything about scary movies, and I was raised in a family and a church where filmmaking was forbidden," so I had no background in film to speak of whatsoever. My whole background was in voracious book-reading.

But when I was a kid, I was taken to something called Telenews in Cleveland by my best friend's father. My own father was gone by the time I was five, I think, but this man would take us to Telenews at the end of World War II. We'd watch all these newsreels, so I had seen film—but I'd seen real stuff. That kind of stuck in my mind. And in college, we were allowed to see documentaries and things of that sort. And then when I was teaching, it was a very intense period of about four to five years when I taught in a town where there was an art theater, and I happened to be plopped down right in the middle of this magnificent burgeoning of European filmmakers. We were seeing Buñuel and Fellini and Truffaut and all of these guys who were making these imaginative, wonderful films, and that's where I fell in love with it. And it was just a matter of a certain point, my department chairman saying, "Stop goofing around with cameras in student-film class. I want you to either get your PhD or you're fired." And I quit on the spot. Finished out my term, but that's when I started going to New York to get into films. I was kind of clueless about that kind of horror film. I just fell in love with film itself. I think all that shows in the original *Last House*.

AVC: So you fell into horror almost accidentally?

WC: It was totally coincidence. My mother wouldn't even let me read DC comics. [laughs] I came from a very strict background. It was just that Sean had some guys with some money who wanted to make a movie that was interesting, and it had to be scary. I literally remember a conversation along the lines of "Sean, I don't know anything about making a scary movie." Sean said, "Well, you were raised as a fundamentalist, just pull all the skeletons out of your closet." And we had this kind of wicked sense of humor between us. I always remember the clarity and purity of the bolstering story—how simple it was and how wonderfully ironic it was, the turning of the tables—and also of the flipping of these very strict Christian parents into very barbaric behavior, especially on the part of the father to the point where it got out of control and he realized he had become what he was fighting. That fascinated me then, and it fascinates me now.

AVC: Were you braced for the reaction the film got from critics? Did you have a sense of what you were putting out there in terms of intensity?

WC: No. And I think that, especially at that time, it was something where we were trying to be a bit outrageous. At the same time, there was the part of me that had graduated from Johns Hopkins writing seminars under Elliott Coleman, the great nineteenth- and twentieth-century novelist. So I had a side of me that wanted to do something worthy of some thought. I wanted to tap into the humanity of the characters and the complexity of what seems to be a simple plot, but the way the bad guys suddenly are appalled by their behavior. And in the end, the parents are appalled by theirs—that sort of stuff was kind of thrust in there despite people's protestations, in a way.

But I don't think either one of us thought it was going to have much impact. We didn't think that it would have such a wide audience. We made it literally for a group of theater owners in Boston that owned, I think, thirty, forty, fifty outdoor theaters. And it was specifically for those theaters and no place else. We never thought we'd go beyond that. Going in, I thought I'd never have to worry about anyone in my past going to see it, which proved to not be the case whatsoever. But at that time, that thought gave me a freedom to be outrageous and to go into areas that normally I wouldn't have gone into and not worry about my family hearing about it, or being crushed. I was always very concerned about the disappointment from the world I'd come from, as someone who had left it in such an egregiously dark manner. That was something that haunted me for a lot of my career, until a lot of those people died off.

AVC: Did you get a lot of blowback in that regard? People you didn't want to see the film seeing the film?

WC: Yes. My marriage had failed at this time. I was living on the Lower East Side in a group apartment, and it was a very rich amalgamation of people. Academics and hipsters and dope dealers and musicians, they all went to see my movie when it came out, and almost all of them were appalled. I literally had people who would no longer leave their children alone with me. Or people that would, when they found out I had directed the film, say, "That was the most despicable thing I had ever seen," and walk out of the room. So there was a very strong, very real revulsion, to the point where I almost didn't want to talk about what I did for a living or what I made. And that lasted a long time.

Last House offended a lot of people. The results in the theaters, even in Boston, reminded me a bit of things from when I was studying Theatre of the Absurd and the rise and the appearance of Ionesco plays and things like that. Thinking, "My God, people actually are getting into fistfights. People are having heart attacks. People are actually trying to get into the projection booth to destroy the print." You know, we set up a separate editing room just to repair prints that had been slashed and diced by people trying to get offensive moments out of them. So there was a very real sense of "Oh my God, what have I done?" And I think both Sean and I . . . Sean also came from a background of humanity. Sean had been a stage manager, and we tried very hard to move away from that. For a while, Sean had some money, and I wrote with and for him. I wrote, I think, half a dozen films that were completely out of genre— comedies, love stories, even one serious film about Vietnam—and we couldn't get backing for any of it. And we both sort of drifted from making, at that time, serious money on *Last House* to going through it all in the course of almost three years and only getting offers to do something scary again. I think that's how Sean ended up doing *Friday the 13th*, and I ended up listening to the urging of another friend, Peter Locke, and going out to California and writing and directing *The Hills Have Eyes*.

AVC: How would you describe the politics of the original film? It feels like the *Gimme Shelter* of horror movies, like the darker side of hippie-dom.
WC: I didn't see it as that, so much as . . . There was a generation of kids who were just kind of emulating distant heroes and wearing peace symbols, and parents who were thinking of themselves as liberal and removed from barbarity, but it also was the era of Vietnam. And not to put too fine a point on it, I very much was influenced—and I think the whole country was kind of in a state of shock—for the first time seeing the horror and cruelty of war. Recently shot 16mm footage was coming back and appearing on television immediately, so there was little censorship of what you saw. And it was just appalling. Then there was this kind of creeping awareness that the government was lying about almost everything and was losing the war and that there was no real definable purpose. Sounds a little familiar now, doesn't it? [laughs] So there's a sort of despair, and I think a sense that the whitebread people, the people who were kind of on the surface of things, good Christians, far removed from any sort of behavior like that, were slipping into it themselves. At the same time, the villainous people that did horrible things had their own personal concerns and uncertainties. And you're to look at that if you're going to have any understanding at all.

AVC: You've always been able to insert a certain amount of political subtext into your movies. Even the recent *Hills Have Eyes II*, which you co-wrote, had a strong Iraq War subtext in that regard. But this *Last House* remake seemed freed from that. Are there resonances I'm not seeing?
WC: No. I think partially, it's that Dennis isn't from the United States and doesn't have quite the same feelings about specific things like 9/11. I've done a few interviews where I realized that 9/11 was the ultimate home invasion, not to be glib about it. You know, where the place that you think is safe and the people that you think are safe and far from evil are suddenly just slaughtered by it, and you

have no control over it. The horror of that, for me certainly, was profound. It just knocked me to my bed for several days, and I think we all were stunned and in disbelief. That, to me, is extraordinarily resonant, but we didn't set out to make a movie about that. That's just in the American psyche now. With Dennis, the movie is much more about a broader feeling of loss, of seeing or sensing terrible things. But over the course of European history, even recent European history, there's a plentiful supply of things that you can possibly reference for when things go terribly, terribly wrong. It's not quite the same as in the United States. And we wanted that broader, more non-pointed view of something more eternal. Dennis very much felt this was an eternal story, of family and trying to defend those that are nearest to you and having to face what you have to do in order to counter these dark forces that have come into your life, your home, and your child's life.

AVC: Having the experience you have now as a filmmaker, is there anything you'd change? Did this remake rectify anything you weren't happy with?

WC: I try not to look back too much. I think the important thing about staying creative and staying sharp and original is not to look back too much and to kind of look to where your vision is going now. But I have felt over the years a definite progression or arc from feeling guilty about what I had done with the first one because certainly there was all that fundamentalist guilt that came pouring back in. Feeling like I'd done something horrible, "I'm a despicable person and I'm perverse," and all these things to a sense of the power and the necessity, in a sense, of horror films and dealing with dark material. And I did have the resource of having taught Greek mythology and the history of Western civilization, and you can go back into the plays of Aeschylus and follow what happens when people seek revenge. There are people plucking their eyes out. And Greek mythology is filled with all kinds of monsters and whatnot.

So I realized that I really, almost by accident, had fallen into a labyrinthine, very powerful paradigm for dealing with these things through genre films. And once I realized that and realized the power of it, and the fact that because horror films aren't, in general, studio products—studios back them sometimes, but they don't try to meddle too much because they kind of don't want to sully their skirts—you have a lot of freedom. And as long as you keep the audience on the edge of their seats, either scare them or keep them guessing, you can put anything in there that you want.

So something like *Nightmare on Elm Street*, to me, was kind of an examination of levels of consciousness and the pain of facing the truth, and how easy it is to fall asleep or want to fall asleep. And only a few of us struggle to stay awake. And you know, you can look at what's happened to America in the last eight years and say a lot of people were asleep. A lot of people were not staying awake and watching what was going on and facing the pain of that and dealing with it. So to me, that goes a long way to making the work important to myself. At the same time, I don't care if the rest of the audience doesn't think along those lines at all because the audience is a huge spectrum of people, from people who are introspective to people who just want to be scared and have fun, and all the points in between. So in that sense, I came to terms with living mostly in a world of horror pictures or genre pictures. I have had a few chances to get outside and do something different, like *Paris, je t'aime* or *Music of the Heart*, but mostly it's been my lot. And to have created with a few shocking films, an awareness or a perception of me as somebody dangerous and scary—that can be sold, but trying to sell me for some other kind of picture, like *Music of the Heart*, was very difficult.

AVC: And it continues to be? Or you just found that this is the genre where you can express yourself best? The great thing about horror films and genre films in general is an ability to respond to the times in a way that most other films can't, at least directly.

WC: They do. And I love the fact that a lot of my audience is people from the inner city. African Americans love my films. Whenever I go to have a meeting at Universal, the security guard just leaps to his feet and comes over, bumps my hand, and says, "Thank you! Thank you, I love your films!" And its people who are kind of at the cutting edge of life and survival, and being near the nitty-gritty, who like my films, and I like that.

At the same time, I think that there has been a slow recognition that there's a mind at work here, and there's a skill and some bit of artistry and that I could probably do other things. Otherwise, I don't know that I would've been given the opportunity to do *Paris, je t'aime*. On that one, I was told, "Okay, we want you to do something around this month that has a big cemetery, but you can write anything you want." So I wrote, you know, a romantic-comedy moment. I pulled it off well, and I think there is a slow perception that I can do all sorts of different material. But I think if anybody had a roll of dice with a lot of money at stake, they would not want Wes Craven and a romantic comedy. It would have to be a small film, and what I've done instead, in the interim, is to insert into my films comedy and romance and moments of tenderness. 25/8, if I do say so, is an extraordinary film in the sense that it just kind of expands what a genre film can be. And I was given final cut on it, so in that way I've reached a place that many directors and filmmakers get to. I'm grateful for that, and I can work within those boundaries. If something comes along that is totally outside of horror, fine, but I find there's an immense amount of freedom within the genre.

AVC: Is that an unusual circumstance for you, having that kind of freedom? Have you had to deal with a lot of constraints in the past?

WC: I think there's been a gradual movement toward a lot of freedom—onscreen, in my head, a great deal of freedom. And I believe with *Scream*, the first test screening determined whether I would have final cut, and if it rated above a certain level, they were perfectly happy to let me have it. I wound up having final cut on all three movies, so I think it was built on years and years of making movies and having a reputation of being somebody who will not be crazy, not descend to doing drugs and spending an enormous amount of money, and instead delivering a product to these people, because that's what it is to them. Something they can sell and recoup their money and make a profit. At the same time, I make something I can look at and say, "That's a good piece of work. There's some terrific directing and acting in it, and you should be proud of it."

Sins of the Fathers

Michael Marano / 2010

From *SciFi* magazine, December 2010 © 2010 by Michael Marano. Reprinted by permission.

I'm really quite bummed by the death of Wes Craven. As a kid of the 1970s and 1980s, the artistry with which he articulated the darkness that was thrashing around in the American subconscious gave me a lot of catharsis. I had the pleasure of interviewing him by phone back in 2010. He was erudite, literate, and intellectually deft. One of these days, I should transcribe the whole conversation. But for now, on the occasion of his death, I'll share the bits that were published.

I was sitting down the road from the marsh where Wes Craven filmed *Swamp Thing* back in '82 when Craven took time out from filming *Scream 4* to phone about his upcoming movie, *My Soul to Take.*

"I very jokingly can refer to it as *Stand by Me* with knives," says the man who picked apart the American id when he brought us *Last House on the Left*, *The Hills Have Eyes*, and *A Nightmare on Elm Street.* His voice is cultured and smooth as a really good whiskey, the kind of voice that'd be perfect for a late-night jazz DJ in a rainy city like Seattle or San Francisco. "It's about a group of young kids, sixteen-year-olds on their sixteenth birthday. And all were born on the same night in the local town hospital . . . on the night that a serial killer who had seven personalities died. Or at least, seems to have died . . ."

"The legend in the town is that this man [is still alive and] is going to come back to take his revenge on the town. But also, it is suspected that he did die and that his [murderous] soul went into one of these kids and that the rest of the kids have his other souls. All of this man's souls were rather benign except for the one that was a killer and that [soul] was operating without this man's knowledge. So, it's a matter of, 'Should we watch out for the friend we have? Or should we be watching out for the killer who is coming to take his revenge on the kids?'"

In this light, *My Soul to Take* almost sounds like a perfect storm of Wes Craven themes. If you look at a lot of Craven's movies, they seem to deal with atonement, even if the people doing the atoning aren't responsible for the initial trespass that's being atoned for. *The Hills Have Eyes*, *A Nightmare on Elm Street*, *Deadly Blessing*, the *Scream* series—all involve some dark wrong committed that fairly blameless people (who often weren't even born when the wrong was committed) have to pay for. And they pay for them real bad. I asked him about that.

"Certainly it's one of the most profound aspects of life itself, when you realize you don't just have to deal with your own stuff and what you have caused but what other people have caused in the past and sometimes in the quite recent past and, in the case of families, maybe even you parents. That's just always interested me."

"This film to me, frankly, feels quite personal. My father died when I was about four, so I do have some memories of him and some of them are kind of scary. Not that he ever beat me or anything. But I think he was a very gruff man with a bad temper. That kind of journey of trying to find out who your father really was and whether he loved you or didn't like you—what were the aspects of his life?—it's a very personal one. And also, you know, I was raised in the Fundamentalist faith, or let's say even more specifically with the bible. And 'The sins of the fathers are visited upon their sons.' That is a profound reality in our lives."

In the context of family dynamics, what Craven is talking about smacks a lot of the same chords as Greek tragedy—how the immediacy of something that happened in your family can rise up and wreck your life. Check out Aeschylus, Sophocles, and Euripedes if you want some familial knee-slappers. Craven has thrown-down with a lot of these themes, too. These family dynamics bubble under *Last House*, *Hills Have Eyes*, *Elm Street*, *Cursed*, *People Under the Stairs*, and all three *Scream* movies.

"Horror films, in my mind at least, are kind of human experience boiled down to the essence and sometimes to a very primal physical threat to the physicality of the body, or the mind or the soul, to the extent that we can understand what that is," Craven said when I brought this up. "These are very, very primal sorts of things. And the family is a great paradigm of that. It's not necessarily that everything in the world is about the family, but in a sense, it's a boiling down of the family of man . . . To take it down to the simplest paradigm, it quite often is the family, or the 'tribe.' Some horror films are about the group of friends who go out to do this or that or some member of the tribe gets killed or whatever. But it is about these very simple entities that have to do with the world we live in, outside of our own bodies, and how that affects us and what those people either have done in the past or what the immediate generation just before them has done. A lot of horror films start out with: 'On this night, one hundred years ago, these sailors died because someone took the lanterns off the rocks!' and then you end up with *The Fog*. I just think that for teenagers, especially, part of the coming into maturity is finding out who your parents really are and what they did and how that affects you. Even wrestling with the question of 'Am I ever going to be distinctly different from my parents?' or 'Am I going to be haunted by realizing, Oh my God, I've become my father?' is something that can happen to you in your thirties or forties."

In this context, the antagonist in *My Soul to Take* seems to combine a couple of elements that have been staples of horror and slasher films of the past few decades: the earthly killer and the supernatural bogeyman. In the early days of the slasher genre as we know it, the killers had no direct connection to the supernatural. They had a level of power and blankness that seemed otherworldly—just look at early Argento movies. Then Jason became an undead superbeing. Michael Meyers became a Druidic spirit being. Then we got Freddy, Chucky from *Child's Play*, the Trickster from *Brainscan*, Horace Pinker from Craven's own *Shocker*. Where does the killer in *My Soul to Take* fall along this spectrum?

"I would spoil the story if I told you," Craven said. "But the possibilities are that this is a man who has died and come back in one of the souls of the children, or this is a man who did not die and who is coming back to take his revenge. Or this is a man who has died and who has come back in his own form, that has kind of been haunting the woods. All three of those are the given options over the course of trying to penetrate the mystery of what really is happening."

Craven has directed in wildly different contexts. He's done episodic TV for the 1980s incarnation of *Twilight Zone*. He's done studio movies like *Music from the Heart* and *Red Eye*. One of the reasons he wrote and made *The Hills Have Eyes* was that it could be filmed on the cheap in the desert, where no permits would be needed. The climactic chainsaw fight in *Last House* was shot in a house that associate producer Steve Miner was renting.

"Even the budgets for *Music of the Heart* and *Red Eye* were modest budgets. I think over the course of making a lot of small films and learning how to make them seem bigger-budgeted than they actually were, we've been able to mount films that have managed to get a lot of bang for the buck. *My Soul to Take* I would say is kind of in the middle. It wasn't a miniscule budget. It wasn't a big budget. But we were dealing with mostly unknown kids—there weren't any gigantic fees on that. We shot in Connecticut, so we got a big tax break. The same guy was writing, producing, and directing, and his wife was also producing [Craven's wife Iya Labunka]. So we kept our costs down. I think the unusual thing about this film is that it falls into the films I've made that were written and directed by me where I've had final cut, which were most of my classic films, possibly with the exception of *Scream*, written by Kevin Williamson, and which also had terrific writing and Carl Ellsworth's work on *Red Eye*—both were scripts that were in terrific shape and had great ideas, and I was able to just step in as director."

"But *My Soul to Take* is very much a personal film. I was given the auteur's version of making a film, so I was allowed to do what I wanted, with great support.

And although we didn't have an unlimited number of days to shoot, we were able to put a film up that was designed to be modestly budgeted but has a terrific look. I don't think anyone is going to look at it and think that this is guerilla filmmaking. But on the other hand, anybody who knows about film would see that we designed it in a way that would be fairly economical to shoot."

Scream 4 Director Wes Craven on Keeping the Franchise Alive

Perri Nemiroff / 2011

From *CinemaBlend.com*, April 7, 2011. Reprinted by permission of *CinemaBlend*.

When I was ten years old I sat next to my mother and watched Casey Becker, sans insides, hang from a tree. Yes, the image made it tough to sleep at night for quite a bit, but *Scream* also left a long-lasting impression in the best way possible. Just a year later, my grandparents were kind enough to take me for not one, but two viewings of *Scream 2*, and finally, by 2000, I found ways to sneak into R-rated movies so I could enjoy the third film minus a guardian. Having grown up with this franchise, getting to speak with Wes Craven about resurrecting the franchise with *Scream 4* is honestly a dream come true.

On the other hand, the pressure is on for Craven. I'm not the only moviegoer who's a dedicated franchise fan, meaning that in *Scream 4* Craven doesn't just have to do the original films justice, but he's got to offer something new. No, the general story of *Scream 4* or the decision to make another *Scream* film for that matter didn't come from Craven, but the director certainly had a strong impact on the project from the moment Bob Weinstein offered him the gig.

Check out everything Craven had to say about bringing the franchise back to life, summoning the old, adding some new and, where we can expect the series to go from here.

Perri Nemiroff: When did you decide to resurrect the franchise? Did you just wake up one morning and decide now is the time?

Wes Craven: No, that's actually pretty far off the mark. The way it worked is that Bob Weinstein called me and said that he was going to remake it or do a *Scream 4*. Kevin [Williamson] was working on an idea that Bob thought was really good, and was I interested and would I like to talk to Kevin about it? That's really how I came into the picture. I had dinner with Kevin; he didn't have a script yet, but he had a very coherent outline of the film. I found it fascinating. But I didn't commit to the film until some months later when the first of the real big chunks started coming. I think it's a matter of Bob Weinstein deciding this. He told us there was not going to be a *Scream 4* for a long period mostly because of *Scary Movie* and because he didn't want us just making it because we could, so I think it was smart of him to wait until we could comment on an entire decade and a decade that was the twenty-first century. That's a significant landscape to set your picture on.

Nemiroff: Considering Kevin only had that outline when you met, did that give you the opportunity to work with him on developing the actual script?

Craven: Yeah, the moment I signed on I'm writing notes, outlines, whatever I can to help the process. Kevin and I collaborated a great deal with Bob also on the script until Kevin left. So sure, I'm a very hands-on director in so far as notes and things like that, not demands, just, "I think this works," or, "I think this maybe doesn't work."

Nemiroff: And how about your returning cast? Did you approach it as though they'd come if you called, or did you have to choose your words wisely?

Craven: No, and again, the man who controls the circus is Bob Weinstein. He owns the franchise, and he pulled the trigger on doing this film. So by the time I came in, he had already spoken to Courteney [Cox] and David [Arquette] and Neve [Campbell]. I can't remember whether people had fully committed or not. I think maybe one had and the two others had not yet, but as soon as it was known that I was going to be directing or considering directing seriously, we all talked and made sure that we were going to be there for each other. I think we all feel very much that we depend on each other to keep the quality good and keep the franchise, whatever iteration of it that it is, strong and powerful and based in the original journey of Sidney Prescott.

Nemiroff: And then how'd you go about choosing your new cast members? A lot of them bear similarities to previous characters, so did you have your eye on certain actors who reminded you of the original casts?

Craven: Within the structure of *Scream 4* there is the film within a film, but that's been part of the *Scream* franchise since *Scream 2* when you had the *Stab* franchise. In our film, *Stab* is up to *Stab* number seven, and the kids talk a great deal about that because we established that the first three *Stabs* basically were based on the life of Sidney Prescott. So then she sued them for using her story and for starting making up crazy qualms and making the one sequel after another. So that's kind of our poking fun at people who just make endless sequels of the film that was originally original. Within the context there is the evil version of people, let's just say, that are aware of original them, a certain emulation of them, a certain copying of them in a way to get at Sid's arriving in town. She thinks having dealt with all the ghosts and perhaps even living in a town in a peaceful way that could put the stuff behind her. So that's part of what those traces are doing; they're saying it's not over.

Nemiroff: Once you had your stars, how'd you go about preparing them? For those newcomers, I assume they were all very familiar with the franchise.

Craven: Yeah, I think a lot of them have watched my films, several of the actors that used to watch it through fingers over their eyes, and they were familiar with the *Scream* franchise and a lot of them went back and watched them again to get refreshed on it. You just find the best actors that you can. There's an inherent drama within the framework of scares and killings and all that. In *Scream* there is very real drama that would be in almost any drama. In this iteration [Sidney's] mother's sister is part of the cast and Sid's cousin, played by Emma Roberts. So there were those family ties. That's straight drama. There's a thousand ways you could do it as a director to guide them, help them, whatever, but this was a very, very experienced cast, really, even though they're young. Emma Roberts, for instance, has been making movies for quite a long time. Hayden Panettiere, same thing. Rory [Culkin] comes from a filmmaking family. A lot of them came with a great amount of professional accomplishment already, so then it was just a matter of approaching it as real life drama and not, "I need to hear you scream." It's never, ever like that at all even though I constantly get asked, "Do you make them scream first?" It has nothing to do with that; it just has to do with people who can really act.

Nemiroff: So how would you compare your directing style overall now to ten years ago? Times have changed, so have your methods—script breakdown, exercises?

Craven: Nothing like that. In general, I don't even have the luxury of rehearsal time on most films that I make. It is just a scene-by-scene full cast read through. It's very much just doing the rehearsal sometimes the day before, at the end of the day, but just on the spot as the scene unfolds. After a take is over going up to them and talking to them and giving my observations, my ideas and working with the thing as a progressive has been the way I've approached it ever since the beginning. The reason we've probably done very temporaneously—in some ways, it's done on practical locations where you're not shooting on sets, where things are much more conventional. You just don't even have that trust to the set until the day the owners who have it move out. It is much more in-flow at the time, talking about directing.

Nemiroff: What's the plan from here? When we first heard about *Scream 4* there was a 5 and 6 there as well. Is that still the case?

Craven: No, there is no *Scream 5* script. Kevin [Williamson], when I first talked to him about this project before there was a script, he had an idea for a trilogy, so we'll have to see what comes out of that. I'm sure Bob Weinstein is open to it if the script or ideas are to his pleasure. He has very high standards. I don't think he's in any rush to do it, particularly; but on the other hand, I think he's open to the idea of a trilogy. So at the point when there is an idea that he's really excited about, I'm sure he will begin launching that next film.

Director Wes Craven: Interview

Christina Radish / 2011

From *Collider.com*, April 10, 2011. Reprinted by permission of *Collider* and Christina Radish.

Fifteen years after the *Scream* franchise ushered a new wave of horror, series creator Kevin Williamson (*The Vampire Diaries*, *Dawson's Creek*) and horror master Wes Craven, who directed the first trilogy, have reunited for *Scream 4*. Reflecting back on where it came from, and taking into account the technological and internet savvy world we now live in, the film reunites its lead trio while introducing a new group of actors for Ghostface to terrorize.

At the film's press day, director Wes Craven talked about taking the internet into consideration for this installment in the horror franchise, the spy work involved with keeping the story secret, how screenwriter Ehren Kruger only made minor changes to Kevin Williamson's script, and why this was the perfect time to breathe life into the *Scream* series again. First, a brief synopsis: Returning home to Woodsboro, Sidney Prescott (Neve Campbell), now the author of a self-help book about survival, is on the last stop of her successful book tour. Once there, she reconnects with Sheriff Dewey (David Arquette) and Gale Weathers (Courteney Cox), who are now married, as well as her cousin Jill (Emma Roberts) and Aunt Kate (Mary McDonnell). But it's not long before Sidney's reappearance also brings the return of Ghostface, starting a new string of bloody killings and putting everyone's lives in jeopardy.

Now, onto the interview:

Collider: How did you and (screenwriter) Kevin Williamson work together to identify and create the new rules for this film, especially with the use of the internet this time?

Wes Craven: Well, we both spend a lot of time on the internet. I think most of our lives revolve around that now. I don't know. We're just clever fellows. Even old fogies like myself, and to a lesser extent Kevin, use all those things now, like it or not. Once you start using them, you have to think of the possibilities of how they could be misused, too.

Collider: Did you think about how they affect the way we watch movies now?

Craven: Very much. If you're in a theater today, people are texting all around you. You have the little glowing screens everywhere. That's just one example. Think of how annoying that can be.

Collider: What made you decide to post on Twitter during filming?

Craven: The tweeting was to do everything from having contests for posters of the film, as they became ready, to having contests for people to identify photographs of weird bugs that we took off of the set, when we were shooting at night and all these strange bugs would fall out of the sky. We just kept the fans aware that we were filming and that we knew they were out there. I have to say that it was very intriguing to see how quickly people answered. Our coproducer, Carly Feingold, got it all rolling for me. People were answering within thirty seconds or sometimes fifteen seconds, from Germany and other parts of the world. It made me realize, even in the process of filming, how different this reality was from even emails. Things are just much, much quicker, and worldwide.

Collider: What lengths did you go to keep the secrets of this film under wraps?

Craven: Keeping things secret was spy work. We did things like, when we did our original casting with hundreds of young actors reading script pages, we couldn't have them read pages from the actual script, so we had them reading pages from *Scream 1*, which was bizarre. I don't think we ever read actors with the actual pages from the script. There were a lot of things like that, which were annoying, but necessary to keep things secret.

Collider: Do you think horror movies will always be bound by rules?

Craven: I think the very essence of the *Scream* films is that we break the rules. We establish or state what the rules are, and then we immediately break them. That started in *Scream 1*, when they said, "If you say, 'I'll be right back,' you'll die," and the person that says that is one of the killers. They said, "If you have sex you'll die." Neve's character has the first sexual encounter of her life, and she's one of the survivors. We like to establish what the rules are, but they're really the clichés. As soon as they're stated in the *Scream* films, we almost always break them. It makes the audience not know what to expect next. If they think they know what the rules are, we immediately say, "No, you don't."

Collider: You're a master of horror, and that's something that nobody can take from you.

Craven: Oh, yes, they can. Have you read the reviews of my last movie (*My Soul to Take*)?

Collider: With the reviews of that film, are you concerned with how people are going to react to this movie? Is that something that still makes you nervous?

Craven: When you do a film like *My Soul to Take*, and people think it sucks, that hurts. We put a lot of work into it. And it's a good film, but you go on. The good feeling about doing this film was getting back with old friends, working on something that I thought was really good and having a chance of being a little bit more recognizable to an audience.

Collider: There was some talk about a lot of changes being made to this script, with Ehren Kruger being brought on, after Kevin Williamson was finished. Are you satisfied with the results of the script that you finally used for the movie?

Craven: Yes, I'm very pleased with the movie. We're all pleased with the way the script turned out. It was the result of Kevin's original master script, and Ehren did a decent amount of work on specific scenes and areas of it. I also wrote sections of the film myself. But it very much is Kevin's concept, characters, situations, and over-arching framework for the film.

Collider: How did this come about, after ten years?

Craven: I don't know how it came about. How do these things come about? Bob Weinstein, of the Weinstein brothers, is the godfather of *Scream*. He's the man who bought the original script from Kevin. He and Kevin were talking about it, and he felt it was time. He originally told us, after *Scream 3*, that there were not going to be any more for a long time because he didn't want it to feel like we were just knocking them out to make money. And, of course, there was the *Scary Movie* series, so we needed to get some distance from that.

But at the end of the decade, there was a feeling that this was the perfect time to look at the first decade of the twenty-first century, and it was quite distinctive from others, with 9/11 hovering over things and the presence of electronic media being brought down to people to the level where everybody is online, everybody is on Facebook, and people are tweeting, all over the world, all the time. It's totally different. So it was time to take that into account.

At the same time, the cinema was changing very much. You aren't just watching movies in the theater anymore. I have a stepdaughter who's twenty years old, and she watches movies on her computer or her phone. The whole business is changing dramatically, and the way fans follow and participate in movies, and make their own movies to emulate those movies, is profoundly different. It felt like it was time to make a screenplay that could reflect all this newness.

The Legendary Wes Craven Talks *Scream 4* with Mr. Beaks!

Jeremy Smith (writing as "Mr. Beaks") / 2011

Originally published April 12, 2011 at www.aintitcoolnews.com. Reprinted by permission of Jeremy Smith.

Fifteen years ago, Wes Craven and Kevin Williamson resuscitated the slasher film with *Scream*. It was slick, smarter-than-average trash in which a stock group of teenagers struggled for their lives against the rigid conventions of a shopworn subgenre. Though the film wasn't as thematically complex as it might've appeared at first blush (Craven had dug much deeper two years earlier with the fascinatingly flawed *New Nightmare*), the Pirandellian conceit gave mainstream critics license to enjoy it as a "guilty pleasure." Powered by surprisingly good reviews and strong word of mouth, *Scream* went on to become the first slasher film to gross $100 million. And a postmodern horror franchise was born!

Though Williamson deserves a tremendous amount of credit for nailing the zeitgeist with his self-reflexive take on the subgenre, it's impossible to imagine *Scream* hitting phenomenon status without Craven at the helm. For a filmmaker who'd been experimenting with horror-comedy hybrids since 1989's *Shocker*, Williamson's screenplay possessed lightning-in-a-bottle potential—which Craven fully exploited in the film's bravura opening sequence. Though he'd pulled off plenty of memorable set pieces in his career, Craven's films had never been this technically polished; shooting widescreen for the first time in his career, Craven seemed reborn as a director. *Scream* was the work of a master performing at the peak of his powers—and while the scripts for the immediate sequels suffered from varying degrees of narrative overexertion, Craven's newfound visual panache at least kept them watchable.

It's been an up-and-down run over the last twelve years for Craven (with both apex and nadir being hit in 2005 with the crackerjack B-movie *Red Eye* and the appropriately titled *Cursed*), so perhaps a return to the *Scream* franchise is just the thing to recharge his creative energies. With a decade under the bridge and Kevin Williamson . . . 85 percent back as screenwriter (Craven attributes the other 15 percent to Ehren Kruger), *Scream 4* could very well do for the fame-obsessed, social-networking generation what the original did for the nascent internet generation.

So how does a once-pioneering franchise reestablish its relevance in a world gone meta? I discussed this and sundry other topics with the ever-eloquent Mr. Craven a couple of weeks ago. For the spoiler-conscious among you, not to worry: I signed a non-disclosure agreement promising not to reveal the big third-act twist, so we talk about the narrative only in the broadest of terms.

Mr. Beaks: When the first *Scream* was released, there had been a real dearth of slasher films. The genre is thriving now. What prompted you to return to the franchise?

Craven: It's not my perception of the genre. There are a lot, but a lot of them are remakes and a lot have come out and not done that well. So I do feel like the genre could use a little boost. Right after *Scream 3*, we all agreed we shouldn't do any more for a significant period of time. We all—while we were making that trilogy—really felt it was a trilogy, and to do another *Scream* would be kind of saying, "Oh, we were just kidding." But after ten years, we felt we were in a place where the first decade of the twenty-first century had gone by, things had changed a great deal in the youth culture, and there was a really legitimate opportunity here to talk about new things and to bring the fans up to date with what is going on right now.

Beaks: *Scream* felt so different at the time. It was self-aware and acknowledged the conventions of the genre—and also respected the audience's intelligence by letting them in on the game. Do you think audiences are now too self-aware?

Craven: I don't think so. *Scream 4* acknowledges that pretty much up front, saying to the audience that we're aware of this, and kids know every detail about it—including everything that's operating on a meta level. That's all part of what we're talking about here. It's not like we have to make things up out of whole cloth; we always talk about the culture as it is and actually exists—and perhaps make it a bit more arch or sardonic. The whole social networking phenomenon is new. It's profoundly affecting the current generation: in the way we deal with people, in the way we relate to people, and in the way we gather news. All of these things are unprecedented and vast in their scope, so I thought, "Wow, here's some really significant stuff we can set our picture amidst and do something that is germane to today as opposed to ten years ago."

Beaks: How has the nature of your collaboration changed with Kevin Williamson over the years?

Craven: The first film was unique in the series in that it was a completed script that Kevin had written as a virtually unknown independent writer; [the script] suddenly came on the market over a weekend and was acquired after a big bidding war—which was won by the Weinstein brothers and Miramax. It's not like I was giving a lot of input to him; he was a writer who'd written a terrific script and was done. He came to script from time to time, and, as he likes to say, sat at my feet and "watched the master." But he was a very quick study—and destined to be doing his own directing and producing as well. So he was much more a person who was there to learn.

By the second one, he had his own television show and had directed his own things. He was a much more accomplished and knowledgeable man than he'd been on the first. That was the biggest difference to me. And in some cases, his attention was divided at certain points of the making of the film between the film and his television show, so that was sometimes something significant. But that didn't really come into play until the third one, when it made it kind of impossible for him to fully participate.

Beaks: How was it reuniting with him on this film?

Craven: It was great. Kevin's a great guy. He has just a remarkable imagination. He's very smart. He can capture in a sentence, or a short moment in a scene, the essence of the zeitgeist of the moment. It's kind of extraordinary. His dialogue is really original and quite shocking sometimes—in a way that just makes it fresh and something that you don't feel like you've heard a million times in other genre films or on television. I like working with him a lot.

But my entry into *Scream 4* was after he and Bob had been working together for some time, kicking around ideas. The original idea for this was not anything I participated in. But on the other hand, once Kevin was writing, I participated a lot: as a director, I'd give pages and pages of notes and so forth. In that sense, it was a good collaboration and went on for some time. I would say that 85 percent of what you see on the screen was there in the script by the time Kevin departed. I think the chief reason for his departure was that he got to the point where his television show was going into production again, and he needed to be there and was being threatened with a lawsuit by the network. (Laughs) That's when Ehren Kruger came in and polished up the loose ends.

Beaks: We hear a lot about films that go into production without a completed script. Was that really the case on this film, and, if so, how did you deal with that?

Craven: I have to say, just looking at the films I've written myself, the [writing] process goes on all the time. In horror . . . and comedy, there is a constant creative interplay that's going on in the making of the film. You can go back to *Casablanca* and read the stories of how they wrote the third act over and over again and shot it the day after they finally got it down on paper. It's not something new, and I don't think it necessarily means the picture is in trouble. It's the core group of people trying to make it absolutely as good as they can and taking every opportunity to do that. The fact that you've started shooting doesn't mean the script needs to be put in a leather binder and not touched; it means you still have time to fiddle with the third act or whatever scene it is that is still days or weeks ahead from shooting.

Beaks: You've been doing this for so long and have pulled off so many terrific suspense set pieces. How did you approach this film in terms of doing suspense beats you hadn't done before?

Craven: I think the opening was more a matter of staging. Kevin's brilliance there was very specific with dialogue. We always shoot on practical sets, actual houses—and every house is different. Almost always, what's written on the page doesn't fit the house that you're in. (Laughs) That sort of thing is constantly being massaged and changed, and then I'll add this and that to almost anything I touch. Nobody tells me you can't touch the script—but at the same time I know not to screw it up by fiddling with something that doesn't need to be enhanced or made a little better.

It's a constant process. The opening was a lot of fun to play with. The scene in the parking garage, that was obviously a scene that lent itself to a lot of suspense. After we filmed and cut the original version, we went back because Bob Weinstein and I had some ideas; I wrote some additional moments in that scene. Sometimes, even quite late in the process, you have an idea where you can make it even more suspenseful. And the scene at "STAB-athon," all of the big set pieces are very much a combination of what is written and what is made possible by the location—and me filling in blanks that need to be filled in.

Beaks: Can you think of a particular instance in the past where a sequence was dramatically improved by reworking it on set?

Craven: It's actually hard to think of a time when that didn't happen. Going back to one of my more obscure films, *Deadly Blessing*, there was a scene written by two young writers that was essentially out of *Psycho*. The heroine is taking a shower, and you see past her to a shadow going past the shower curtain. And then a snake appears in the bathtub—something like that. I knew that was too Hitchcock, and it would not be original. Up to the day before we shot it, I literally, before I fell asleep that night, got a concept for a totally new version of that scene. That's what I ended up shooting, and I think it made it really fascinating because it was something you'd never seen before, so the audience didn't know what to expect next.

I think continuously you're watching every scene thinking, "Have I seen this before? Is this a repeat of someone else's look? How can I do it originally? How can I take advantage of this particular house?" In one of the opening scenes, when we did a location scout for the house, we discovered this passageway that led from the upstairs hallway into the garage and down a set of very rough stairs into the garage itself. Based on that, I wrote the chase up the stairs and then through the sort of back way down to the garage—based entirely on the location and knowing that, cinematically, it would be very interesting.

Beaks: Over the years, do you feel that the things you find frightening—or what you think audiences find frightening—has changed?

Craven: This film's a good example of some of the vulnerabilities that have been brought about by the internet—and the fact that people can watch you remotely very easily and record you. All of that stuff is pretty new. There are older variations of it, but this film was built on new situations like that that could be frightening; we looked at that while we were revising this film. But on the other hand, I feel like a suspense scene . . . kind of what's going on on the exterior is almost not as interesting to me as what's going on in the interior of the character and what changes the character just before they go into a scene where something is going to happen. I think when someone is doing a good suspense scene, it's as much the interior mechanisms that are taking place with the character as it is the exterior stuff of who jumps out of what building.

Beaks: There was talk last year of a *Deadly Friend* remake at Warner Bros. Do you have any idea where that stands?

Craven: None whatsoever. Honestly, there was a period when we were doing the sequel to the remake of *The Hills Have Eyes* when everyone was talking about me doing remakes of all my films—and a lot of people that owned various properties were suggesting it to me. But I reached a point in that whole process—between *Last House* and the two *Hills* pictures—that I was kind of disappearing from the cinematic scene, especially as a director. So I vowed to myself that I'd done enough of that. The situation with *Last House* and *Hills* was different in that we discovered—by "we" I mean Peter Locke, who I did *Hills Have Eyes* with, and Sean Cunningham, who I did *Last House* with—that we actually owned those properties after thirty years because that was built into the contract. So we had the opportunity to remake those films having total control. It wasn't like someone else was remaking my films. On the other hand, my contract with *A Nightmare on Elm Street* was that New Line Cinema owned it forever and ever so that remake I had nothing to do with. It's kind of a case-by-case thing, but I certainly felt at a certain point that if I want to remain an active and growing artist, I shouldn't be remaking my own stuff; I should be making new movies.

Beaks: Well, there's a very good chance *Scream 4* will make a good deal of money, which would then necessitate another sequel. But it sounds to me like you'd rather follow this up with something original. What would you like to do next? Would you be open to doing another *Scream* film?

Craven: It might be easy to forget, but my previous film, which we completed literally while we were in preproduction on *Scream 4*, was *My Soul to Take*. I poured two-and-a-half years of my life into that. It's a film that was very, very different, and I think a lot of people just didn't get it. I felt like I'd done something very original, very personal with that. So when *Scream 4* came along, I thought it was going to be fun and interesting and would kind of put me back on the map in case I was in danger of disappearing with [*My Soul to Take*] not doing well—and before that, producing remakes as opposed to directing. There were also films in that decade, like *Cursed*, that took an enormous amount of time to make and almost didn't break the surface at all. I have done something original very recently, and I will, when we're done with this, be taking time off with my wife to rest and then maybe start writing something new. But we're also reading scripts and deciding if and when we want to do another film. There's a lot else out there in our lives now, and we're not going to rush into a film unless I'm really intrigued by it.

Scream 4 opens wide this Friday, April 15.

Faithfully submitted,
Mr. Beaks

Wes Craven Screams Anew

Bryan Reesman / 2011

From *Moviemaker* Magazine, April 15, 2011. Reprinted by permission of *Moviemaker* magazine, all rights reserved, www.moviemaker.com.

Wes Craven has unleashed incredibly influential horror films over the last four decades, including *The Last House on the Left*, *A Nightmare on Elm Street*, and *Scream*. His movies have resonated with audiences not only because they tap into our primal fears, but also because they often dip into the mainstream zeitgeist and hit upon social issues. His excursions into fright films have inspired many to label him "The Master of Horror." In recent years Wes Craven has taken some time off from directing, but even though some are calling last fall's *My Soul to Take* and the upcoming *Scream 4* a "comeback," in truth he never really went away. But times have certainly changed.

The return of *Scream* comes more than a decade after the *Scary Movie* franchise (ironically, they're both produced by Dimension Films) transformed the lightning-fast, knife-wielding Ghostface from an icon of terror into a figure of mirth. It also follows a massive horror renaissance that has spawned endless remakes, reboots, and sequels of classic films. The original, semisatirical but still deadly *Scream* trilogy certainly became more self-aware as it went along, and by the third installment the eternally besieged heroine Sidney Prescott was being pursued by a new Ghostface on a movie set version of her home from the first film. It became a meta-meta-horror film that was akin to being caught in a room full of funhouse mirrors. As Craven sagely notes, "That doesn't mean you can't die in the funhouse."

Yet given the irony inherent in the series and the bloody imitators spawned in its wake, one wonders if *Scream 4*—which finds self-help author Prescott (Neve Campbell) returning to her Woodsboro home, where she reconnects with her cousin (Emma Roberts) and is stalked anew by Ghostface in the wake of a new *Stab* movie—will build further upon the irony or be more earnest.

Craven laughs good-naturedly at that philosophical query, responding: "It is, and it isn't. I think there is a very strong central family drama with the Emma

Roberts character because it's a very deeply written role of this kid who is part of Sid's family and doesn't know her intimately but gets to know her and lives in the house of Sid's aunt. That story is very naturalistic and carefully drawn. On the other hand, there is a comment on the last ten years and where we as a society are now that I think is more analytical than ironic."

Wit has always been integral to many of Craven's films through characters like Freddy Krueger and *Shocker*'s Horace Pinker. Horror and humor often go hand in hand, but the director has learned to be careful when injecting chuckles into his cinematic carnage.

"I found that out quite hideously with my first film, when I cracked jokes very close to a scene where somebody was dying," recalls Craven. "The audience felt a lot, then you had two goofy sheriffs walking around, and that was resented. So I learned that you have to take what you're doing seriously if it's a serious moment, but at the same time it's a very natural human tendency to joke between, before, and after times that you're scared. It's like combat humor; it's just a way of coping. You just have to be careful you're not wink-winking too much. It's a judgment call in every scene that you do. You have to be aware that you can't be too funny, or the audience will say, 'Oh, come on now.' Hopefully we walked that line in *Scream 4*. There are times when it's just flat-out kick-ass, and there is nothing funny about anything. But there's lot of laughter, too, so hopefully we got everything right. It feels like we did."

The *Scream* series took an eleven-year slumber after *Scary Movie* emerged. Craven says that even Dimension's Bob Weinstein thought that they should let it lie for a while, letting the parody series run its course before returning so that a new generation could discover the original.

Craven admits that watching the first *Scary Movie* was painful for him, not simply because it poked fun at a franchise that he had worked so hard to create, but also because they replicated exact shots from the original, and he did not even have a financial piece of it.

Scary Movie gave Craven the resolve to move on and do new things. He helmed the werewolf movie *Cursed* (its PG-13 theatrical release hurt the film in some people's eyes; the bloodier, unrated cut is better) and the taut psychological thriller *Red Eye*, both of which were released in 2005. He also produced successful remakes of his early films *The Last House on the Left* and *The Hills Have Eyes* (parts one and two), executive produced *Feast* and *The Breed*, wrote the 2006 sci-fi thriller *Pulse* and directed a segment of the romantic anthology film *Paris, je t'aime*, which was certainly a nice detour.

People associate Craven with just one genre, and when *My Soul to Take* emerged last October, it had been five years since the world had seen a new directorial effort from the horror maestro. The reaction, both artistic and commercial, was not good.

Critics and fans alike trashed the film, which quickly dropped off the mainstream radar. Needless to say, Craven, who also wrote the screenplay, was devastated by the harsh criticisms. "As hunters say, I went to ground," he reveals. "That's when an animal gets shot and goes as deep as it can into its burrow and just sits there to see whether it's going to die or live. It was shocking to me."

He stresses that the film "had a terrible history of birthing." *My Soul to Take* was made between Hollywood strikes, and the moviemakers were pressured into going ahead with production before they were ready. They lost their leads the weekend before they were to start shooting. "I think we went through three changes in administration at the key studios," adds Craven. "Rogue was bought away from Andrew Rona, who was our patron, and suddenly we were in the hands of strangers. They didn't even look at the film for three months. We sent in the finished film and never heard anything. We couldn't even get them on the phone. It turned out they were in a big, long, drawn-out battle with Universal over who owned what because [Rogue's parent company] Relativity had been a financial partner with Universal for several years and had backed about 50 percent of their movies. It was very complicated."

Regular changes in executives and a lack of awareness about the film—Craven says no poster was released until two weeks before *My Soul to Take* hit theaters—led to problems with both completion and promotion. Even worse, a last-minute edict to retroactively make the film 3-D hampered not only *My Soul to Take* but *Scream 4*, as well. The whole situation was turning into a real-life horror show for this cinematic purveyor of fear.

"We were shooting *Scream 4* at the time, so on weekends in the middle of this quite exhausting shoot, we had to go forty miles away to a town that had a screen big enough to do 3-D passes on *My Soul to Take*," explains Craven. "Every single shot had to be looked at. People would fly in from California to take notes, then go away, and come back the next weekend with revisions. That went on for months.

"*My Soul to Take* is one of the toughest films I've done," Craven admits, "but I'm proud of it, and I think it's going to be looked at again and reappraised. I tried to do a whole different kind of horror film, not who really has schizophrenic elements to his own life."

War in various forms has always had an impact on Craven's films, from the influences of the atrocities of the Vietnam War on *The Last House on the Left* and *The Hills Have Eyes* to that of the Reagan-era social and economic policies on the *People Under the Stairs* and the "War on Terror" on *Red Eye*. It sounds like Craven might have a war movie to make.

"I guess I would have to consider it," he muses, "but in a sense I feel like I'm doing war movies. The war on civility and the war on normal living is carried out by people with violent tendencies. In a sense, both horror and war movies are about that polarity of life—the way lunatics or nations act. I think that struggle is going on within the human race all the time. It happens at the family level, it happens at the schoolyard level, it happens at the national level, and none of it necessarily has to be typical combat, if there is such a thing anymore."

In spite of his recent creative battles, Craven is quite pleased with *Scream 4*. "It's been a lot of fun," he declares. "It's been great working with Courteney [Cox], David [Arquette], Neve . . . and the new cast is fantastic."

Assuming that *Scream 4* is a hit (and Craven feels confident that it will be) and assuming that the studio would then greenlight a project of his choice, where does the seventy-one-year-old director think he might venture?

"I could say something totally different, like a romantic comedy or whatever, but even *My Soul to Take* taught me a very hard lesson that if you go too far from your audience's expectations they'll stab you in the back faster than you can say, 'Jack,'" he admits with a laugh. "I did *Music of the Heart* and Meryl Streep got a nomination for an Academy Award. In test audiences it got one of the highest ratings for a Miramax film ever . . . But they had a very hard time getting people into the theaters because of my name. I guess I would love to do a thriller or something that is a little bit more grown up.

"Until *My Soul to Take* I thought I kind of knew my audience," Craven continues, "but there were some very vitriolic and nasty reviews and a general response that said, 'Fuck you, Wes Craven.' I actually ran across things like 'R.I.P. Wes Craven.' I opened up a book on filmmakers and saw my name, and it said, 'Won't somebody please tell this guy to retire?' There was a vein of viciousness that I had really never [experienced] before. At this point I don't have any illusions about it. I think *Scream 4* is going to do very well and maybe some of those people will say, 'Wes Craven's back,' but I know I can't trust them anymore. And in the horror community it doesn't feel like there's a big search for something more complex than just more scares and blood, and that's kind of disappointing."

Craven's oeuvre is held in such high regard because there are still horror fans who crave something deeper than a series of mutilations, eerie ghosts, or outright bloodbaths. Mainstream perception of the horror genre is another matter. Many people see the basic building blocks but not what the structure ultimately represents. Hollywood routinely passes over fear films at the Academy Awards, although last year they paid the genre lip service with a half-assed movie montage that included clips from the *Twilight* franchise.

Why is Oscar so disdainful of horror? "I think because in some ways the material isn't that deep," Craven replies bluntly. "If you look at *The Silence of the Lambs*, they are willing to [go there], but it has to have adult intelligence to it in order to be nominated for something by adults. If it's just there pushing all the bells and whistles of sensationalism, then it probably won't make it up to that next level. In some ways that's its charm, and in some ways that's its limitation."

Those are sobering words from the man known to many as the master of horror. Then again, that's not a title that Craven feels comfortable with. "I'm sure every other horror director curls their lip at that," he confesses of his unadopted appellation. "I think in a way it's that I've been around a long time, and I've made a number of influential films. But I just like to think of myself as a working stiff, as a director who has a pretty consistent output and has been doing it a long time and tries to keep the standards as high as he can."

Wes Craven Talks YEAH TV, *Nightmare on Elm Street*, and His Future

Eric Walkuski / 2013

From www.joblo.com, March 15, 2013. Reprinted by permission of Paul Shirey, *JoBlo*.

Wes Craven is going back to Elm Street . . . well, in a manner of speaking. The director is revisiting *A Nightmare on Elm Street*, as well as *Scream*, as part of AMC Network's new online streaming service Yeah TV, which offers the audience a plethora of information while they watch a movie. Think of it as a commentary, but not just an audio one, an interactive one. Craven is providing all new information for fans who want to dig deeper into the worlds of *Elm Street* and *Scream*, and he took the time to chat with yours truly about it briefly while he was in Austin, Texas, promoting the new service.

Of course, we also found some time to chat about *Elm Street*, the future of *Scream*, and his new comic book series.

Eric Walkuski: What can you tell us about your involvement with Yeah TV?
Craven: Well, the first contact was I got contacted by a friend about some people who wanted to interview me about *Nightmare on Elm Street*, and then they also said they'd love to do *Scream*. So I did the interviews, which were both very good. Then I kind of forgot about them, and then a year later they called me back—this was just recently—and they were offering me two slots on this new site. I went and saw what they were doing, and I was just delighted. When they asked me if I wanted to come to SXSW, I said, "Great." I think it's very state of the art and unique. I went to the site just to watch ten minutes of *The Exorcist*, and I was so excited about all the information that was coming, I ended up watching the entire film. And I've seen that film many times, but I learned a lot of new things. It's a great way to immerse yourself in other aspects of the film aside from what's on screen. If you want the behind-the-scenes tour, when my face pops up on the screen, you can tap on my face and the movie stops and the interview portion

begins. And you have time as a director to tell the whole story, as opposed to DVD commentary when you're sort of racing to get through the story before the scene disappears and you're onto something else. It's a much broader, deeper look at the films.

Walkuski: Does doing something like this make you appreciate *Nightmare on Elm Street* all over again? Are you able to reassess it, or is it always the same movie for you whenever you look at it?

Craven: Well, there were a few new things about *Nightmare on Elm Street* that I learned, believe it or not. There was a piece of information that came up on the screen that said, "Freddy Krueger's entire screen time was only seven minutes." And I went, "What, really? Wow!" (Laughs) I didn't even realize it, but I guess the less you show of your villain, the better. You don't want to grow tired of him. So, things like that gave me an appreciation of the craft of the film. And then watching the commentaries of the actors and actresses saying I did a good job, that felt really good, it always helps when you feel like you're doing your job well.

Walkuski: Do you think the future of movies and series is on the web?

Craven: I think the experience of going to a theater and seeing a movie with a lot of people is still part of the transformational power of the film, and it's equivalent to the old shaman telling a story by the campfire to a bunch of people. That is a remarkable thing; if you scream and everyone else in the audience screams, you realize that your fears are not just within yourself, they're in other people as well, and that's strangely releasing. But on the TV, you can still watch it with friends. We watch films on so many different mediums now that I think they'll complement each other for a long time.

Walkuski: For the people who are aching for another *Scream* film, is there hope for *Scream 5*?

Craven: So far I have not heard anything about *Scream 5* from Bob Weinstein. There is some talk about a television series, but I don't think anything has moved forward on that yet. That's what I'm hearing more than anything else from the guys at Dimension. It would be them picking up the phone and asking me if I wanted to play with them, so . . .

Walkuski: And what's next for you?

Craven: I'm doing a five-issue comic-book series called *Coming of Rage*, which is about a teenage kid who is born into a family of vampires and doesn't know it until his coming of age, so to speak, which comes in the middle of a bar fight when he's gone into a place he shouldn't have. He's helped by a guy and a girl, and she turns out to be a zombie. And the guy turns out to be a werewolf. It's a road picture, believe it or not, sort of "them against the world." And it turns out each one of them has one human parent, so it sort of bridges both worlds. It's a coming-of-age—or coming-of-rage—story; what can I say? I wrote the entire outline with Steve [Niles], and now he's off writing the entire first drafts of all the issues.

Walkuski: And that could become a feature film one day?
Craven: Oh absolutely, that's part of the deal. I have first dibs on a feature of it.

Walkuski: I remember years ago when you directed *Music of the Heart*, which you wanted to make for a change of scenery, so to speak; do you ever have the urge now to do something outside the horror genre?
Craven: There's always the fond hope that someday I'll get to do something else, but I've come to terms with the fact that I'm very good at making genre pictures. And I can express basically anything in them anyway. Making *Music of the Heart* was a great experience, but I probably won't go back in that direction again. Unless I get a chance.

Walkuski: Thanks so much for your time, good luck with everything!
Craven: Thanks!

Father of Freddy

W. Brice McVicar / 2014

From *Fangoria* 337, 2014. Reprinted by permission of Joseph A. Sonnier IV, CEO of *Cinestate* and *Fangoria*.

Nightmares. We all have them. They're one of the few universal elements of the human experience and have been the subject of paintings, books, and films, inspiring images of terror, cold sweats, and many sleepless nights for those afflicted. In other words: They're the perfect basis for a scary movie.

However, the idea of people's fears taking form in their sleep remained a mainly untapped resource for decades when it came to celluloid. Dream sequences, certainly, have played pivotal roles in films for decades, but it wasn't until thirty years ago that a small, under-the-radar film that many studios took a pass on dove headfirst into the unexplored waters of nightmares.

Prompted by a newspaper story about a man who could not sleep or he feared he would die—which came to pass—writer/director Wes Craven struggled to get the story out of his head and onto paper. Having already made a name for himself with the gritty *The Last House on the Left* and *The Hills Have Eyes*, the Cleveland-born filmmaker shopped his script around before finding a willing risk-taker in New Line Cinema. Company topper Robert Shaye loved Craven's vision of a burned, razor-gloved pedophile stalking his victims via their dreams—and unbeknownst to both at the time, they would launch what became one of the highest-grossing series of horror films in history.

A Nightmare on Elm Street opened to an unsuspecting public in November 1984 and immediately gave a whole new generation a reason to be scared. Freddy Krueger became a household name, and the movie, modestly budgeted at $1.8 million, slashed its way to success, netting $25 million in American theaters alone. On this, the thirtieth anniversary of the film's release, *Fangoria* reached out to Craven to discuss his masterpiece, its impact on the genre, and whether or not Freddy Krueger has become a nightmare or a dream come true for his creator.

Fangoria: Is *Nightmare* a gift or a hindrance to you now?

Wes Craven: It's both. When you look at all the films I've made, the two really big ones are *Nightmare* and *Scream*, and there are a couple of clunkers in there too. It certainly was successful for me, and I'm sure it'll be on my gravestone: "Father of Freddy Krueger" or some such thing. It's great to have done something that is still so much a part of the public language. It has become part of the culture out there. It's pretty amazing to have something that you struggled to pull out of your brain still around in the conversation. When you look at the whole pile of stuff I've done in forty-odd years, it's the most significant film I've made, and the most personal one.

Fangoria: You say it was successful for you intellectually; can you expand on that?

Craven: (Pauses) Coming up with the movie, and the idea that somebody was having a dream they had to wake from or they would die, came from a story I read in the newspaper. His situation was that he had to stay awake or he would die, and when he eventually did fall asleep, that actually happened. That was a true story.

But what do you do with it? The whole situation was profoundly moving to me, but I struggled with what type of story comes from that. My decision to base it on a metaphor of awareness of reality and the willingness to face reality—as opposed to living in denial—and constructing that around a young girl whose parents had done something horrible and (she's suffering) as a result of that, without knowing why, because the parents were keeping this horrible secret—that process was something I just hammered and hammered away at in my head. The final thing was to figure out how to avoid what happened to the guy in the newspaper article. How do you either stay awake long enough, or how do you take the enemy and bring him into your own territory?

That process was really arduous, and I wrestled with it for years. It was very hard, and I believe I came up with a really good solution based on the writings of a Russian philosopher who was a mystic and wrote about pain as facing reality, and how it was similar to whether you were awake or asleep: A person who is awake faces reality, but it becomes increasingly painful as you become aware of what reality is. And most people will back down away from that and go into sleep.

Fangoria: While writing it, did you realize how big an impact the film could have, not only on your career but on the genre?

Craven: No. I believe Bob Shaye did, but I didn't. I thought it was a really good story, and when I told it to friends, their eyes would light up and they'd say, "I'd love to see that movie." I should have put two and two together a little bit more because I would have hung in there and followed my agent's advice and not have signed the contract I did, because I basically signed everything away for the rest of my life and all of eternity. I lost an immense amount of participation in prof-its and everything. The idea of making a sequel, I kind of had a stick up my butt about that and didn't like the idea of it. . . . not that I had any control over it. Bob Shaye knew it was going to be very big and make lots of money, but I had no idea that was going to happen. I was very, very surprised. I'd done a bunch of pictures, and some of my earlier ones—*Last House* and *Hills*—had seen successes, but I had done pictures that hadn't done well at all, so the idea that I was suddenly going to make a hit picture was just . . . My mind was already telling me I should go back to teaching.

Fangoria: You've said the ending wasn't exactly what you envisioned.
Craven: That was Bob. We had a very interesting relationship, very friendly. I was trying to get the picture funded, and he was not able to raise the money. And I wanted to make it for more. Now, the figure seems minuscule. I think I had it budgeted by a friend, and it came in at $2.5 million. We made it for far less than that. But there was a part of Bob that wanted to be a director. He had directed one film, and there's always something I call "pissing on the post" in the film industry, where the studio people want to somehow put their imprint on the film creatively. And they'll do it in various ways. With Bob, he wanted to set up the sequels.

The ending I had, and it was just a page in the script, was that Nancy comes out of the front door and it's very misty, and she just sort of goes off into the mist and you're not quite sure if it was all a dream or not. Bob wanted something sort of spectacular, or a hook. He wanted to have Freddy driving the car. That's almost exactly the opening of *Nightmare 2*, which Bob had complete control of. It was a matter of compromise, and a sort of nod to Bob that he had busted his guts to get the funding because it was no easy task for him to do that.

Fangoria: Shaye took a chance on you, right? A number of other studios turned it down . . .
Craven: I was turned down by everybody. I took *Nightmare* to all the majors in Hollywood. I still, in my writing studio, have a framed letter from one of the big studio heads saying, "We're not so sure we want this at this time, but when you get it done, we'll take a look at it for a negative pickup." Meanwhile, Bob was try-ing to raise the money and raise the money, and it went on for years. I wanted to have the budget to do it right, and Bob was initially talking about making it for $100,000, which was the world we were coming out of.

That was the struggle, and it still sort of is. I remember meeting Bob in some club in New York. I went with a guy who was doing some projects he wanted to get me involved in, and my friend had said Bob was a very smart guy and a real up-and-comer. Bob said, "If you ever want to do anything, let me know," and I told him about my idea for *A Nightmare on Elm Street*. He thought it was great and kept in touch with me for years. He got it instantly, and quite frankly, nobody else did. My tip of the hat has always been to Bob for immediately understanding it.

Fangoria: Your collaborators frequently praise you for the way you've treated them on set, and your approach to filming . . . What was it like on the *Nightmare* shoot?

Craven: I'm not a director who wants to be best friends with everybody and let them throw in their ideas and follow whatever they say—I have a script, and I know exactly where I want to go—but at the same time, I feel like they're all collaborators and everybody is working their butts off. Everybody wants to help you get your vision on that screen, and a lot of them, especially the actors, put themselves through emotional anguish and pain and physical discomfort making these films. I always try to have a set that is safe for the actors and where the crew feels appreciated. It's such a glorious place to be. There are a lot of creative people, and everyone's giving 100 percent or more. I'm not someone who would ever think of screaming at an actor or a crewmember. That's just not who I am.

Fangoria: Any particular memories from that set?

WC: You relive every moment, but the rotating room was pretty amazing. We got some really big shots out of that.

When we did Johnny Depp's blood coming out of his bed, the whole set was inverted, and once the blood had come out I wanted to have the room slowly rotated so the blood would not only hit the floor but start slowly pouring down the walls. Once we started to do that, that immense amount of fluid shifted and the whole thing started spinning on its axle twelve feet up in the air. All the lights were bashed to bits and shorted out, the whole set went black and there were electrical sparks. The director of photography, Jacques Haitian, and I were sort of bolted to the walls in these chairs with five-point harnesses. So we were inside while all this was going on. We hung upside down for half an hour before they got the set stabilized and the electricity turned back on, and it was safe for people to come in. That was pretty remarkable.

There are a lot of wonderful moments in the film. I thought Heather did a tremendous job, and it was fun watching Johnny Depp. Obviously, I had no idea he'd go on to become what he did, but I was watching the struggle of this young guy trying to overcome his fear. He was always sweating; he was just so intensely unsure he'd be able to do what he had to do. I remember he had a friend coaching him, and it has been incredible to see that scared kid turn into this very confident and dedicated actor.

I could go on for hours and hours about the wonderful stuff that happened on that set. One funny story involving Gregg Fonseca, the production designer, was that he and this grip—I can't remember his name—were always fighting, and I think this involved the rotating room. There was a doorway that didn't have enough space for the grip to get his equipment through, and he was screaming at Gregg. And Gregg was saying, "I'm not going to change it." So the grip said, "Fine, I'll change it," and he stormed off and literally came back with a chainsaw and went onto that set. Everybody was sort of aghast, and we heard this (makes chainsaw noise). And he came out and said, "Problem fixed." He'd chainsawed this hole so he could get his stuff through. Gregg was screaming at him, and I eventually told them to get off the set. (laughs)

Fangoria: Robert Englund wasn't your initial choice for Freddy.
Craven: My recollection is that I wasn't originally looking for anybody who looked like Robert Englund. I was looking for an older man, like a creepy old man. Robert had come in and read, and he was so enthusiastic that after I had gone through old man after old man after old man and not found the person I thought could pull it off dramatically—and having gone through a lot of stuntmen too, because I thought we needed someone very physical—I went back to Robert. He was the only person who had shown enthusiasm for the role, really, as opposed to someone just looking to get a job.

Fangoria: Did Robert play it the way you saw Freddy to your head?
Craven: No, but that happens all the time when you cast someone. Another example is David Arquette because he said he wanted to play the deputy in *Scream*. And we had asked him to be one of the teenagers. He said, based on the description that he could play the character in a way that would be different, and I took that chance because there was something in David's enthusiasm.

That was the thing with Robert. He had an almost balletic way he moved as Freddy, and that's what you depend on with great actors: to take the role and enhance it and expand it and make it their own. All those gestures and the way he used the claws were all the things you hope for in an actor.

Fangoria: What can you say about Heather Langenkamp's performance? Did she capture the innocence you were looking for?
Craven: I think she has that quality. There's nothing artificial about her. I wanted someone who looked like she just walked off the streets of Cleveland—an ordinary person who you wouldn't, in a sense, rely on if a fight were to come. This would be a person who could keep a level head, tell you the truth, and come up with solutions. She believed what she saw and then figured out a way to confront it because there was no way to run from it.

Fangoria: So why is it that in 2014, we are still talking about *A Nightmare on Elm Street*? Why didn't it become like so many other slasher flicks and fade from memory?

Craven: I think it's eternal. It's classic. In my best films, I've tried not to make them about the moment and what gadgets people are using or what words they're saying—it's ordinary language. I just wanted to make something that could be true for all ages and that anyone in any culture could relate to, with sleeping and dreaming and nightmares being an eternal subject. It's about a very primal, trans-cultural, trans-time sort of thing, and I believe that what it takes to make a great horror film is to take the medium seriously and aspire to go beyond just scaring or titillating people, and do something that really makes your brain work and that will hold up for a long time. Those of us who are horror fans can feel proud that we love the genre because it does things that have significance.

Fangoria: Are you done with Freddy?

Craven: The intellectual property-thing is in the hands of whoever has that. There's a part of me that would love to do it again, to do something with Robert as Freddy. That would be fun, but I don't see it happening.

R.A. Interviews Wes Craven (R.I.P.)

R.A. the Rugged Man / 2015

From https://ratheruggedman.net, June 1, 2015. Reprinted by permission of R.A. the Rugged Man.

A while back I got to discuss film with the man behind *Last House on the Left* and *A Nightmare on Elm Street* as well as the commercial franchise *Scream*. With the recent news of Craven's death from brain cancer, I decided to repost the interview in his honor.

R.A. The Rugged Man: What are some of your favorite horror films?
Wes Craven: *Frankenstein. The Exorcist* is stunningly powerful. *King Kong. Texas Chainsaw Massacre*, when Leatherface kills the guy with the mallet. I jumped out of my seat. I also like David Cronenberg's early work.

R.A.: Like *The Brood* and *Rabid*?
Craven: Yes, remarkable. And *Scanners*.

R.A.: What's the most brutal kill in a Wes Craven movie?
Craven: When they killed the best friend in *Last House on the Left* and she was being stabbed and crawling away. That was pretty brutal, especially for that time. That scene caused fist fights in theaters.

R.A.: In *Last House* when the girl was forced to pee on herself, did she actually pee on herself, or was it a tube?
Craven: It was a tube. That was to establish the villain completely in charge. Peeing on oneself goes back to everyone's childhood. It's an ancient no-no, and when you're forced to do it, it's really degrading. It's also shocking with no gore.

R.A.: A child molester brought to justice by townspeople. . . . Is Freddy Krueger a homage to Fritz Lang's *M*? No one seems to acknowledge the similarities.

Craven: 'Cause you're probably the only interviewer in the genre that studied. I was trying to think of a crime that would cause parents to commit murder. It wasn't a conscious thing, but I had seen *M*.

R.A.: I think you're most kick-ass kill scene is in *Deadly Friend* when they throw the basketball through the old lady's face and her head explodes.
Craven: That scene was cut down. After her head gets knocked off, she ran around for quite a while like a chicken with its head chopped off. They forced me to cut a lot of gore from that film.

R.A.: You made your first serious drama *Music of the Heart* starring Meryl Streep. If you could spice that film up with a couple grisly murders, how would you do it?
Craven: (laughs) Oh, God. Uh, I don't know.

R.A.: I was thinking, maybe beating Meryl Streep to death with a trumpet.
Craven: Maybe she kills her ex-husband. Maybe she'd strangle him with a violin cord. I'm not sure.

R.A.: *Scream* doesn't have that "mean-spirited-raping-and-murdering-mommies-vibe" like *The Hills Have Eyes*. Do you think you've calmed down a bit?
Craven: It's different. *Scream*'s more ironic and self-reflected. It's actually one of the more sophisticated films I've made in the genre. It just wasn't as primal.

R.A.: In your long career of chopping people the fuck up, what actor or actress did you have the most fun killing?
Craven: Umm. Drew Barrymore. She was fun to kill 'cause she was so intense. You know, people ask me how I can defend filmmakers putting murder and torture on screen, and I say start by looking at the president—he's really torturing people. We're just making movies.

R.A.: When I was thirteen, I made a Freddy glove out of duct tape and steak knives.
Craven: Interesting.

R.A.: Then I got naked at a party and tried stabbing people with it. I was a young kid. Do you take responsibility for my actions?
Craven: (laughs) Absolutely not. I'm just glad you didn't try to jerk off later that night. You would've cut yourself to shreds.

Wes Craven: One Last Scream

Jennifer Juniper Stratford / 2015

From *The Front*, November 4, 2015. Reprinted by permission of Jennifer Juniper, author, and Thalia Mavros, CEO of *The Front*.

Wes Craven had an incredible life—half the things that have happened to him as a result of following hunches are completely unreal, which may be exactly the reason why he was able to change the horror genre, having inadvertently invented a whole surrealist framework for it. As campy and goofy as *A Nightmare on Elm Street* is, it's actually very surreal. The way it bends what feels ultrafamiliar, following characters who are relatable, made it even scarier. You can watch that film a million times and laugh your ass off and cheer Freddy on, and then without fail have horrible, sweaty nightmares.

Just last November, two days after Thanksgiving, Wes Craven and his wife invited me over to their home to take Polaroids and record an interview documenting his life. Sitting in their Zen, airy home on Mulholland Drive, they made me lunch, and we talked about everything, starting from the beginning, when he was on a fast track to selling rare coins for a living.

In a way, this film was made to ameliorate the very first he wrote and directed, *The Last House on the Left*. It featured an incredibly brutal scene in which two women just trying to have a good time in life are raped, slashed, and mutilated—a story line that seems to have haunted Craven throughout his career because he realized he took it too far.

Women in horror films are often fetishized for their bodies and victimhood. Craven effectively changed this narrative, writing the female protagonist of *A Nightmare on Elm Street* as a strong, intelligent young woman who knew how to outsmart the villain.

Throughout our conversation, Craven stayed present and kind, behaving as if there were no difference between us, even though he was famous and spent half the year in Martha's Vineyard. Never once did he mention his illness, lavishing me with time as if it were to last.

The Front: You didn't start off being a filmmaker.

Wes Craven: No. I had an interest in the arts without thinking of them as "the arts" for a long time, though. I grew up in the Baptist Church, so no listening to records or watching movies, along with alcohol and dancing and everything else. Disney films, those were okay, that was the one exception. So I saw every Disney film that came out, and at first I wanted to be a Disney animator. I drew and drew and drew. Around junior high I got on the school paper and started writing. Then I went to college and chose literature. I was a lit major and nobody in my family ever went to college, so I was kind of an odd duck. My mother always encouraged me and my brothers to take a safe job—she was suspicious of books. She read ravenously but exclusively *Reader's Digest*.

I got a double master's degree in philosophy and writing, and by that time I had wanted to be a novelist. A friend of mine told me that a master's qualifies you to teach college. I said, "Really!?" So I applied to a bunch of colleges, and this is how my whole life was at the beginning, blindly following instincts and leads. I didn't get in anywhere, and I was being trained to sell rare coins at a department store in Baltimore.

The Front: Rare coins!

Craven: I was getting into rare coins not because it was what I wanted to do, but I thought I could also write at night. Some English teacher in a college in Pennsylvania dropped dead in class two weeks into the semester. The phone rang asking if I could come tomorrow. So I packed my bags and went out to the woods of Pennsylvania and taught English there, and then the next year I got a better job in upstate New York and taught English at Clarkson College. And there I was, writing and trying to get stories published, and nothing was happening. But the extraordinary thing that happened was that I got a chance for the first time to watch movies.

The Front: So you didn't start watching movies until after college?

Craven: I went to an interdenominational school, Billy Graham's alma mater. If you were caught in a movie theater you would be expelled. They had almost the exact same rules I grew up with. Sex was not mentioned. Senior year, I decided to move when my literary magazine was cancelled because of something I published about an interracial couple. I was denounced from the pulpit in chapel. I was semiradicalized. So I went to go see *To Kill A Mockingbird*.

The Front: What a way to commemorate being kicked out of school.

Craven: It hit me like a thunderbolt. If this was a sin . . . it was clearly not. So then I went on to grad school, and there was nothing to do there but read and write.

The Front: How old were you then, when you saw the film?

Craven: I was probably twenty or twenty-one. I lost a year of school because of paralysis. I got paralyzed from the neck down when I was a freshman in college and had to drop out; it was a long recovery on that. I was laid up for half a year and then worked half a year to get out. Then I went back to college. The college town had an arts center. It was the mid-1960s; I was twenty-four when I got married. So I was twenty-five, and I already felt old.

I found myself more preoccupied with film. I saw *Blow-Up*, and then I went back and saw it six more times. Nothing else had ever affected me like that. As a teacher, you get a lot of sample textbooks. All of us in the faculty would sell them at the end of the year, and I sold enough to get $300. I bought a nonsound Revere crank camera in New York and started taking pictures and reading film magazines. Some students saw this and asked me to be a faculty advisor to a film club they were starting. I agreed, and we ended up making a series of small films. For one of them we had a budget of about $300, and it was forty minutes long. We made almost $1,000 showing them around the local colleges.

Right in the middle of that, my department head called me in and said, "I don't know what you're doing with this bullshit making movies. You were hired to teach English. You need to get your PhD and publish or else I'm not going to have you back next year." I thought about it overnight and went back and said, "Fine. I'm going to go figure out how to make movies."

The Front: Thank God, right?

Craven: At that point I had a wife and child, so we were paid through the summer. I went to New York and didn't find a job. I had to come back and teach a year at a local high school, which was kind of a letdown. I talked it over with my wife, and she told me to try again. So I went back and slept on my brother's couch in New Jersey.

One of my students told me he had a brother in New York who was making movies, something called "industrials" for IBM. At the end of the second summer, still without a job, I went and saw him. He told me he didn't have a job for me, but he could show me what he was doing. There, he taught me the basics of editing. I just sat by him and sucked it all up. His name was Harry, and my student's name was Steve Chapin. And it was two years before he became the folk singer Harry Chapin.

I was watching him, learning, and the guy who ran the postproduction house that Harry was running a room in fired his sixteen-year-old messenger. He asked Harry if he had anyone to fill in, and I said I would do it. He said, "Are you the guy with the master's degree who is a professor?"

It paid something ridiculous, but I agreed. That was my first paying job. It was the ticket. Once you get your foot in the door you can show your skills. I worked my way up, first learning postproduction, then I moved into syncing up dailies and working in editing rooms. Then I met a guy whose tiny little film I worked on got an offer by some theater owners to make a scary movie. He told me to go write something scary, and if they liked it I could direct it. He owned a little Steenbeck editing table, he said, so I could cut it on that and direct it; he'd produce it. That was Sean Cunningham, who did *Friday the 13th*. That's how I got started making scary movies. It was *The Last House on the Left*. Before that, I had no impulse. I immediately tried to move away from it.

The Front: From the horror genre?
Craven: Yeah. That film was especially brutal and scarifying.

The Front: I heard a rumor that you were never able to watch it.
Craven: No, no, I've watched it. It's just not pleasant to watch. The suffering feels very, very real. It's mean. The bad guys are mean-spirited and very personal. Just total rage and take no prisoners.

The Front: But you wrote it.
Craven: Oh, I wrote it. I get that all the time, "Where does this come from? You seem like such a nice guy." I don't know. Now I know most of the major guys and girls who make horror films, and they are a jolly bunch. We've all talked about it amongst ourselves, and we were scared in school or bullied or whatever, or had scary fathers. It's partially a way to immune yourself from terror and fear. And I'm sure there is a certain amount of anger and even rage in being raised in a way that says half of the great sources of inspiration and joy in life are sins and you burn in hell forever. I'm sure that had done a lot of psychic damage.

The Front: Did you want to get out of horror because you didn't like the subject matter?
Craven: I don't think Sean or I knew quite the power of the enraging element of *Last House*. It was all scary. There were fights in theaters, citizen's groups formed, projectionists set fire to the reels. We had to set up editing rooms in New York to restore prints from other prints that were destroyed. Among my friends in New York, my girlfriend at the time—my marriage had ended—was a PhD candidate. She was around academic types, and they backed away from me. A lot of people were repulsed by it. That's a big word, but I felt like I had done something almost heinous. I knew that wasn't all I was, so Sean and I wrote another five or six scripts. None of them was able to get backing.

The Front: So they weren't horror movies?
Craven: They were comedies and American beauty contests. A father raises his

half of the kids after a divorce, things that I was going through as an adult. No interest. Finally, I had a friend who encouraged me to do another *Last House*. He was in Las Vegas and said there were deserts. No one asks for permits, so I should write something about the desert. So I wrote *The Hills Have Eyes*. Once that came out and it did very well, I was a horror film director. It soon became clear that I wasn't going to do anything else unless it was scary, so that's kind of how it was for a long, long time. Then I wrote the script for *A Nightmare on Elm Street*.

The Front: Did you make a conscious decision to change the constructs of the horror genre?
Craven: I never did anything to rewrite horror; I just tried to do something interesting. So it wasn't that grandiose. It was just that I had no hesitation about writing something that was parallel to what I was studying at the time—Eastern religions and meditation, Sufism.

There was something about me that was always drawn to dreams. I had nightmares when I was a kid. My parents had a contentious marriage. My father had a hair-trigger temper, and then he died when I was five. There was a lot of *storm and drung*. There was one germ that *A Nightmare on Elm Street* was based on—nightmares—and I was terrified to go back to sleep.

In my child's naiveté I asked my mother to come to bed with me, and she said that's the one place I can't come with you. And I was totally awake, just like, "What!? What do you mean!?" She said she would be there when I woke up, but I would just have to be brave. I remembered that moment for a long, long time.

The Front: So dreams and making horror!
Craven: At the time I was reading about a level of consciousness in sleep where you are not really aware, yet are essentially fully awake; you need to go down a few levels or you need to lose your ego and break through [to a dream state]. That seemed like a perfect metaphor for a person trying to stay awake in order to face an overwhelming horrible truth that needed to be dealt with. As long as I scared the shit out of people every eight to ten minutes, I thought, let's try it!

The Front: Were other people into it, too?
Craven: No one thought it was a good idea except for Bob Shaye [founder of New Line Cinema, a top independent film distribution and production company]. I have a pile of rejection letters that I go through from time to time just to remind myself. If you are ahead of your time, you are not in a good position. But Bob Shaye was in New York. He was totally independent; he wasn't part of that Hollywood scene.

The Front: What did he like about the script?

Craven: He just got it right away. Someone took us to an old men's club with beautiful wainscoting and people bringing you drinks. He told me he loved *Last House* and asked if I had anything else. I said I have something about a guy who exists only in dreams and he can kill you if he comes into your nightmare. So you have to stay awake and get him to get on your turf, although I didn't know how at that point. I sent him the first draft, and he immediately went out and tried to raise money for it. And it took him a really long time. I showed it to everyone in Hollywood and nothing happened.

That was the second time I was completely broke. I was on the verge of selling my house, which was the last thing I had left. Then Bob got the money. You know that Grateful Dead song, "What a Long Strange Trip It's Been"? That seems to be like my life.

The Front: I've heard a lot of filmmakers say that you have to get used to the anxiety between projects.

Craven: You operate without a net and that also means that you can die at any moment. You always feel that anything can happen at any time, but that's true for all of us. Look what happened to the American middle class. They had pensions up the wazoo that just vanished. It's the cliché of how long you are doing something—at least you're following your passion.

The Front: In *Nightmare*, you made Nancy an intelligent character and not a bimbo.

Craven: Part of it was having a daughter who was fourteen at the time. When I was casting for the role of [Nancy's boyfriend] Glen, just by quirk Johnny Depp came in. His friend had a role of coroner who later got cut out of the film.

There are times when you're not really ahead of things, but my daughter was. I had the quarterback, the surfer-looking guy, and I had a picture of Johnny Depp that I happened to toss into the car and showed my daughter and her friend. I put the three pictures on the table and asked them which they liked best for Glen and they instantly pointed to Johnny. I asked why; he had greasy hair and nicotine stains! They both said because he was beautiful. So I was smart enough to say okay.

There was something about having a daughter . . . When I was doing *Swamp Thing* there was a scene with Adrienne Barbeau, and she tripped—it was something I've seen in a lot of horror movies, the damsel getting caught. My daughter saw the film and said, "Women don't fall when they run." And I saw the truth in it. Women's liberation was going on, and I realized it was true. Going back to *King Kong*, it's all so slanted. It seems like we're going backwards. My daughter now has a five-year-old and is fighting this princess thing. In all the stores everything for girls is pink and princess. The force that wants to push women back is so strong. I felt with Nancy and Sid in *Scream*, I wanted to do normal, strong women, not Hollywood big boobs and blond hair and speaking the latest teen slang. I wanted someone who you could picture living next door to you who has that strength of character.

The Front: *New Nightmare* supposedly brushes up against the fourth wall. What was your idea to do that?

Craven: It came at a point of frustration. Bob Shaye called me up; I hadn't talked to him in years. We already killed Freddy Krueger, but he said there was an audience for one more. He asked if I could come up with an idea for Freddy to come back.

We were in the middle of dealing with a lot of strict censorship. We asked ourselves what these films give or take away from culture. Do we really make kids go crazy and kill their baby sisters? It's like boot camp for the psyche. This is the way humans deal with the horrors of existence. If you forbid this kind of art, the actual, real horror is unleashed in a sense. The way humans deal with the horrific is to put it in a narrative and cloak it in character. So by censorship and not being able to make any more films about Freddy, he will be unleashed. That was the concept that came out.

Smartest thing I said was that Bob would have a part in it, and he liked that. I was steeped in nineteenth- and twentieth-century literature of the absurd, so it was in my intellectual bag. But in that time people had the same reactions as with *Last House*, fights in theaters and what have you. So I felt like, why not get past this fourth wall and talk about how music and art affect people . . . and what about the people who make music and art and how it affects them?

The Front: Why didn't you direct the sequel to *Nightmare*?

Craven: They showed me the script, and it was terrible. They just wanted to get it out the following year.

The Front: How do you feel when a character you created has a trajectory that's out of your grasp?

Craven: It's an interesting thing, you can fret about it, or you can just leave. There was always a creative give-and-pull about who was in charge because after the original contract Bob owned everything. He had creative control. I can't take anything away from Bob; he was very influential on the script, erudite, and he was a Rhodes Scholar, a very interesting man. Robert took something and made it his own, and I chose to leave. Then I came back ten years later and did something.

The Front: It's one of the top three Halloween costumes. Do you get a kick out of that every year?

Craven: It's not too bad. At a certain point you realize that on your tombstone it will say, "I gave birth to Freddy Krueger." I wrote and directed it, and that's what I did. A lot of people love it; a lot of people got inspiration from it. I got a lot of letters from young women saying I empowered them. It could be worse, you know? The things that came out of me that never would have come out of me if someone didn't tell me to make them a scary movie. . . . I told my friends that I never even saw a scary movie. Sean said that growing up as a fundamentalist Baptist was enough, just go pull the skeletons out of my closet.

Additional Resources

Abrams, Simon. "Wes Craven: I Always Encouraged Robert Englund to Make Freddy Krueger His Own." *LA Weekly*. January 16, 2014.

Anderson, Martin. "Interview: Wes Craven on *Last House on the Left*." *Den of Geek*. 2009. http://www.denofgeek.com/movies/14465/interview-wes-Craven-on-last-house-on-the-left.

Barkan, Jonathan. "Wes Craven Looks Back on *Scream* Franchise." *Bloody Disgusting*. September 3, 2010. http://bloody-disgusting.com/interviews/21549/wes-Craven-looks-back-on-scream-franchise/.

Benshoff, Harry M., ed. *The Companion to the Horror Film*. London: Wiley-Blackwell, 2017.

Benson-Allott, Caetlin. "Wes Craven: Thinking Through Horror." *Film Quarterly*. 69.2 (Winter 2015): 74–76.

Cane, Clay. "Q & A: The King of *Scream*, Wes Craven, Talks Race and Horror." BET.com. April 14, 2011.

Clover, Carol. *Men, Women and Chainsaws*. Princeton: Princeton University Press, 1992.

Dargis, Manohla. "Meeting Mr. Fright." *The Village Voice*. 39 October 25 (1994): 65.

Garris, Mick. "Wes Craven." *Post-Mortem*. October 20, 2014. https://youtu.be/qjmb98M70Tk

Goldman, Andrew. "The Horror of Being Wes Craven." *The New York Times Magazine*. April 15, 2011. http://www.nytimes.com/2011/04/17/magazine/mag-17talk-t.html?mcubz=3.

Gross, Terry. "Wes Craven." Fresh Air. WHYY/NPR. February 18, 1998.

Krohn, Bill. "Le territoire, c'est votre corps: Entretien avec Wes Craven." Trans: "The Territory, It's Your Body: Interview with Wes Craven." *Cahiers du cinéma* (April 2011): 90–100.

Kruszelnicki, Fabien. "Horror Maestro Wes Craven on *Scream*, Freddy and Bloodying the American Dream." *Hero Magazine*. November 14, 2014.

Kutzer, Dale. "Making *Wes Craven's New Nightmare*." *Imagi-Movies* 2. 1 (1994): 14–16.

Leeder, Murray. *Horror Film: A Critical Introduction*. New York: Bloomsbury, 2018.

McCarty, John, ed. *The Fearmakers*. New York: St. Martin's Press, 1994.

McDonagh, Maitlin. "Wes Craven." *From Filmmaking on the Fringe: The Good, the Bad and the Deviant Directors*. New York: Citadel Press, 1995.

Merchan, George. "Exclusive Interview: Wes Craven (*The Hills Have Eyes*)." Chud.com. March 13, 2006. http://www.chud.com/6125/exclusive-interview-wes-Craven-the-hills-have-eyes/.

Muir, John Kenneth. *Wes Craven: The Art of Horror*. Jefferson, NC: McFarland: 1998.

Netburn, Deborah. "Wes Craven on the Disturbed Dreams of a Society." *LA Times*. March 23, 2007.

Persons, Dan. "Wes Craven." *Cinefantastique* 29 n4/5 (1997): 87–88.

Prigge, Steve. "Constant Craven: The Franchise That Doesn't Die (Unlike Everyone in It)." *Interview Magazine*. April 2011.

Prince, Stephen, ed. *The Horror Film*. New Brunswick, NJ: Rutgers University Press, 2004.

Rausch, Andrew. *Fifty Filmmakers: Conversations with Directors from Roger Avary to Steven Zaillian*. Jefferson, NC: McFarland, 2008.

Rodowick, D. N. "The Enemy Within: The Economy of Violence in *The Hills Have Eyes*" in *Planks of Reason: Essays on the Horror Film*, Barry Keith Grant, ed. London: Scarecrow Press, 1984.

Robb, Brian J. *Screams and Nightmares: The Films of Wes Craven*. New York: Overlook, 1998.

Rose, Charlie. "Wes Craven." *Charlie Rose*. WNET/PBS. February 17, 1997.

Svehla, G. J. "Wes Craven's Exploitative World: The Horror of Family Violence." *Midnight Marquee* 34 Fall (1985): 7–11.

Wee, Valerie. "The *Scream* Trilogy, 'Hypermodernism,' and the Late-Nineties Teen Slasher Film." *Journal of Film and Video*. 57:3 (Fall 2005): 44–61.

Wooley, John. *Wes Craven: The Man and His Nightmares*. Hoboken, NJ: Wiley, 2011.

Index

About the Editor

Shannon Blake Skelton is assistant professor at Kansas State University, where he teaches classes in theater history, film studies, and dramatic literature. He is author of *The Late Work of Sam Shepard*.

CPSIA information can be obtained
at www.ICGtesting.com
Printed in the USA
BVHW030905251019
562044BV00002B/6/P

9 781496 825964